John Allen was born in 1942 in Knightswood, Glasgow. After graduating from Heriot-Watt University he spent the early part of his career in Edinburgh, in pharmacy. With his wife, Anne, and their two young children he moved to Strathspey in the Scottish Highlands to manage community pharmacies in Kingussie and Newtonmore. There John's interest in mountains and mountaineering increased until, after the Cairngorm Plateau Disaster of 1971, he joined the Cairngorm Mountain Rescue Team. He became Team Leader in 1989, remaining in post until retiring from the Team in August 2007. He was closely involved in well over 1,000 rescues, and received an MBE for services to mountain rescue in 2001.

Chris Bonington was born in Hampstead in 1934 and is considered by many to be Britain's most distinguished living mountaineer. He has led many expeditions including the successful one in 1972 on the hitherto unclimbed south-west ridge of Mount Everest, and in 1985 achieved the summit personally. He has travelled and climbed all over the world and is the author of many successful books.

Robert Davidson is a writer, editor and experienced hillwalker who lives in Highland Scotland.

CAIRNGORM JOHN

A LIFE IN MOUNTAIN RESCUE

10th Anniversary Edition

JOHN ALLEN
with Robert Davidson

Introduced by
SIR CHRIS BONINGTON

First published in Great Britain by
Sandstone Press Ltd
Willow House
Stoneyfield Business Park
Inverness
IV2 7PA
Scotland

www.sandstonepress.com

The publisher acknowledges subsidy from Creative Scotland towards
publication of this volume.

ISBN: 978-1-912240-64-7
ISBNe: 978-1-912240-70-8

Jacket design by Ryder Design, Sheffield
Typeset in Garamond by Iolaire Typesetting, Newtonmore.
Printed and bound by CPI Group (UK) Ltd, Croydon, CRO 4YY

This book is dedicated to all members and supporters of the Cairngorm Mountain Rescue Team, past, present and future.

CONTENTS

ABOUT
The 10Th Anniversary Edition

In 2009, at the time of writing *Cairngorm John*, I had reservations about any book reporting on mountain rescues and Mountain Rescue Teams. Having agreed to write the book I attempted to justify it by outlining my three main reasons for putting pen to paper. Since then I have become convinced that it was the correct thing to do. There are a great many books written on mountaineering and the 'great outdoors'. Whether the climber takes part in mountaineering in the Scottish Highlands, the European Alps, or the great ranges of the Himalayas, all participants in this sport have one thing in common – they may have an accident and they may need to be rescued. The thread of rescue runs through the whole range of outdoor pursuits and, in that case, the book *Cairngorm John* has its rightful place in mountain literature. This was acknowledged at the Kendal Mountain Festival in November 2009 when it was shortlisted for the Boardman Tasker Prize for mountain literature.

Towards the end of 2018 it was apparent that *Cairngorm John*, after a number of reprints, was again out of print. Due to the success of the original book, instead of another reprint, Sandstone Press was keen to bring out a 10th anniversary edition with some updating to recognise the changes in the Cairngorm Team and in mountain rescue generally in the last ten years. There have been rapid and extensive developments in all aspects of modern sports during this time, and mountaineering is no exception. Appropriate additional chapters could include: the privatisation of the search and rescue helicopter service; the advancing technology of rescue equipment; the use of smart phones and apps; and the formation of the Independent Mountain Rescue Service – a group of four Rescue Teams who gave up their membership of the Scottish Mountain Rescue organisation.

I found it very gratifying to note that the original book was generally well received. I was also aware that some mountaineering instructors suggest it as recommended reading to their students and some suggest to their clients that if they wish to learn some of the dos and don'ts in the mountains then real-life stories about real-life incidents are a good way of remembering some of the main points of safety.

One well-known mountaineer went as far as to say, 'That book should be on every climber's shelf.'

Ten years is a long time, accidents are forgotten, and there is a new generation of climbers out there who may benefit from the message in this book.

John Allen
Kingussie, 2019

THREE REASONS
for writing this book

As a guide to the media

In my years as a Team Member, Deputy Leader then Leader of the Team, I was acutely aware when dealing with the media that many researchers and reporters had little understanding of mountaineering. This often led to poor and inaccurate reporting. For example, the press in both TV and newspapers would report an incident in two or three lines:

> '…two injured climbers were airlifted from the Cairngorms to Raigmore Hospital in Inverness where they have been kept in overnight.'

Frequently no mention was made of the 20 or 30 Rescue Team Members who had spent ten hours rescuing the two climbers from a difficult location and then carrying them to below the cloud level to a point where they could be airlifted off the hill!

To share the experience

I benefited from being a member of a Rescue Team. I saw at first hand the mistakes that could be made and this in turn made me a more careful mountaineer.

This document of my many years of experience in search and

rescue may be of some value to those still actively involved in mountain rescue in Scotland.

It is of course understood that what worked for the Cairngorm Mountain Rescue Team may not be applicable to other Teams.

I am aware that there may be some sensitive issues raised by my decision to put into print some of the stories of rescues which took place in the past, but for any book to reach a broad spectrum of readers it has to be interesting. This requires a good deal of detail, rendered as accurately as possible to take the reader into the rescues and into the minds of the rescuers and rescued alike.

To raise the profile of mountain rescue

Mountain rescue in Scotland is the responsibility of the police. Unlike the police, the fire brigade, or the ambulance service it is an emergency service operated by unpaid civilians with limited funding. I was always surprised by the number of casualties whom we rescued who believed that we were a paid service.

I believe that in order to obtain and maintain funding it is necessary to keep mountain rescue in the public eye. One of our most important sources of funding in the past has been the goodwill and generosity of those individuals who have supported our work through donations, fundraising and legacies.

My hope is that readers who share my lifelong love of mountaineering in Scotland will sympathise with my sincere wish to raise public awareness of the volunteer nature of mountain rescue.

John Allen
October 2008

ACKNOWLEDGEMENTS
to the First Edition

For supporting this project and for their many reminiscences, corroborations, elaborations and permissions John Allen thanks Anne Allen, Willie Anderson, Sarah Atkinson, Denise Barley, Helen Brebner, Peter Cliff, Peter Finlayson, Nick Forwood, Roger Gaff, Alistair Gilmour, Peter Grant, Paul Gray, Jas Hepburn, John Hall, John Lyall, Duncan MacDonald, Neil MacDonald, Heather Morning, Paul Hyett, Dave Pierce, Rod Pimm, Mollie Porter, Fran Pothecary, Martin Robertson, Uiga Robertson, Willie Ross, Malcolm Sclater, Jimmy Simpson, Dave Snadden, Simon Steer, Wes Sterrit, Chris Stuart, Tim Walker, Margaret Wigham, Roger Wild, Donnie Williamson and Hamish Wylie.

Robert Davidson thanks Iain Gordon of Sandstone Press for first suggesting this project and Iain and Brigit Gordon for the use of their cottage in Kingussie where much of the first draft was written. John Allen made his eco-cottage near Boat of Garten available for the rest.

Great thanks go to the Committee and Team Members of the Cairngorm Mountain Rescue Team for their welcome and co-operation. Team Doctor Peter Grant contributed hugely to Chapter Eleven on hypothermia in a three-way internet conversation between John in Kingussie, Robert in Dingwall and Peter in Uganda, on the upper reaches of the Nile where he was working on an AIDS/HIV project with Voluntary Service Overseas.

Special thanks go to the eight other Team Members who allowed themselves to be interviewed: Willie Anderson, Peter Finlayson,

James (Jas) Hepburn, John Lyall, Duncan MacDonald, Heather Morning, Simon Steer and Donnie Williamson. Paul Hyett has been a friend of Cairngorm Mountain Rescue Team since his dramatic rescue on Ben Alder and contributed greatly to Chapter Twelve.

Moira Forsyth applied her acute eye and sensibility to all the book's many drafts.

Very special thanks go to Anne Allen who gave her practical support to the project from the outset, read early drafts, assisted with proofing, engaged in discussions on mountain rescue and provided her unique insight into the motivations and character of mountain rescuers.

Sir Chris Bonington's generous Introduction is acknowledged with particular gratitude.

ACKNOWLEDGEMENTS
to the Second Edition

It seems that almost as much work has gone into preparing this new edition of *Cairngorm John* as went into the first, with almost as many people contributing their time and experience. My wife, Anne, has again gone over the text, correcting many minor errors that had somehow found their way to publication first time around.

In addition, I am happy to acknowledge Team Members, present and past: Willie Anderson, Iain Cornfoot, Al Gilmour, Nick Forwood, John Lowther, John Lyall, Dave Rutledge, Heather Morning and Donny Williamson, who all consented to be interviewed not once but several times. Chris Stuart contributed the dramatic image from which Ryder Design developed the book cover. Chris has also contributed images to the second (new) plate section, especially the beautiful landscapes. Pictures of Fingers Ridge were generously donated by Steve Broadhurst. The Scottish Avalanche Information Service supplied the dramatic image of a cornice collapse and I happy to put my thanks on record.

I am also grateful to Chief Pilot John McIntyre and his air crews at Inverness Coastguard Base, Damon Powell of Scottish Mountain Rescue for sharing their views and experience, Ron Walker of Talisman Mountaineering, the legendary figure David 'Heavy' Whalley for sharing his research into the Beinn Eighe disaster of 1951, and to Mark Wilson, who contributed greatly to the general summary of the S92 and to 'triggered lightning'.

LIST OF ILLUSTRATIONS

First plate section

Second plate section

Almost all of the photographs in this book have been supplied by members of the Cairngorm Mountain Rescue Team and are of actual rescues and training exercises. Author and publisher gratefully acknowledge Denise Barley, Steve Broadhurst, Jas Hepburn, John Lyall, Cathy Mordaunt, Martin Robertson, Simon Steer, Chris Stuart and the Scottish Avalanche Information Service as authors of these images. Otherwise, every effort was made to identify and contact the authors.

INTRODUCTION

by Sir Chris Bonington

The Cairngorms are a magnificent mountain range lying roughly at the centre of the Scottish Highlands. Within their wide open spaces four of the five highest peaks in Britain can be reached on foot in a day. Reached, that is, by physically able and experienced mountaineers. I had one of the best days I have ever had on skis reaching those four wonderful summits. They are crossed by several great passes which, while much lower than the summits, are at a higher level by far than that at which most people will survive comfortably.

I have had many great days in the Cairngorms. Back in the sixties I did some truly enjoyable winter climbs with Tom Patey, that great character of Scottish climbing, who pioneered so many first ascents and celebrated them and his companions in song, verse and brilliantly witty prose. In the eighties with Jim Fotheringham we climbed many of the great Classics, among them Steeple and Needle on the Shelter Stone Crag in summer and we had a 24-hour epic on Creag an Dubh Loch trying to climb Labyrinth in thin conditions. After being turned back just a few feet from the top we were faced with a terrifying abseil descent in the dark with very poor anchors.

More recently, on Parallel Gully B on Lochnagar, with my brother I had one of the closest calls of all, when he fell as second and pulled me off my inadequate axe belay in the upper snow slope, giving a 50m clear fall onto the one runner I put in place on the pitch. Fortunately, it held both our weights, and with broken ribs I managed to top out of the climb.

I have never had to be rescued but have had quite a few close calls over the years. It has made me very aware of how all of us climbers and walkers might well need the help of a Mountain Rescue Team and indeed, may owe our lives to their skill, stamina and courage. Nowhere more is this the case than in the Cairngorms where the heights, distances, and ferocity of the weather, particularly in winter, are of a more serious scale than anywhere else in the British Isles.

These mountains have a unique beauty which some say is an acquired taste but which, once gained, is never lost. They are the single malt whisky of landscapes and have generated a literature which sits comfortably on the long shelves of mountain books from around the world. *Cairngorm John: A Life in Mountain Rescue* now joins this amazing library.

Newly arrived in the Highlands from Edinburgh with his wife and young family John Allen was to develop a successful chain of community pharmacies, but when he joined the Cairngorm Mountain Rescue Team in 1972 he truly found his niche. As far as family and business commitments would allow he immersed himself in mountain rescue and, in 1989, became Team Leader, remaining in position until early 2007. The rescues he participated in, led directly, or organised from either Glenmore Lodge or the new Mountain Rescue Centre at Inverdruie number easily more than a thousand.

The title of this book, *Cairngorm John*, refers to the call sign he used throughout his career when speaking to the Air-Sea Rescue helicopters. His steady voice over the radio must have been a reassurance to the crew of the legendary Rescue 137 as it hovered over Aviemore, waiting for the break in the weather that would let them into the corrie, or plateau, or deep glen, where John and his fellow rescuers were struggling against the elements to save a life. The same steadiness arises from these pages but carries with it other qualities such as observation, humour and empathy.

Although frequently in the news Mountain Rescue Teams are not well understood. Surprisingly few people know the rescuers are unpaid or that they achieve, to put it in John Allen's words, 'the most professional standards possible within an amateur ethos'. Why then, do they require such large sums to function, and where does the money come from? Likewise their relationships with other, full-time, emergency services are not well understood. Few, even among mountain enthusiasts, know they act on behalf of the police and that it is the Team Leaders who co-ordinate all aspects, including the use of helicopters.

One of the least understood groups to go to the hills, the mountain rescuers are an enigma to the general public who all too often label them simply as heroes. No dedicated rescuer feels this way. Nor do they see the casualties as the public too often does, as feckless and foolish. John Allen's book does much to explain the motivations of both, the trials the rescuers put themselves through to come to the assistance of others, and the crafts and science developed through their work over the past half-century.

Often the rescuers are required to meet and work with people during the worst experience of their life, experience that will alter their futures utterly. Sometimes they have to deal with people in what will be the last few hours of their lives. In the course of a long search they will often interact closely with the relatives of a casualty. Relationships are developed, grief is shared and sometimes long friendships are established.

Filled with anecdotes and compassion this book takes the reader deeply into the world of mountain rescue, more deeply into the hills themselves than many more direct appreciations. *Cairngorm John: A Life in Mountain Rescue* is by turns exciting, funny, informative and wise, an indispensable addition to the literature of the mountains.

CAIRNGORM JOHN

A LIFE IN MOUNTAIN RESCUE

10th Anniversary Edition

PROLOGUE
The Mountains

The Cairngorms in Scotland are a mountain range, a hard reality, a unique and sensitive environment, a playground, a sanctuary, an idea. The name 'Cairngorm' is a modern development taken from the name of a single mountain. A Gaelic word it means 'blue hill', with 'cairn' implying a high degree of rockiness. It is not the true Gaelic name of the range, which is 'Am Monadh Ruadh', but those puzzling 'dhs do not sit well in the mouths of English-language speakers.

The name is also applied to wider areas with boundaries that vary depending on the authority involved. The area as described in the Scottish Mountaineering Trust's guidebook, *The Cairngorms* by Dr Adam Watson, covers Ben Rinnes in the north to a line drawn between Pitlochry and Montrose in the south, with the west side boundary running down the centre of the River Spey. Against this, the Cairngorm National Park Authority crosses the Spey to place its boundary along the crest of the Monadhliath hills ('liath' means 'grey'). The heart of the matter though, is the mountain range which has its own history, literature, songbook, human ecology, plant forms, animals, birds; it even has its yeti figure in the Great Grey Man of Ben MacDhui. If ghosts exist it most certainly has ghosts.

Even in planetary terms its rocks are old. Five hundred million years ago masses of molten rock emerged from the earth to form mountains many times higher than those of today. Glaciers, wind and water gradually eroded them to their foundations, the three relatively flat plateaux of the Cairngorm massif at around 1,200m above sea level. The westernmost of these plateaux has the most peaks with seven designated as Munros – mountains attaining a height of 3,000ft as measured in imperial units. The wide flat area between these peaks is termed the Great Moss, the name it gives to the whole plateau.

The central plateau has two Munros, Cairngorm and Ben MacDhui, with the two outliers known as Beinn Mheadhoin and Derry Cairngorm, and takes its name from the most famous of them to be generally known as the Cairngorm Plateau. Although the most celebrated peak, Cairngorm is not the highest. Before the hills of Scotland were surveyed with modern accuracy Ben MacDhui was thought to be the highest mountain in Scotland. In fact, it is the second highest after Ben Nevis. In Ben MacDhui, Cairngorm, and across the Lairig Ghru, Braeriach and Cairn Toul, this range boasts the next four highest peaks in the British Isles.

Granite does not allow for tremendous fertility and neither does the almost constant south-west wind that blows unhindered from the Atlantic to trouble the gravel and short spiky grass of the tundra. Across Beinn a'Bhuird and Ben Avon, on the easternmost plateau, these processes have formed weird rock shapes that could pass for modern art sculptures.

On the plateaux themselves there is much to be seen, although it tends not to be noticed by the untutored eye. A herd of reindeer was introduced in the 1950s, tiny alpine plants blossom in their seasons, the bare, exposed rock faces take all manner of forms, and flocks of a most charming little bird, the snow bunting, arrive each year from the Arctic to nest among the boulder fields. The robotic weather station on Cairngorm was built for the use of mountain rescuers as a radio shack, but everyone who uses the mountain professionally knows it as 'The Igloo'. Provided it is in sight a rescuer can be in contact with others who might be below the horizon. Effectively it is a repeater station. Its location though, makes it ideal for long-term studies so Heriot Watt University adapted it to test outside conditions every 20 minutes or so. It is a good, practical example of co-operation between bodies with a substantial overlap of interest, although unwary hillwalkers have been known to jump out of their boots when a gleaming cylinder of plastic and steel grinds noisily out of the roof.

The area features three great mountain passes that have been used by travellers since human beings first arrived in these parts. Glen Feshie links Strathspey in the north with Deeside in the south. The Lairig an Laoigh, the Pass of the Cattle, was used in earlier times by Highland drovers herding their beasts to the markets at Crieff and Callander.

Most famous of all is the central pass, the Lairig Ghru that joins Coylumbridge and White Bridge, dividing the Great Moss from the Cairngorm Plateau. At its crest the Pools of Dee at 760m are usually taken to be the source of the River Dee that runs ever widening to Aberdeen and the sea. However, the Wells of Dee, high on Braeriach, to my mind have at least an equal claim. In former times traversed by cattle, but too rugged to be paved for vehicles, the Lairig Ghru remains more or less unspoiled and one of the world's great mountain walks.

Equally distinguishing are the huge, bowl-like corries that have been carved by glaciers from the sides of the mountains. Photographs do not do justice to the scale. For a full appreciation it is necessary to go there, especially into the Lairig Ghru, to stand beneath the Highland sky and look up. Eagles live here, as do ptarmigan, and dotterel lay their eggs on the high tundra.

The mountain features carry names that bear testimony to the primacy of Gaelic in former times and act as a repository of lore, but the language has long since been displaced by English. In the nineteenth century the Highland Clearances took their toll when the native people were evicted in favour of large estates and sheep. Those remaining suffered the imposition of a class system such as had been unknown to their ancestors and was contrary to their traditions.

Theirs is a great and important story but it is not this story. Rather it is one factor in what the Cairngorms have become, to be acknowledged as an irreversible tragedy but otherwise accepted. Different people live and work here now and have made their commitments to remain and to build.

In Glen Feshie and Glen Derry, in Rothiemurchus to the north, around the Dee to the south, are stands of Scots Pine and mixtures of broadleaved native trees, birch, alder and willow, remnants of a much greater woodland environment. The forests have been attacked and diminished by man for centuries, but much good work is now being done to preserve and extend what remains. Even what we have teems with birdlife, redwing, goldeneye, the rare Scottish crossbill, capercaillie. They are also home to red squirrels, hare, red deer, many kinds of moth, dragonflies.

The Northern Corries are more rugged than the corries to the south and are a magnet for climbers and rough walkers. The four greatest are Coire na Ciste (of the Chest, or Coffin), Coire Cas (of the Foot), Coire an t-Sneachda (of the Snow), and Coire an Lochain (of the Lochan, or Tarn), and several of the massif's notable summits are situated on their edge, including Cairngorm itself. Each of these peaks is marked by a cairn, and all are important wayfinders in low visibility, none more so than the unnamed Point 1141 between Coire Cas and Coire an t-Sneachda.

The years after the Second World War saw an increase in the steady growth of popularity that outdoor pursuits had enjoyed for several decades. As a consequence, in 1947, the Glenmore Lodge Outdoor Centre was established beside Rothiemurchus Forest in the foothills of the Northern Cairngorms, providing training for anyone with an interest in the outdoors. From the outset its instructors raised the levels of knowledge and standards of competence in all sorts of outdoor activities, winter hillwalking, rock climbing, kayaking and more.

Through the decades Glenmore Lodge has developed from no more than a few huts into a sophisticated complex of buildings and technical equipment. In the same period its reputation for progressive outdoor education has widened from a relatively small group of enthusiasts in Scotland into an international circle of appreciation and acknowledgement. Parallel communications systems have been created between this complex and the Cairngorm Mountain Rescue Team's new Rescue Centre near Aviemore and, on those occasions when a mishap occurs in the Northern Corries, the Rescue Team will often use Glenmore Lodge as its Control Centre. With the full and active support of successive Glenmore Lodge Principals, instructors make themselves available for mountain rescue operations in these areas if at all possible. Due to their location they are often first on the scene and, in these circumstances, the two Teams work almost as one.

In 1960 and 1961, two years before the foundation of the Cairngorm Mountain Rescue Team itself, a new road was built onto the mountain from near the Outdoor Centre, with chairlifts to hoist skiers onto the higher snowfields and to the new Ptarmigan Restaurant only 150m below the summit. From that time access into the corries has been made easier and walking and climbing activities have increased to a significantly higher level. Between 1999 and 2001 a funicular railway was constructed from the road's end to a new improved Ptarmigan Restaurant against a background of much environmental discussion, and has proved a popular tourist attraction.

The area to the south and south-east has always been more populated because nature made the land more fertile. It takes more of the sun, and the same ice sheet that shattered the northern faces 10,000 years ago made easier slopes and created a richer soil. It enjoys the presence of royalty which brings its own sub-culture of ceremony and style, and encourages tourism, and the Dee is one of the world's great salmon rivers. This is where herds of deer roam and grouse fly low over banks of heather, and where the hunters come to be guided into the hills to shoot them. The improved road system brings caravans and cars to the hotels, guest houses and campsites of both north and south.

The Estates use Land Rovers and four-wheel drive vehicles, but otherwise the mountains are mostly spared motorised transport. Sometimes helicopters have occasion to land. Mostly though, people travel on foot and to do so it has always been necessary to plan and go prepared.

From whichever direction the walker enters there is a fair way to travel before anything like real solitude is found, but eventually the crowds clear and the silence deepens. Under these circumstances the streams make a singular music and it is a wonderful thing to sleep beside them when the weather is right. All of Cairngorm is a photographer's paradise with subtle shades of purple and green, brown and grey that alter with the seasons and shift with the angle of the light.

The area looks like wilderness and many people consider it to be so, but human influence is everywhere. The grouse moors are as much a made environment as is a high building and require almost as much maintenance. There are Estate houses in Glen Avon, Glen Feshie and Rothiemurchus. Some rivers are bridged and the tops of the plateaux have erosion tracks created by generations of walkers. There are ski tows in the Northern Corries, and a funicular railway that climbs to near the top of Cairngorm Mountain. The winding road that leads to the ski areas gives drivers the choice of three high car parks, the topmost at almost 650m, more than half the elevation of the summit.

Winter strikes hard with temperatures falling well below zero even in the glens, and on the plateaux the snow can lie deeply enough to make walking next to impossible. In these circumstances even a slight wind can produce a chill factor that will take the effective temperature well below freezing. The same wind will turn even a light snowfall into an impenetrable wall of white, and the snow can fall heavily while the wind can be a hurricane because there is nothing to break it on its passage from the ocean. With your footprints filling behind you, direction comes down to compass work alone, and disorientation is a moment's doubt away.

Here and there in the passes and corries are shelters, some of them little more than a rickle of stones, others strongly made buildings constructed for sound economic reasons. The bothy at Corrour, for instance, in earlier times was used by deer watchers.

That is to say, it was used by gamekeepers looking out for poachers. Changing times have removed that usage and the Mountain Bothy Association now maintains it as an unlocked shelter for mountain travellers. As such it becomes not just an emergency shelter but a social centre, albeit one with severe toilet inadequacies.

The shelters have saved lives but have also tempted the less well prepared into the mountains at times when they were likely to be overwhelmed. There have been tragedies.

Across the Lairig Ghru from Corrour is the Tailors' Stone where, according to legend, two local tailors met their end in pursuit of a bet that they could travel to Coylumbridge from Braemar overnight. If the bothy had been available, it could have saved them. In 1800, at Gaick in the wider Cairngorm area, five men were killed in bed when their hut was struck by an avalanche. In 1804 five soldiers out of seven returning to Abernethy from their barracks in Edinburgh died of exposure in the Lairig an Laoigh.

'Exposure' is a frequent cause of death in these mountains. To be more specific, the word implies demoralisation, exhaustion and hypothermia. Snow, rain, low temperatures are all contributors, with the wind a multiplying factor. Add these to inadequate clothing and inexperience and it can be a lethal combination.

In November 1971 two parties of children from Ainslie Park School in Edinburgh set out with their leaders from Lagganlia Outdoor Centre. One of the parties consisted of six children at 15 years old with two instructors, Cathy Davidson and Sheila Sutherland, who were not much older. Making a relatively late start they drove to the high car park on Cairngorm and from there took the chairlift close to the top of the Cairngorm Plateau. Intent on reaching the Curran Bothy near Ben MacDhui, they had a long distance on the Cairngorm Plateau to traverse in what soon became nightmare conditions, so bad they failed to reach their destination. Their companion party did reach the Curran and must have spent an anxious time of waiting and hoping that their friends would appear. When the weather relented sufficiently this other party returned to Lagganlia and, finding their friends overdue, raised the alarm. By this time the missing party had been outside for two nights and a day.

The Cairngorm, Glenmore Lodge, RAF and Braemar Rescue Teams were turned out, as was Grampian Police. The Teams went through their procedures, but conditions made the search almost impossible. The group was eventually located from above when a helicopter crew was at last able to take advantage of a break in the weather. Cathy Davidson and one of the boys had set out from where the rest of the party were now buried in snow. Cathy was soon reduced to crawling on her hands and knees and it was her bright orange jacket that called the crew's attention. By the time the rescuers reached her she was barely able to speak but managed to point the way to her charges. Once again, the rescuers went through their procedures, this time applying first aid and doing what they could to warm the casualties until the helicopter could lift them away.

The decisions and events of the day were analysed and reanalysed. The parties had started out late, leaving them less time to adapt and readjust their plans as they travelled. On a short winter day the economy of time was a particularly decisive factor. By using the chairlift they were deprived of the benefits of a long walk in, loosening joints and getting into their stride. There was little opportunity for an assessment of the conditions against the strength of the group before they stepped onto the plateau and into the blizzard.

Sometimes, the bravest decision is to turn back, to leave the adventure for another day, to write off the time and expense of reaching the tipping point. On this day the group continued, eventually becoming disoriented and misplaced. Demoralisation, exhaustion and hypothermia naturally followed. On the hill or later in hospital Sheila Sutherland and five children died. It was the worst disaster in Scottish mountaineering history.

The scale of the losses sent a shock wave through the wider public who had, for the most part, not understood that a disaster of this magnitude could occur on home shores, especially within the education system. An inquiry was instigated into what became known as the Cairngorm Plateau Disaster that had a profound effect on outdoor activities in the UK. Purposes and methods were re-evaluated, training methods and certification schemes tightened. Very few voices were raised in favour of ending such activities. The values and skills to be developed in the same difficult, exquisite environment were understood and appreciated, but safety on the hills, and training, were recognised as having to attain a new level of thoroughness and sophistication. The Mountain Rescue Teams and their associates also re-examined their methods and procedures, as well as their resources.

No rescuer ever rushes to judgement, far less blame. Everyone involved knows that under different circumstances, in different times, it could have been them. There is always a back story, a combination of circumstances, history, decisions made by others, character. It is true of the mountain itself, whose story goes back into geological time, of the casualties and the strings of decision and coincidence that bring them to grief, and it is true of the rescuers.

ONE

The German air crews who flew across these islands in 1942 looked down on a blacked out land, trusting in their navigation systems and whatever natural features moon and starlight might pick out. Those on their way to bomb the River Clyde, the fading Empire's great factory of shipbuilding and marine engineering, will have looked to the north and the sparsely populated land of the Highlands. They will have picked out the relatively low hills of the Trossachs, the more rugged terrain around Loch Lomond, on a particularly bright night the higher hills to the north, Ben Nevis and the Grey Corries, the Cairngorms, all of them white in the longer, colder winters of the time. Much lower in height than their own Tyrol and German Alps they were, and remain, a unique landscape that once seen is never forgotten.

The bombs they discharged shattered much of the city of Glasgow, and the adjacent, shipbuilding town of Clydebank was substantially destroyed. Only a few miles away, in Knightswood, on one occasion a bomb exploded close to our home and our doors and windows were blown out, but we were more fortunate than many. It was there, at home as was customary at the time, that I was born, on the dining table according to family lore. I was the baby in a family of three children and always our mother's favourite, or so I believed.

My sister, Helen, was seven years old and my brother, Bill, two. Our home was a two-bedroom, semi-detached Council house and we considered ourselves privileged to live in it. In our early years all three children shared one bedroom while our parents had the other. When the sirens sounded we took refuge in an Anderson hut in the garden, our family bomb shelter.

My father, Duncan, was 34 when I was born and my mother, Mary, 32. My mother gave up her job on marrying, again as was customary at the time, and I believe we children benefited, relying on her constant presence, and her discipline.

She had been a secretary with the Prison Service in Barlinnie, Glasgow's largest jail, where some of Scotland's most dangerous criminals were incarcerated, and Helen and I still treasure a photograph of her from the 1930s, taken with the uniformed staff. A tiny woman in comparison to all those huge, uniformed men, it was through her we learned respect for our elders and the police, for authority, and our wilder tendencies were kept in check. Nowadays my son, Michael, and his partner, for reasons entirely of their own, have elected to raise their children in the same way and I have to say I am impressed by my grandchildren's attitudes and behaviour.

Time moves us all on. I lean on the fence around our office in Kingussie, looking across the shinty pitch and the fields, across the River Spey to the Cairngorm Mountains and understand that memory must be more than a vehicle for nostalgia, but when I think of my grandchildren I naturally think of the many changes that have occurred since I was their age. Computer games and television, DVDs and downloads mean that many children remain indoors or only venture out under conditions of close supervision. This means that the values and challenges of the outdoors are at an even greater premium. Change has also occurred on the planet itself.

I begin this book one February in the early years of the twenty-first century. My office is a box-like building close to the railway station from which, for many years my wife, Anne, and I used to manage our community pharmacies located around the Eastern Highlands, to organise goods and staff, and as a store for some of our stock and equipment.

When we arrived in 1970 it was to manage two pharmacies. By

dint of hard work and good business practice we not only achieved ownership but increased the number of shops to six. The hills were white with snow in the winters of our early years in Strathspey, and the stream beside the road, the Gynack, was frozen and silent. Today it runs freely and noisily. It is a joy to hear but it also signals climate change that will serve us all much for the worse in time.

Visitor numbers to the area increase steadily as do the number of accidents on what is a beautiful but dangerous terrain. The standard of 'readiness' for the hills grows greater but increased numbers and a wider range of user ambitions, such as ice climbing, skiing and snowboarding, endurance walking, hill-running and Award schemes ensure that accidents are not long between. The mountains are now part of the vast Cairngorm National Park and may soon be recognised as a UNESCO World Heritage Site, concepts that were unknown in the immediate post-war years when my father worked as a shipping clerk with William Sloan and Company of Glasgow.

Sloan's ran a fleet of small cargo ships that traded around the British coast. Named after Scottish rivers such as the Beauly and the Findhorn they travelled to Belfast, Swansea, Bristol, trading with all the seaboard cities. It was Dad's job to arrange for cargos in each port so that the boat never travelled empty, and sometimes, when school holidays permitted, I was allowed to travel with him. Always treated as a favourite I was shown round the engine rooms and taken onto the bridge to hold the wheel and sometimes pull a lever. I spent very little time indoors when not studying and all of my primary school years seem in memory to have been given over to football. Only two years older than I, my brother, William, always known as Bill, was my best friend and we remained close all of his life. Helen, seven years older, lived a rather different life. She had, and still has, a love and gift for music, particularly singing, inherited from our grandfather who sang with the Glasgow Orpheus Choir.

Bill and I joined the Boys Brigade and Helen joined a number of choirs. Our parents were religious and we accompanied them to church. Each Sunday morning we would make the two-mile journey to the Church of Scotland at Anniesland Cross, usually by bus or tram, sometimes walking. I would go as often as three times, to morning service, Sunday school in the afternoon and Youth Fellowship in the evening. Religious attendance and belief at that time were unquestioned.

I began attending what was known as the Tent Hall, an Evangelist centre, and was struck by the sense of 'life lived fully and joyously'. People attended as a pleasure, not a duty and it was their 'place to go' on a Saturday night. Not only that, the duty of charity was taken seriously, and down and out men, of whom there were many in those years, would come in for soup and sandwiches. I was very moved by their plight and felt that I must do something for them but could not bring myself to do so directly. Instead I would buy bars of chocolate with the money I earned from my various jobs. On my way home I would drop the bars into the litter bins that were banded to bus and tram stops in those days, knowing the men would rake around in there for what they could find. With good intentions but from a rather superior moral position that was in no way justified by knowledge and experience, I had given them food, not money which might have gone on drink.

Life has been good to me. My parents could not have envisaged the home and lifestyle my wife and I enjoy here, four-wheel drive vehicles, television, computers, my boat, the physical space we enjoy or the material wealth, any more than the partial knee replacement that has freed this latest phase of my life from much pain. Theirs is the generation on whose shoulders we stand, but we also made our own lives and, to some extent, luck.

I took on several jobs because, in those days, supplementing the family income was close to a necessity. I was able to keep some money for myself though, and since my friend Ian Young introduced me to cycling I was desperate to buy a bicycle. I took a job delivering groceries on Fridays and Saturdays and made a sort of challenge of getting three loads into the basket and so shortening the round. In time I got to know the people who gave tips and served them best. This way I usually had money on a Saturday night.

Later I took a second job selling papers. A friend had two stances and could not keep both going, so I took over, standing outside the shipyards when the workers came out and giving them the call. 'Eve-eh-ning Times! Eve-eh-ning Ci-ti-zen!'

This was even better for acquiring tips and soon I was cycling back and forth on an old bike. Soon a third job appeared selling warm bread rolls on the street corner close to the No. 9 bus terminus.

The old bike also allowed me to get away more, and further, and fed into my desire for freedom.

From the Tent Hall I joined the Scripture Union and in time was invited to attend their camp at West Linton on the east coast. This was an old army camp of Nissen huts and cement roads, left vacated after the war, and was for boys only. I asked Mum and to my delight she agreed. After that first adventure I went to a second camp run by a Church of Scotland minister, a Mr Meiklejohn, at Scoughal Bay near North Berwick. The camp was organised along more or less military lines, part of our war heritage, with competitive tent and hut inspections that we tried desperately to win. Six boys shared each tent with one put in command of the rest, ensuring they kept the place tidy and clean. We had no sleeping bags, instead gathering straw from a local farm we stuffed sacks to make hessian-covered palliasses. I loved all this, the discipline and teamwork as well as fresh air and exercise, comradeship, games.

The following year Mr Meiklejohn invited me to advance camp. This meant entering an empty field to dig the latrines, erect the marquee and in every way prepare the site. Groups arrived for two-week stays but the advance group remained for the whole six weeks. Mr Meiklejohn invited me to be quartermaster of the tuck shop and so I found myself in charge not only of Penguin biscuits and Irn Bru but also the budget. This was my first exposure to the retail trade and I carried out my duties enthusiastically and well.

Between this and my various jobs it was starting to look as if I might have a talent for business.

I came out of Tent Hall activities aged 15, still without a decent bicycle. With two friends I had been cycling further and wider, and more quickly, and my interest and hunger for touring and racing grew ever stronger. This was in contrast to school where, although I studied and did reasonably well, I had no sense of direction or purpose.

The qualification exam of that time served to separate us three children, at least in terms of education. Helen had as good a brain as either Bill or I and earned the right to attend the Girls High School of Glasgow but decided to let the opportunity pass so that she could attend the local secondary school with her friends. Many years later she would tell me that, even then, she was also aware of having two younger brothers coming along behind with attendant costs. Bill excelled and won a scholarship to the fee-paying school, Allan Glen's.

When my turn came I attained only what might be thought of as 'second prize' and a place at Hillhead High School. I had little interest or enthusiasm but my parents were keen and I arrived just too late to befriend probably the school's most famous old boy, Menzies Campbell, the future leader of the Liberal Democrat Party.

It meant a sort of severance with old friends and the establishing of new relationships and, in this sense, I suppose, was character-building. The great drawback, as far as I was concerned, was that it was a rugby playing school and I had been a footballer, player and supporter, since my father took me to see his team, Queens Park, play Clyde. He asked me, his small son, which side I would support and I told him, 'The winning side!' Clyde won and I have had a soft spot for them ever since.

At rugby my relatively short stature set me out as a scrum-half and that is the position I played most Saturday mornings. I continued to play football in the afternoons though, and whenever else I could. Looking back from the latter stages of life I understand I did not much enjoy school. Nor did I have any notion of a future. I studied so as not to let my parents down, but I did not really have purpose, nor did I have any guidance.

The Tent Hall, football, cycling and my three jobs were the meaningful parts of my life but soon the jobs had to stop. The energy and time they demanded affected school performance too much, and by now I had put enough money together to buy a fine racing bike. I started cycling to school, regarding it as training, and made a point of beating the bus and tram.

Exercise was a discipline in my life, allied as it was to ambition as a cyclist. Work, real work, was more a part of my character than study, and character has a way of asserting itself. Having given up my jobs I found I missed them, and missed the income, so I acquired another paper round. This meant getting up at 06.00 and cycling to the public baths with my friend Ian. I would swim lengths for a mile, including every so often a length under water, and then pick up the papers for my round. With the papers delivered I would cycle to Hillhead and a school career that, unsurprisingly, failed to improve.

Thinking back, the level and range of activities seems almost impossible. Strangely and without planning or intent, the development of physical stamina and business sense were preparation for later phases of my life. No one could have foreseen this, least of all my parents, from whom it seemed I was becoming estranged. They must have been at least slightly disappointed in my academic progress but, more significantly, their Christian commitment remained four-square where my 16-year indoctrination had begun to waver. Their belief in the Sabbath Day, to keep it holy, and my developing independence would soon divide us.

When I was 16 I went on a cycling and hostelling tour with three friends. In the course of Easter week we cycled, on Day One, from Glasgow to Loch Lochy near Fort William, on Day Two to Ratagan in Kintail, then on to Inveralligan in Torridon, Carbisdale in the Eastern Highlands, Inverness, finally Braemar and home. This tour amounted to several hundred miles and gave me my first close look at my country's mountains, lochs and coastline. It altered my view of the world forever and I never stopped returning.

I had become an adult but was still without ambition or direction. I guess I was a slow developer, unlike my brother and sister. Bill now attended the Royal College of Science and Technology, one of the world's great centres of engineering instruction, later to become

Strathclyde University, where he studied chemical engineering and would eventually take an honours degree, going on to a PhD.

Helen had long since left school and worked as Secretary to Willie Allan of the Scottish Football Association, but by now an important young man had entered her life. She had known George Brebner from their childhood at Sunday school, but when they joined the Church Badminton Club something clicked between the shuttlecocks. Her membership of the Scottish National Orchestra Chorus (later to be named the Royal Scottish National Orchestra Chorus) led to working in the Orchestra's administration department which, in turn, led to her becoming personal assistant to their conductor, Sir Alexander Gibson, working from an office in his home. The Brebners and the Gibson family became good friends and, in time, I was introduced to Sir Alex and also became a friend.

At the time I felt I could do no better than concentrate on racing and time trials and keeping myself at the peak of physical condition. Differences with my parents grew greater. I retained their Christian values but eschewed their disciplines and doctrine. Much of my cycling took place on Sundays. I could neither disappoint them nor obey and found myself lying to them instead. I would invent excuses to be away so that I could continue in secret. It was a sad development but a necessary one. By acting in this way there were no truly harsh words between us. Nothing was said that could not be retracted and nothing done that could not be healed.

My time at school was coming to an end. I was physically and mentally strong but directionless and confused. Fortunately, change was coming. I stand now in Kingussie looking at the Cairngorms and listening for the next train. That will do as a sort of metaphor. It had all been preparation for what was on the way.

TWO

The geese that fly over Strathspey have always carried messages to human beings. Deeply embedded in our understanding of the world they speak of return, reliability, faith. Their image was absorbed into the Celtic church and can be found as ancient stone carvings and in stylised, illuminated form in the Book of Kells. If one is shot it can be heard calling to its comrades as it falls and they can be heard calling back, but they continue, holding to their formation. In those last years of my school life the children who would die in the Cairngorm Plateau Disaster were being born. Their lives would be lived in some way parallel to my own although we would never meet, yet their early deaths would change the direction of my life.

At that time, when I was at the age when they would die, I was still without purpose. A slow developer socially and academically I still raced, but I had come to prefer touring and regularly covered prodigious distances. On one occasion I cycled from Knightswood to Oban and back in a day. I visited Skye for the first time and here, in Strathspey, had my first, awestruck look at these great mountains, the Cairngorms. Between these activities, my jobs, and a general lack of interest in studies, I did less well at school than I should. Exam results meant university was out of the question.

I left school at 18 without a job, a situation that could not continue for the most practical of family financial reasons. Bill was doing well at Strathclyde and Helen was set fair in life, but I had no ambitions beyond the day until I read an advertisement that proved to be fateful. Boots, the giant High Street chemist, was looking for counter staff. I was interviewed by the area manager and taken on as a shop assistant with the vague notion that I might become an unqualified dispenser.

Soon a new shop was to be opened in Drumchapel, near our home, but at first I was sent to the St George's Cross branch. There I stacked shelves, dusted, moved things around. My experience of advance camp helped as I was not afraid to tackle any task, however menial. I met shopfitters shop-fitters for the first time and assisted them in their work, experience that would stand me in good stead here in Kingussie.

In the new shop I was put in charge of 'Pets and Gardens' where I built in my own systems and procedures. I must have impressed the store manager because he soon extended my small empire to include 'Photographic'. This suited me very well because photography had already entered my touring life. We worked a five-and-a-half-day week with Sundays off and a half-day on Tuesday.

Eddie Brown, the pharmacist in charge, recommended I take an internal course in dispensing. Eddie must have seen something more in me because he invited me into his office to 'give me a hand'. Soon I was helping him balance the daily and weekly ledgers, important work that required thoroughness and accuracy.

It was from Eddie I learned the importance of delegation and the management skills necessary to remain in touch with the shop floor. Whenever errors happened I would call him in and he would clear my mess without rancour or temperament before returning to his rounds. He was always calm, always steady, and mostly seemed unoccupied. When I asked him how he got such a job he told me he was a qualified pharmacist and if I wanted to enjoy a life like his I must become one too. I still had not thought of a career and this advice sounded as good as any.

Two years had passed since leaving school and I was already much changed from my directionless youth. Working at Boots had not only brought me focus but also made me something of a company man. I went to night school and took the qualifications that would allow me to apply for university. That achieved, I looked around for a university that would take me into its pharmaceutical course but did so without great enthusiasm. The outdoors remained my heartland, and pharmacy's challenges seemed, at that time, to be entirely in-store and behind a counter. Against that, a Boots career offered steady income, and I had great liking and respect for the men I worked for.

Unknown to me, and against the grain of all my thinking, someone was about to enter my life who would bring still more change. Helen had been president of our church's Youth Fellowship and Bill had followed in her footsteps. My own faith had waned, but church involvement continued and in due course I too became president. There I met a young woman named Marjory Millar who picked me out as a likely boyfriend for her sister, Anne. How any woman can predict and engineer such a match will forever be a mystery but when Anne began to attend she took my eye. She was younger than I by a few years, slim, very attractive and bright. I took an immediate shine but she had already attracted a good deal of male interest and it was clear I would have to move quickly. Before long we were going steady.

In those days we did not go to pubs as is normal now. Life was more constrained by lack of money and space, and we had no car. We went to the cinema a lot, and to cafes, and soon I had to take her into consideration when thinking about the future. By this time I felt a strong need to get away from home and when Heriot Watt University in Edinburgh offered me a place I accepted. It meant being away from Anne through the week but I would be home at weekends and there were long holidays to look forward to.

At the end of First Year I came home for the summer, keen on earning some money. My cycling friend, Ian Young, told me of labouring work that was available in Glen Fruin. I had cycled there as part of the Three Lochs Route and was familiar with and greatly appreciative of the landscape. By now the nuclear age had arrived and bunkers were being created at Faslane for the storage of Polaris missiles, the nuclear arsenal that was already hotly contested by

CND in marches and demonstrations. The construction site would be no easy billet but I had already decided to avoid any comfortable indoor job in favour of a wider experience.

Ian advised where the site buses uplifted the workers in the mornings. All that was necessary was to turn up on time and all the rest would fall into place. I arrived at the appointed location at 06.30 and climbed aboard for the one-and-a-half-hour journey to a Glen Fruin that was utterly changed. The tree-covered hillside and narrow country roads were destroyed and where once there had been streams there were now underground culverts. Rustling leaves and birdsong had been replaced by the roar of machinery and the cries of working men.

I checked in at the site office where the foreman assigned me to a labouring gang and the toughest physical labour I would carry out in my life. I was given a pneumatic jackhammer so heavy I could hardly lift it, and sent down into a deep, rocky excavation. There I toiled, raising the hammer to the wall or forcing it into the ground, gunning the machine so that my whole body shook and the noise was deafening. In the days before the Health and Safety at Work Act we had no ear protectors and I sometimes wonder if the hardness of hearing I suffer today dates back to the hammering my eardrums took then.

Rock and compacted earth, once loosened and broken, had to be shovelled up and out of the excavation. At the end of the first day I was shattered. With pain in my back and across my shoulders, and in my thighs which had acted as shock absorbers, I had never endured such agony, but was determined not to give in and continued to work as hard as I could. The shift ran from 08.00 to 18.30. This, combined with the journey to and from the site, meant I had neither time nor energy for any other activity.

It was a life of work and sleep, and my plans for more time spent with Anne foundered on the necessity of income. She did not waver though and it became more apparent than ever that we were committed to each other.

I drilled and dug all week, not realising how out of step I was until one day we were sent to unload and stack heavy bags of cement. I was giving the task all I had, as usual, when one of the other labourers hissed at me, 'Slow down!' The more experienced men knew the value of pacing themselves where I had been surviving on youth and fitness. I was also breaking the team by forging out on my own. It was another lesson learned.

Many of the men I worked with were former convicts. They had no great future and would naturally gravitate to whatever work paid the most in the short term. Their only lawful talents amounted to the speedy resolution of the *Daily Record* crossword and the strength of their backs. At that time a wage of £100 a week was exceptional, but the work was hard and relentless. To tackle it over a lifetime, rather than my limited holiday period, must be soul-destroying. For me though, the limited ten-week period was invaluable, widening my experience of human nature. It also made me more appreciative of my advantages, and more determined to succeed.

The following year I took another job on a building site, the construction of high flats in Maryhill, starting as tea boy, and later clearing the completed flats of debris, hurling broken loos down into refuse skips far below. It was hard enough work but, in comparison with Glen Fruin, not back breaking.

By 1966, the year before my graduation, Anne and I decided to marry, and within the year our daughter Joanne was born. Anne found a garden flat on the outskirts of Edinburgh's New Town and there, while she was nursing Joanne, I completed my studies. Boots, to whom I was still indentured, provided a loan and our Bank provided the rest. We were saddled with debt, but life had meaning and purpose at last.

Looking back from retirement I recognise those final years as a student as among the best of my life. The two years I had taken out of the system had provided a grounding that students who arrived straight from school did not have. Beside this, work in construction had hardened me physically and mentally. Now I found I was ready to take on responsibilities and to thrive with them, to live life to the full in ways I would not have thought possible.

In 1967 I took my Diploma in Pharmaceutical Chemistry, just a few months after my father had died of a heart attack on New Year's Day. Our son, Michael, arrived the following April. Sadly, my mother's health deteriorated when she contracted osteoporosis.

I returned to Boots, as I had promised, served the year of post-graduate training that was necessary to finalise my professional status and, on 18th July 1968, received the certificate that hangs on the wall of my office to this day. I was still very much the company man, but understood that promotion depended greatly on the filling of dead men's shoes. In my post-graduate year I worked in the dispensary of the huge Shandwick Place branch, in the West End of Edinburgh, and as was usual in any period of traineeship, was given a project to pursue. I was asked to redesign my area, which was considered to be inefficient. I asked my brother-in-law, James Robertson, husband of Anne's other sister Elisabeth, to help me. James was a draughtsman and between us we produced an excellent scheme which I submitted. To my surprise no acknowledgement was made either by the area manager or head office. When I was fully qualified I worked as a relief manager throughout Edinburgh while I also worked as a pharmacist at Shandwick Place. Later still, my refit scheme was used without reference or credit to me and, at about the same time, a post came up in Campbeltown for which I was not considered.

I was a restless man when I noticed an advert in the *Pharmaceutical Journal* in 1969. A Mrs Buchanan in Kingussie was looking for a manager for her shop there.

There was nothing to lose but my security so I applied, and very soon found myself at an excellent lunch not only with Mrs Buchanan in her beautiful Highland villa but also with her lawyer and accountant. It would be an understatement to say I was overwhelmed but more was to come. Mrs Buchanan, a woman in her sixties, had been widowed a few years before and had to run not just one, but three pharmacies in Kingussie, Newtonmore and Aviemore. It had become too much and she had recently sold the Aviemore shop. Now she wanted a partner to buy in to the business and manage the remaining two.

This was beyond our aspirations. We had no capital and owned nothing but our heavily mortgaged flat. For another thing, the security that Boots offered, and the pension, represented a safety net I was reluctant to give up however dissatisfied I felt. Back in Edinburgh I discussed it with Anne to find she was happy to go along with whatever decision I made.

I took this sense of solidarity to our Bank manager and between us we gave the matter a good airing, with me feeling very much the 'wee lad with no money'. To my surprise he was insistent that we should go ahead. The Bank would repay Boots' share of the loan, and such money as we could realise would be put into the new business. He put me in touch with a firm of lawyers who could act for me.

Among much else we agreed with Mrs Buchanan's advisors that I could buy out the business at its then value if at any time I could afford it. Such a development seemed unlikely and I entered the agreement with no great hopes for the future, but a great deal of determination. I moved into digs in Kingussie in January 1970 while Anne remained in Edinburgh to sell the flat. Then all four of us moved into a holiday cottage for the remainder of the winter months.

As a pharmacist I was considered to be an essential worker and so would qualify for a Council house. Anne and I would have preferred to own our own home, but the most important thing was that we were together again as a family. In dealing with housing matters we met Martin Robertson, the tall Town Clerk who was about my own age and would become one of our greatest friends.

The shops' turnover and profit were steadily improving when a stone built villa in Kingussie came onto the market. The Council, with Martin assisting, offered a 100 per cent loan with a high, but fixed, interest rate. Wary of the debt we agreed a price and, as so often, fortune favoured hard work and preparation. The country was struck by inflation and what had seemed a high interest rate became quite moderate. In a period of inflation the house value also soared. We were making friends, making a new life and soon felt wholly committed to the area and to the business.

Now all my experience of creating systems and procedures, begun at advance camp with the Scripture Union, advanced in the early years with Boots, and later during my post-graduate period, and my experience on the building sites, all came together to a single end, the success of these two pharmacies. In fact their improvement was speedier and greater than I had dared to hope. Once again I discussed matters with Anne and, this time, took the company's improved figures to my Bank manager in Edinburgh.

We had decided we would buy Mrs Buchanan out if we could, as had been agreed. He looked at the figures, adjusted his spectacles and asked how much we wanted. In no time the business was ours and we were working entirely towards a future of our own and for our children. With this incentive Anne applied herself to the company's financial administration and we became full business, as well as life, partners.

We were now set fair for the future but it had not all been plain sailing. In November 1971 Anne had to go into Raigmore Hospital in Inverness for an operation. At that time Raigmore was little more than a collection of old army huts adapted as best as possible, and not the advanced centre of medical excellence it is today. Even now no surgical operation can be taken for granted, and the state of the hospital at the time did not inspire confidence. Nor did the road I had to travel with the two children to visit her.

It was snowing heavily and I was perhaps too impatient. By the time we reached the Slochd summit, the exposed high point on the A9 above Inverness, visibility was down to a few metres as the snowfall continually defeated the windscreen wipers. Suddenly the wheels lost traction, spun wildly and we found ourselves in the ditch. Making sure the children were safe, I stepped into the biting wind where big flakes of snow quickly covered my jacket and froze while our vehicle tracks filled behind us. I recall my sense of wonder at the depth of cold and thinking how much worse conditions must be on the mountain tops.

When a Royal Navy Land Rover happened along the crew kindly stopped and attached a rope to our car, hauling us out of the ditch and straightening us. We continued to Raigmore to find Anne comfortable and looking forward to coming home. Next day she watched from her ward window as a Rescue helicopter ferried in the only two survivors from the Cairngorm Plateau Disaster.

THREE

At the head of the Kyle of Tongue in the North West Highlands stands one of the world's most beautiful mountains, which is also one of its great viewpoints.

Ben Loyal has several tops that project almost like a goat's horns around the summit. It is not high, at 764m falling well short of Munro status. The mountains of West Sutherland, all unique and fascinating sculptures, range across the landward sides. To the north though, the observer looks down the long stretch of the Kyle to a cluster of rocky islands inhabited only by seals.

The land slopes steeply up from the shore to the village of Tongue, a brief scattering of dwellings with, immediately below, farms, grazing sheep, cattle, here and there some patient horses. When the tide is out it leaves the Kyle more or less dry, a sandy feeding ground for wading birds. When in, its waters take the colour of the sky at that moment, the whole picture painted in a rich palette of greens, blues and browns.

I was in my teens and cycling round the country with my pal, Dougie. More interested in speed than scenery I would sometimes stop to look around. I had already climbed Ben Hope from the road. Now I stood on the summit of Ben Loyal. My motivation was simple:, to see what was there. At that time I had little in the way of equipment but well-founded confidence in my own physical fitness. I had no map other than my road map, no compass, and would have had no idea how to use them had they suddenly appeared in my hands.

From the roadside I had launched myself directly, almost frivolously, for the summit wearing my vest and shorts, my feet protected only by the flimsiest of cycling shoes. By the time I reached the cairn they were almost destroyed. My eye took the scene in and inside me it remained as memory; never, in fact, to be forgotten. I descended and continued to Durness and the south, my first experience of hillwalking completed.

In December 1971 I was still finding my feet as a pharmacist, creating the procedures that would serve the business well over the years. Anne and I were thoroughly established in our relationship, the parents of two healthy and delightful children, and like me she was finding her place in life. At that time our confidence in the world of business was only at its beginning and we had no idea of the sort of decisions that lay ahead. Decisions such as how much time to commit, 'work' against 'whole life', and how much material gain is 'enough'?

I knew I missed the exercise and challenges of my earlier life but I was also enjoying new friendships. Late in 1971 I had read a short article in the local paper. The Mountain Rescue Team was seeking new members. If anyone living in the area was interested now was the time. I called Martin and we agreed that this might be for us. I had written to the Secretary and now we were invited to attend a meeting in Aviemore Police Station, just a few miles along the A9 from Kingussie.

On Tuesday 14th December we went along to the station, upstairs to the recreation hall, where chairs had been laid before an impromptu stage, to take our places among a crowd of about 70.

Committee member Dr Neil MacDonald, a local GP and coming to the end of his period of Chairmanship, placed the mountain rescue effort in a regional context and outlined its history and structure. We learned that the local Mountain Rescue Service had two parts, as it still has, the Association and the Team itself, founded together in 1963. The Association had 12 committee members, two of whom were the Team Leader and Depute. The rest was made up of local people with an interest in the mountains and the Mountain

Rescue Team. It was their place to raise money, form policies and liaise on the needs of the members.

For many practical reasons the police are heavily involved in mountain rescue. Sgt Ian Boa, the policeman then responsible for mountain rescue in Aviemore, went on to discuss the Team's workings and methods, outlining the day-to-day matters that would soon occupy so much of Martin's life and mine. The Team itself consisted of many members but was presently at a lower than healthy level. Only after our early rescues did we properly understand why so many members are required. In addition to mountain rescues its activities included searching for lost children and dealing with attempted suicides. It is surprising how many people choose to take their lives in beautiful and remote places, almost in defiance of their life-enhancing qualities. In those colder winters people often had to be rescued from cars stuck in snowdrifts on the A9.

Its area included the Great Moss and Cairngorm Plateau, but not the easternmost plateau, and also included the Drumochter and Ben Alder hills, and the Monadhliaths all the way south to the Creag Meagaidh group where the Lochaber Team took over. It was and remains a formidable landscape.

The Team Leader at the time was Alistair McCook, a press photographer, and his Depute was Mollie Porter, a professional mountaineer who had climbed in many challenging and remote parts of the world as well as spending time in the Antarctic. In time I developed an enormous respect for both. Mollie is the wife of Jo Porter of the Countryside Commission and together they are a tremendous outdoor couple. She was particularly expert and particularly fit. In the coming years I would often walk uphill beside her while she talked easily, self-possessed and in complete command of her breathing, while I desperately gulped in air, unable to answer as we climbed.

At the end of the evening we were invited to think about whether we were interested in joining and, if so, a training programme would be devised in which we would be invited to participate. Martin and I were very decidedly interested.

Early one Sunday in January 1972 we met as a large party in the Coire Cas car park on Cairngorm, the same car park the Ainslie Park group had set out from the previous November. Winter still had its grip on the land, even down below, but at this level it was diamond hard. Snow lay all around and the burn was frozen and silent. I wore a duvet jacket more suitable for lower levels and a pair of jeans, and my footwear was woefully inadequate. My rucksack was a small thing, suitable for carrying sandwiches and little else. Martin was dressed similarly. Neither of us carried map or compass or had any idea how to use them. Our one piece of effective forethought was to bring plastic sheeting to wrap around our trouser bottoms and boots.

Alistair and Mollie assessed the volunteers and divided us into two groups, those with some experience and, the rest, the absolute newcomers. Mollie led the more experienced party around the Cairngorm–Cairn Lochain ridge. As an experienced Leader she would have eased up for their benefit and very few would have realised the standard of fitness she maintained as she led them onto the heights and around the rim of the Northern Corries before descending again at Cairn Lochain. On such days the view from these heights can change lives.

Alistair led us along the path the others would eventually return by. This meant we could look into Coire Cas and Coire an t-Sneachda before rounding into Coire an Lochain. It was a high-pressure day of long views and great clarity. The snow was relatively dry after we left the car park but it would slip down into our boots and melt there, soaking our feet. Martin and I would stop to adjust our plastic leggings and at the same time note Alistair's proper, well-fitted gaiters, and how they worked to keep his boots and socks dry.

That led to further examination of his equipment. He wore a sophisticated cagoule, and used a rucksack with a comfortable carrying system. Much of the body's heat is lost through the top of the head so he used a cosy balaclava rolled up and tucked over his ears. When the wind picked up he rolled it down to protect his face. When the glare from the snow increased Alistair put on his sunglasses and we realised they were a necessity at this level, not a style statement.

He carried three pairs of gloves: a lightweight pair that allowed him the use of his fingers. Over these he wore woollen mittens impregnated with oil against damp, an intense insulation. If conditions should become more extreme he carried stormproof gauntlets he could pull over the whole arrangement. Protection of his body core was built up in layers of vest, shirt, pullover, stormproof jacket. Soon the arrival of Gore-tex and other modern materials would serve to lessen bulk and weight but, at that time, they were not foreseen by many climbers.

This great contrast with our own equipment exercised Martin's thinking and mine as we walked, but not so much as Alistair's use of map and compass. He had carefully folded his map to show the area we were walking in and encased it in a clear plastic holder. Only later did I learn that a single outing in bad weather can destroy an expensive map, and that a sodden map is unusable on the hill. Every so often he would take out his compass and apply it to the map. Since it was a fine day and he certainly knew the area like the back of his hand Alistair's purpose must have been demonstration.

For Martin and me the message went home. By these means, and with developed skills, you can find your way around on the hill. You can find your way back in low, or even no, visibility. You can always know where you are. You can be not only safe but comfortable.

Under his leadership we rounded into Coire an Lochain, past the shelter known as Jean's Hut to the cliffs. Neither of us had seen anything like this before. The shelter was a crude wooden structure with a corrugated iron roof held in place against the wind by wire ropes attached to bolts concreted into the rock. All around was white. High above us the snow stood out from the corrie rim in slender, fluted cornices. Mollie would keep her charges well away from it, Alistair told us, or they might fall through and we would have surprise visitors.

We broke out our flasks and sandwiches and sat for a while

beside the frozen lochan, in the white but looking across Strathspey to the Monadhliaths, along the River Spey and down to the villages and towns. It was an exhilarating and moving experience, and its effect, against the effect of Ben Loyal so many years before, marked how I had travelled as a man. It seemed I had changed. I found I wanted not only to be part of all this, but also to contribute.

We had no crampons or ice axes, and would not have known how to use them, so continuing onto steep ground was out of the question. As we returned to the car park I resolved to equip myself properly and learn all I could of the ways of the mountain.

Even then I did not think of mountain rescue as heroic or dangerous or anything more than a job that must be done. In fact, later experience would tell me that mountain rescue is remarkably safe. In the many call-outs across the Scottish Highlands in my time I only know of two fatalities among rescuers. On 1st February 1987 Harry Lawrie of the Killin Team was thrown from a crashing helicopter on Ben Ledi. On another occasion Phil Jones, Leader of the Assynt Team, struck his head against a rock in a training accident. Both were fine men and their deaths were tragedies, but this low number of fatalities considered against the high number of call-outs represents a good safety record.

Safety and learning were in the organisers' minds from the outset. Regular meetings were held on Thursday nights in Aviemore Police Station where the tutors and guides from Glenmore Lodge taught us navigation and first aid, explaining that the masterclass can only be given on the hill. Glenmore Lodge was already deeply embedded in the mountain rescue scene. Fred Harper, the Principal at that time, was often first to be notified of an event, and a first decision on whether the Lodge tutors should attend or the Team called out was made by him.

Doctors lectured on more complex health matters and we were introduced to the other professionals whose interests overlapped with ours: the ambulance service, Air-Sea Rescue, the police. Given our part-time, amateur status the period of training was intense but, of the 70 or so who attended that first meeting, 47 continued into actual rescues.

In fact we were expected to participate early in the training process without being asked to perform any task that might have been beyond us. Our first call-out, Martin's and mine, was to the Creag Meagaidh range but since it speaks strongly of Mollie Porter I will leave it until the next chapter. The first call-out to a fatal accident came in late summer.

A 20-year-old man from Greenock had been climbing the Citadel on Shelter Stone Crag with a companion when he fell for almost a full rope length. He was wearing a hard hat but the blow against the crag at the extent of the rope, where he swung uncontrollably, cost him his life.

The two men had been climbing the prescribed route, the leader hammering in pegs as they went, passing the rope through each one to ensure a shorter, survivable fall should he come off. Under those circumstances it is vital that the lower man keeps the rope tight at the belay, and equally vital that the leader puts in a sound peg every time. In this case it seemed he had probably failed to properly secure the last peg before he came off, the pegs below were put under too great a strain by his descending body mass and popped out one by one as he fell. Whatever happened, the survivor was stranded at his position unsure of his friend's fate and unable to move. Other climbers in the area made the journey over Cairngorm to telephone Aviemore Police for help.

I was called out and asked to take the Team's Bantam radio up onto the plateau to a position above Stag Rocks where I could look down on the rescuers and report back to the Lodge. This way the arrival of the ambulance could be timed and I could also report on any other occurrence or setback. The Bantam was considered to be small at the time, but now would be looked on as quite a monster. It had a 15cm square box to contain its battery, a long whisker-like aerial and a handset sized like a telephone of the time. I carried it up over Cairngorm and across the plateau to a hollow above Stag Rocks where I could look down into the deep trench of Glen Avon, the moonlit loch and the cliffs with their many climbing routes.

From here I watched the rescuers abseil down to the body, secure their positions and lower it down into the glen. When they were down the rescuers and some others volunteers put the body into a bag and strapped it to a stretcher. As they carried it round the head of the loch to Coire Domhain and the rough path that leads onto Cairngorm I radioed a progress report to Glenmore Lodge. I met the party when it reached the top and assisted with the remaining carry.

The Team was still short-handed when another fatality occurred in Coire an Lochain, the same winter wonderland we had walked into with Alistair McCook. A party had gone in to attempt an ice climb called The Vent that started close to where we had sat looking across Strathspey. From here the ground sloped steeply up to the bottom of the cliff and the start of the technical climb leading up onto the plateau.

At this point they would naturally pause to take their technical equipment from their rucksacks and put it on. This would mean adjusting crampons, putting on hard hats and warm clothing. They would have to step into their harnesses and rope themselves together before they made their start. Stepping into a harness means taking one boot off the ground, and at that stage a young woman lost her footing and fell, sliding down the steep slope for about 200m, unable to control her descent without her ice axe, picking up speed. At some point she struck her head on a rock and the likelihood, since she was wearing a hard hat, is that her neck was broken.

Through the series of lectures we were attending, as well as walks and conversations with more experienced rescuers, more than ever with these early experiences, the realities of mountain rescue were becoming apparent. Among the first realised was how much time an operation might take, and how long a casualty might have to wait on the hill. When an accident occurred a companion had, first, to recognise that help was required and then, in the days before mobile phones, undertake the journey back. This in itself might take hours with the rescuers' involvement starting late in the day, removing themselves from whatever they were doing to assemble at their agreed point. This time it was the Coire Cas car park.

Twenty-five of us gathered around one of our McInnes stretchers before setting out for Coire an Lochain, a journey of between one and a half and two hours. On the return journey we were to learn the reason for this high number and come to appreciate the value of leadership.

The young woman's body lay close to the lochan. It was not a terrible sight as these findings can sometimes be. On this occasion there was no visible injury, but a doctor had already diagnosed her as dead. Her companions were close by, distressed and no doubt wondering what they would say to her parents. There are many challenges around a death in the hills and informing the relatives is one of the worst. On this occasion our task was the relatively simple one of removing the remains.

I found I could handle the body with calm. There was a job to be done and the first part fell to Martin and me. We had an orange bivvy bag, that is to say a body-length bag of strong plastic, coloured to be easily picked out in snow. We slipped the open end under her legs and moved it upwards, folding her arms inside, pulling the plastic up around her head and tying it. I had no strong emotions. It was a necessary task, nothing more. There was to be no midnight reaction, no nightmares. Neither Martin nor I felt any need to discuss it at length, far less pour our hearts out. We did the job and between us placed the bag onto the stretcher and tied it in place.

In those days the Team possessed two McInnes stretchers, invented by the great mountaineer and rescuer in Glencoe, Hamish McInnes. It came in two parts with telescopic poles, used as handles that fitted together with the support canvas attached. To comfortably carry a mountain rescue stretcher in winter conditions it takes a total of 24 people in three groups of eight. The lifts are restricted to five minutes duration. Men and women both carry; no distinction is made between the sexes. Having completed their carry, the first eight go to the rear to await their turn coming round again.

The second eight carry for their five minutes and the procedure is repeated with the third eight stepping forward.

Most important is the Team Member appointed to walk in front, lighting the way with his head torch as conditions demand, finding the best route for the carrying group, avoiding holes in the ground, noting river boulders that might be fallen over, assessing snow conditions. If the snow has a crust it can be almost impossible to walk. The foot takes a solid stance but when the weight goes on it crashes through and twisted ankles often occur. In these circumstances five minutes is a long time.

Five minutes, with pauses for personnel changes, is also a long time for the following carriers. They are required to hold their formations of eight while moving at a snail's pace. The weather might be cold, the wind blowing. They may have things to do at home or elsewhere. This combination of working, waiting and slow movement is testing, and the personality and skills of the Team Leader are crucial. A simple operation, such as that first carry out from Coire an Lochain, can take five or six hours. In fact, we were on the hill from 15.00 to 20.00 and returned home dead tired.

An ambulance was waiting at the car park to take the remains away and there we took our leave of other people's lives. Some we had spoken with briefly, others we would never meet. Bereaved parents have to contend with grief, brothers and sisters to continue their lives without a loved one. The loss of a life in the hills, especially a young life, is no slight matter, but our job was done. The next lesson was how frequently these events happen. We had two further serious incidents in the same corrie that winter.

Nine years after its founding the Team still had very little equipment. We had two stretchers and the means to lower them down vertical faces, body bags and casualty bags. We had ropes but the members were required to equip themselves. In 1972 Alistair retired and Mollie took over. It had taken a great effort for the Cairngorm Mountain Rescue Association to advance to this point, but now the whole aspect of funding and improvement had to be examined.

Progress had to be maintained and there was, perhaps, an amateur mindset to be overcome. Indeed, the whole argument of approach – professional or amateur in all their ramifications – would be addressed through the coming years. Meanwhile new and better equipment became ever more necessary.

FOUR

Cruise passengers in the Antarctic these past few years may have found themselves in conversation with a slim, very fit-looking woman with an immense store of outdoor tales. Her knowledge is founded on experience as much as reading, her enthusiasm fired by love of wild places. Like a good writer she chooses her words with care, her voice coloured by the accents of her native Hertfordshire and the soft tones of Strathspey.

Fascinating as she is on the subject of the Antarctic she might as comfortably speak of the Andes, North America, the High Arctic or the Cairngorms. She might also have mentioned the Cairngorm Mountain Rescue Team. Almost certainly she will not have mentioned her own central role in its development. Mollie Porter would be too modest for that but, supported by her husband John, known as Jo, she gave a substantial part of her life at a crucial time to ensure its survival and promote its effectiveness.

The Team was founded on 1st April 1963 with an initial £1,000 that had been raised locally – the April Fool date has not gone without remark over the years. The first leader was Tommy Paul, the second Peter Bruce, the third Alistair McCook, with an average duration of three years each. Mollie and Jo moved into the area in 1962 to work as instructors at Glenmore Lodge. Through the following years both Jo and Mollie were members of the British Antarctic Survey. After his last summer on South Georgia, Jo joined the Countryside Commission for Scotland.

They entered the Cairngorm Mountain Rescue Association and

the Team together and the ever-industrious Mollie soon became Secretary of one and Depute Leader of the other. From her earliest days she understood the need to improve the quality of both equipment and expertise and recognised the requirement to raise funds. Some others on the Association also recognised these things but the constraints of amateurism, meaning the more urgent demands of family and work, must have limited their efforts.

Mollie gave herself to it wholly, writing no fewer than 59 funding request letters to Highland businesses in a single posting. These had some success, but a larger and steadier income was necessary. Different methods had to be devised. Her greatest talents would always be on the hill so additional willing and able hands were required. It was to Mollie I addressed my letter of interest. Later she told me she had especially noted one qualification, 'in possession of an estate car'.

Though she said little at the meeting in Aviemore Police Station she took a more proactive attitude on that first walk, when Alistair took our group into Coire an Lochain and she led the more experienced volunteers around the rim of the Northern Corries. It was only on our first call-out, Martin's and mine, that we saw her true mettle.

On Saturday 11th March 1972 at 20.00 I received a call to turn out, if possible, at Creag Meagaidh. Martin and I got there as quickly as we could along with other members of the Rescue Team and walked in the 6km from the Mountain Rescue Post at Aberarder to the glen's terminal loch. Coire Ardair is a typically U-shaped, glaciated valley that curves sharply westwards, first through sheltered woodland, then increasingly through broken and rocky ground, until the two sides close at an almost circular tarn in the heart of the corrie.

This location marks the boundary between the Lochaber Team's area and Cairngorm's, and either Team might turn out. A steep upward slope leads to the foot of the cliffs and a relatively simple climb known as Easy Gully. Surrounded by cliffs on three sides our only illumination came from the stars directly above.

Two young climbers from Aberdeen had completed a new route

close to 59 Face Route. In their elation and fatigue at the top one had taken a wrong step backwards and fallen for about 150m. Unconscious with severe head injuries, fractured ribs and legs he had become wedged on the cliffs above Easy Gully.

Bill March, an instructor at Glenmore Lodge, and Mollie were already on the cliff, engaged in the technical rescue with members of the Lochaber Team who had arrived before us. We stood below, looking up at their head torches as they climbed efficiently into place, listening in the cold air to the *chink* of metal on rock and to their voices as they assessed the casualty's condition and planned their next moves.

It was obvious that Mollie was as adroit on the hill as any of the men and that, in fact, her being a woman made no difference to anyone involved. In the early 1970s this could not be assumed so much as it can today. She spoke with confidence and moved with assurance. In the course of the drama I became more than ever convinced that I wanted to acquire the expertise and confidence of Bill March and Mollie, and that I wanted to increase my involvement.

In mountain rescue there were endless technical problems to be solved and physical demands to be met. A world of discovery and challenge was opening before me.

Eventually they harnessed, belayed and lowered the casualty into Easy Gully, and from there to the low end of the route where we waited with a stretcher. His hard hat had preserved his life but not saved him from severe head and other injuries. Several ribs had been broken as well as both legs and he would have been in great pain had he been conscious. With as much care as possible we manoeuvred him onto his side on the stretcher and strapped him securely in place. We set off for the car park with Mollie monitoring his breathing as we went. Fortunately for the casualty the path in Coire Ardair was, even then, well made with few obstacles, making for a relatively smooth carry.

In December 1972 Alistair McCook stepped down as Team Leader and Mollie took his place with Morton Fraser taking the Depute role. It was an inspired choice. Mollie's impact was immediate and welcome. Proactive in every way her principal aim was to turn the Team into a single highly competent and efficient unit.

At that time funds were low and we possessed too little equipment. There was no regular income stream and no vision beyond 'keeping it going'. It is probably fair to say that the good people who had founded the Cairngorm Mountain Rescue Team eight years before were running out of energy, although Dr Neil MacDonald was an exception. He had already been Chairman between 1967 and 1970 and, following the rush of enthusiasm that was about to be injected, would fulfil the role again between 1974 and 1977.

Apart from the rescues themselves Mollie concentrated on training and fundraising. It was she who planned our training evenings at Aviemore Police Station, collaborating with Glenmore Lodge where she and Fred Harper had a very sound working relationship. In addition to being Principal of Glenmore Lodge Fred was central to its mountain rescue capacity and his instructors were blessed with levels of expertise and knowledge, in addition to physical fitness and hill hardiness, that few outside their number could match. In those days the Glenmore Lodge Principal was the most frequent first contact for the police and first to react to any emergency. What Glenmore Lodge could not manage, however, was a constant guaranteed response since the Lodge was neither open nor constantly staffed all year round. In time the Leader of the Cairngorm Mountain Rescue Team would be established not only as first contact but as rescue co-ordinator.

As a preliminary Mollie established the absolute foundation of any great *esprit de corps*: discipline. She insisted on attendance at these training sessions. Risking a negative reaction and a drop in numbers she warned and dismissed those who did not attend regularly. This, in fact, had the effect of increasing numbers and, by dint of removing negative elements, also improving team spirit.

She also insisted that the Team must take its financial destiny in its own hands. By raising its own income it would be free to spend as it saw fit and not be bound by the thinking of any central authority, whether it was the Mountain Rescue Association or the Scottish Office itself. This meant the Team socialising together and bonding all the more powerfully. Mollie believed in delegation within the Association, and a whole series of small fundraising events was organised.

At this time our business was expanding and I was working for five and a half days a week. We took over a pharmacy in Beauly, on the north side of Inverness, with the intention of making it financially viable and reducing my working week to five days. Eventually I would reduce my shop time as a pharmacist to only one day. The remainder of my working week was dedicated to the business side of the operation. This time was more flexible, and the Team benefited accordingly.

I found accommodation at Crask of Aigas, not far from Sir John Lister-Kaye's field centre and spent my days fitting out the new shop and accustoming the staff to new ways, laying out the procedures that had proved so successful in Kingussie and Newtonmore.

With Highland roads as undeveloped as they were at that time there was no question of my coming home except at weekends. From this location I still turned out for rescues when it was at all possible, but my connection with the Team became more tenuous for a while.

Meanwhile Martin immersed himself more deeply, not only in rescues but also fundraising. I helped when I could, then later, when I was properly home and less wholly committed to the development of a single shop, in more concentrated fashion. Raffles, dances, sponsored stunts: all of these things were organised. Other local groups were sympathetic and supportive and helped where they could. One group even organised a crochet evening. All of these activities were successful in raising awareness and bonding the members; successful, in fact, in everything but their primary purpose, raising funds for the Team.

Enormous efforts had been expended but very little gained. For me it came to a head with the simple task of collecting a two-litre whisky bottle from the pub where it had been filled with customers' loose change. Money raised was small and we expended fuel in picking it up. In addition, we found ourselves socialising with the customers and it would have been cheaper for us, and more profitable for the Team, if we had simply written the cheque ourselves. Some new approach had to be found.

At our first meeting Sgt Boa had floated the idea of a sponsored walk through the Lairig Ghru. Martin and I were getting round to discussing the idea when the Gaelic organisation An Comunn Gaidhealach stole a march on us. Showing enormous ambition they set about organising and publicising a walk of at least 20 miles across rough terrain and wild country. Walking north to south as they did, it meant climbing up through the pine woods of Rothiemurchus onto the increasingly narrow path that leads onto the boulder fields around the Pools of Dee, descending into the area around Corrour Bothy, to finally traverse the rich landscape of Royal Deeside and Mar Lodge.

For people who might never otherwise venture into the hills it was a walk of huge ambition. If the weather was kind they would be exposed to the rugged beauty of one of the world's great wild places. If unkind it might expose them to possibly the worst of summer weather. By way of explanation, it is possible for the Pools of Dee to be frozen over on midsummer's day. Equally it might be scorching. In either case it is without the comforts of shelter and shade.

The many people who loved wild land generally and the Cairngorms in particular laid back their ears. Wouldn't all those marching feet cause tremendous erosion? Wouldn't all those laughing, talkative people frighten the wildlife? How about safety? What if someone dropped dead – or even twisted an ankle? An Comunn went ahead and no one was hurt, no damage done and they had a reasonable financial success.

Our committee looked on with admiration and perhaps some envy. The Lairig Ghru was very much our territory and we felt we had a measure of moral authority where it was concerned. My only worry was that An Comunn, by carrying the idea through first, had an equal moral authority. I contacted them, by now taking on responsibility, but got no reply. This felt like a green light but I was unwilling to repeat the walk because of its high level of challenge and instead suggested a walk to the Shelter Stone.

The route we organised ran roughly eastwards from Glenmore Lodge to Bynack Stables. At that point the going changes from vehicle track to narrow footpath, travelling almost due south through Strath Nethy, between the steep sides of Cairngorm and Bynack More, crossing streams and eventually boulder fields, uphill to a viewpoint known as The Saddle. From there the path cuts steeply down and westwards to the head of Loch Avon and the Shelter Stone. Walkers reversed the route to return. We set about organising checkpoints and refreshments and arranging the necessary permissions. I agreed to man the checkpoint at The Saddle where I could see both walk's end at the Shelter Stone and well down Strath Nethy.

Word began to spread and one day I was approached in Kingussie High Street by a retired Principal teacher of science at Kingussie High School. Mr Morrison, affectionately known as Corky, had been a keen walker of the Cairngorms in his youth and middle age. Shaky knees, powers reduced by the passage of time, and sound common sense had prevented him going out for many years. Now he saw our walk as one last chance. Privately I wondered about his ability to complete the route and cautiously pressed around this point as we talked. He was determined though, signed on the spot and set about arranging his sponsorship.

The day dawned fine and the walk went well without casualties or complaint. I arrived early at The Saddle to count the walkers through and direct them down the final slope and around the loch to the Shelter Stone and lunch. The speedier ones had already begun their return journeys, and in fact were passing through my checkpoint again, when I saw a lone figure advancing slowly up Strath Nethy, occasionally pausing for breath and to wipe his brow. It was Corky, travelling at his own slow pace to ensure he reached the end of his walk safely. It wasn't to be the Shelter Stone though, not on this occasion. When he reached my checkpoint on The

Saddle he told me he had come far enough, but from here he could see the Shelter Stone again and his heart was glad.

I do not know the thoughts that went through the old man's head at that point. All I can be sure of is the joy on his face. He drank in the scene to the full and returned under his own steam to Control.

Martin and I put our heads together afterwards. The walk had taken a good deal of effort; that was true. It had also generated a certain amount of resistance from the environmental lobby. However, the £500 or so it had brought in was almost pure profit, and it all went into the Rescue Team's coffers. Compared to the great efforts and scant returns of our earlier fundraising it was a gigantic success. The work the Rescue Team did was, literally, a matter of life and death, and here was the most effective means of support we had yet discovered.

Mollie was completely supportive. She was also the intermediate figure between an Association that was tired and a Team that was younger than ever and increasingly vital. When the Team Members became rather dissatisfied and began to complain among themselves she gave the wisest counsel possible. If you want something done, she said, do it yourself.

With this in mind we got together privately and agreed to put a large number of our members forward at the next Association AGM. In fact we put forward enough candidates to fill all the posts. We were all elected and it must have appeared as something of a coup, but it was perhaps also evolutionary in that fresh energy and new methods now prevailed.

The thought of an even more ambitious event was on our minds from that point and the Lairig Ghru was the most obvious choice. I contacted An Comunn Gaidhealach and this time received a reply. They had decided not to repeat their walk, mostly because they felt the element of risk was too great.

In 1975 we took the project on, this time raising our ambitions both in terms of the degree of challenge and what sum we might raise. Martin and I accepted the bulk of the organisation, deciding to walk north to south, feeling this would be more aesthetically pleasing as well as giving a great finish point at Mar Lodge. Beginning in Rothiemurchus Forest the walkers would travel through high, rocky wild land to the summit of the pass, gazing into the great corries and ending in the very different landscape of Deeside, open, tended, with buildings at Luibeg and Derry Lodge and, finally, at Mar Lodge itself.

We prepared a descriptive application form that also had space for the walkers' sponsors to make their financial commitments. We prepared line drawings and I typed up our text on the same typewriter the pharmacy used for prescriptions.

The army agreed to help us by trucking the walkers through the forest from Coylumbridge to Rothiemurchus Lodge, and Mar Lodge did, in fact, prove to be the perfect place to end. At that time it had a bar and a log fire so the walkers and organisers could relax together, ease their aching feet and discuss the sights and sounds of the day while waiting to be bussed back to Strathspey. Bringing experience from business, and earlier life, and from observing Mollie's methods, I had taken no particular tasks onto myself on the day of the walk. Instead I delegated everything to willing, competent people and left myself free to deal with the unexpected.

Once again, we had organised a successful event and the Team's funding was assured for yet another year. So successful was it we felt that we could fund the Team by repeating the Lairig Ghru walk every second year. In time we would improve our organisation and our photocopied, typewritten form would evolve into beautifully designed and printed colour brochures, collectible souvenirs of a day that many of the participants would never forget. Now, with a great many walks completed, some participants take pride in possessing them all.

In the years following we would vary from the Lairig Ghru route into the Lairig an Laoigh, the Pass of Gaick and Glen Feshie. All was not only well but improving. Unfortunately other eyes were on us.

In 1978 the Rotary Club of Spey Valley organised a similar walk and repeated it for several years following. In addition, the environmental lobby became increasingly vocal in its disapproval. Ten years into the future we would have to deal respectfully but firmly with the points they made.

The only negative aftermath to this first walk through the Lairig came from the owner of Mar Estate, who wrote from an address in Cheshire. He complained about not being informed of the event and of a number of alleged incidents. Mollie replied personally, assuring him that all relevant members of the Estate staff had been visited in advance and that all necessary permissions had been gathered. There had been an unfortunate encounter with a gamekeeper who she understood had been personally abusive of her, although they had never met.

The keeper's attitude was perhaps an echo of times past, when relations between men and women were of a different nature, and the owner should certainly have been kept informed by his staff. Mollie's letter was courteous but firm. It was the last such complaint we were to hear and relations with landowners were placed on an even sounder base as a result.

Mollie's many talents included the writing of very effective letters when required, as well as her competence in every aspect of hill craft: walking, navigation, technical climbing. Her level of personal fitness was superb. She easily handled the responsibilities and challenges of leading a Team that consisted mostly of men, dealt with the press which was also mostly male and, indeed, took press relations to new levels of organisation and co-operation. Being the first woman in Scotland to lead such a high-profile Mountain Rescue Team she generated quite a bit of publicity without having to try.

It was in her time that the principle of the Leader of the Cairngorm Mountain Rescue Team being 'in charge' of rescues in our area was established beyond argument.

I sit now at my desk in Kingussie with the records of the Cairngorm Mountain Rescue Team all around. Here before me are letters generated by the sponsored walks, elsewhere the accounts she kept of the Team's rescues. In another file are press releases and newspaper clippings and I find myself sifting through all kinds of correspondence, stories told in outline, evidence of forethought, discipline and compassion. In these ways she created conditions in which comradeship and pride could flourish. Mollie Porter's time as Leader was the time of essential change that made the rest possible. I wonder if the lady in the Antarctic truly understands the measure of her own achievement or how well remembered she is; how her memory is, in fact, revered.

FIVE

The bothy known as Peanmeanach is situated on the shores of Loch Ailort, an area rich in Jacobite associations and that has, indeed, a long history of changing peoples. Picts lived here, later Celts and then Vikings. In the nineteenth century the resident population suffered eviction during the Highland Clearances and, in the twentieth and twenty-first, economic circumstances are effecting still more changes. Today it is isolated and beautiful, lonely if you are of that turn of mind. Few these days would call it 'unspoiled' since its woodlands have been substantially reduced across the centuries and the land grazed hard by sheep. It faces onto a beach of white sand, sea and, in the evenings, unmatchable sunsets.

In 1978, as now, the bothy was maintained by the Mountain Bothies Association. Dedicated outdoor people of various kinds, walkers and climbers, birdwatchers and geologists, the members take it on themselves to refurbish and maintain abandoned buildings located about the Highlands. Their mission statement is simple but exact: '…to maintain simple shelters in remote country for the use and benefit of all those who love wild and lonely places'.

The buildings are kept unlocked and might be used as emergency shelters for those walkers who find themselves caught out by fading light or rapidly changing weather. Again, they might serve as base camps for further ventures, where food supplies can be stored, sleeping bags laid out and the evening hours whiled away. Yet again, they might be used as simple getaway locations that afford shelter from the worst of the weather.

Generally, the buildings are old, long disused croft-houses, sometimes gamekeepers' houses, sometimes stables. Very often the walls are lined with pitch pine because that is how Victorian buildings in the Highlands were made. Set away in lonely places they are little chunks of Highland history that would otherwise lie abandoned and rotting, now recycled for present requirements with the permission of the owners, often with their active support.

The word 'refurbish' might give a wrong impression to anyone unfamiliar with the Highland scene. By attending to roofs and windows the MBA renders the buildings watertight and that is, just about, that.

Typically, there will be two ground-floor rooms and two rooms at the top of a narrow wooden staircase. There will be no wall decoration unless someone has pinned a poster to the wall; a poster that, likely, will identify rock formations or wildlife or other natural features. Some, like Peanmeanach, have sleeping platforms. Otherwise you lie on a hard floor that might be wood but is more likely stone or concrete. Furnishings will amount to a kitchen table and two wooden seats. A couple of broken-down, unhygienic easy chairs might lie vacant by the hearth.

There is always a visitors' book, usually containing lengthy entries by people who have had a wonderful time, perhaps a miserable time, or just been passing through. In an area whose principal weather characteristic is wind-driven rain there will be no drying facilities other than the hooks on the door. These hooks are not only for wet clothing though, as no one needs many visits before they learn to hang their food where the mice can't reach. Accept these rough-edged characteristics and you can have a grand time, as Martin and I, along with Team Members Frank Saunders, David Pierce and Dave's dog, Spey, did at the end of January in that year.

I had left the business in good hands with Anne, knowing my presence would not be required until Monday. Martin could have said something similar. Frank was a teacher in Grantown and had the weekend off.

Dave's position was rather different. He worked for the Council's

Water Department and had recently committed quite a bit of time to mountain rescue. His employer was about to transfer Strathspey's water supply to a new source in Glen Einich, a deep trench similar to Glen Avon where it bites into the Cairngorm Plateau. There were concerns about the change in pressure and how it might affect water mains and household plumbing, and it was important for him to be around in the event of an emergency.

At a pub in Spean Bridge on the Friday night we noted from the weather forecast that a deep depression was coming in from the North Atlantic. Afterwards we slept in our cars in a lay-by at the end of Loch Eil, Frank and Dave sharing with Spey. In the morning we drove to the end of the rutted track that leads to the bothy, walking in the remaining six or so kilometres.

Our plan was to stay overnight, doing not much. The great idea was just to get away for a while. We carried in fuel and kindling and our more or less idle Saturday was spent beachcombing for driftwood. Saturday night was spent by a roaring fire with drams, stories flowing, and candlelight within mirrored by stars without – as we noted when nature forced us to a respectable distance from the building.

Through the night the depression arrived. We lay in our sleeping bags, listening to the wind, and in the morning awoke to find snow on the beach and the mountains draped in white. This was a topic of conversation, but not alarm, as we walked out and drove east to Fort William.

The road was clear until we reached Spean Bridge where it divided to head either along the Great Glen to Inverness, or eastwards past Loch Laggan to Newtonmore and home. By the time we reached this point though, the snow was falling ever more steadily and beginning to make driving hazardous. At Laggan Dam it was high at the sides of the road, so high it had brought a minicar to an enforced halt. The driver, who was wearing town clothes and stylish town shoes, in contrast to our own hill gear, was busily digging at the snow with a rectangular tray. Thankfully he did not need too much persuasion to turn his car round and head back to Spean Bridge.

Our cars were bigger and we were better equipped. Since home was no more than an hour away, in normal conditions, we felt it was worth continuing. Not too much further we reached the snow plough that had been clearing the road ahead of us, now halted and unable to dig further, and at last learned how serious the weather conditions actually were. At this location the snow was chest high, soft fluffy stuff that drifted in the wind.

'I'll be going no further along this road tonight and neither will you,' the driver said.

'We haven't that much further to go,' I told him.

'Then you'll have to find some other route. This is the worst snow in years and it's filling in behind me as I go. Best turn around.'

We drove carefully back to Spean Bridge where we phoned our wives before continuing even more slowly along the Great Glen. The plan now was to get to Inverness and then turn south and homewards along the A9 trunk road. From the radios we learned that roads were blocked all across the Highlands. People were trapped in their homes. One train was snowed in somewhere between Inverness and Perth, another north of Dingwall. A snow plough had been abandoned somewhere in the area of Carrbridge.

In Inverness we dropped in on ex-Team Member John MacDonald and his wife who took us in and gave us tea while we talked things through. Our plan had already been stymied by snow blocking the road south at Slochd summit where police were simply not allowing vehicles through.

Obviously we would not get home that night, which alarmed Dave. The radio news got no better. Farmers were struggling to feed their beasts. Helicopters had been turned out to drop food to isolated, cut-off crofts. As we talked Dave became increasingly determined to return until, against everyone's advice, he declared, 'The road's closed to vehicles? Well, *dammit*! I'll walk.'

Next day we drove him in full mountain gear to the police road-block at Daviot on the A9 and watched him as he strode off bravely with Spey trotting at his heel. He was experienced and physically fit but had to cover about 40km. If anyone could get through it was him.

The three of us who remained returned to the MacDonald house where we tried again to phone home. By now the lines were down and there was nothing else for it: we had to concentrate on the situation as we met it. From the radio reports we had a good idea of how the relief operation was being organised. Confident that Anne and the children would be safe in Kingussie I found myself enjoying the situation.

'We are what we are,' I said to the others, 'mountain rescue types,' and they had to admit it sounded like fun. We would offer our services and join in if we could.

At Police Headquarters, close to Raigmore Hospital, so many army and navy helicopters were going in and out it looked as if World War III had begun. When we marched inside in our mountain boots and gaiters the first man we met was Chief Inspector John Maclean of the Badenoch and Strathspey force. 'What took you so long?' he asked.

The snow had caught him out also and he was anxious to get back to co-ordinate the relief effort in his patch.

'Och, never mind that,' he went on, 'they're taking me back in a navy army chopper. You'll be of more use there than here and I've got just the job for you. Want a lift?'

Did we?

We took our rucksacks and other kit from the boot of my car and parked it safely out of the way. At the Raigmore landing strip all four of us piled into a Royal Navy Sea King and took off. In these conditions though, nothing mechanical could be assumed to work, at least not perfectly. The Sea King has two engines and can change from one to the other if necessary, but it has only one gearbox to control the rotors and ours had a problem. After only five minutes aloft the pilot told us to brace ourselves for an emergency landing, and down we went into a turnip field.

Of necessity we had put Dave and our families out of our minds. In fact, they were doing very well, and in Anne's case rather more than well. She and the children were safe and warm at home, but she hadn't understood the severity of the snowfall until she opened the door on Monday morning and found it piled as high as the lintel.

Sometime that night the telephone lines had gone down and the Kingussie to Newtonmore road had become blocked. The snow stopped falling as she dug her way out of the house, but continued to drift around Dave and Spey as they made their way down the A9.

The going was far from easy. Dave cast a thoughtful eye on the railway line. A locomotive and plough had swept it clear and it looked as if he could make better progress by leaving the road. Walking between the rails was quite laborious so he soon found himself tiptoeing along one rail. When he found himself in a cutting with walls of hard packed snow up to his shoulders on both sides he realised he would be in trouble if a train should get through. There was no going back so he transferred his rucksack to one shoulder and brought Spey to heel. If a train should come along, he decided, he would throw rucksack and dog up and follow himself. Thankfully he did not have to put this idea into practice.

On and on they trudged, over embankments and through more cuttings. A family called them down to their cottage for a cup of tea, and no doubt a drink for Spey, but the climbing down and back up again would cost at least an hour.

On Findhorn Viaduct they paused high above the valley where Dave looked onto a scene of hills and snow such as only a few railway workers can have enjoyed since the structure's tall, slender columns were built.

Shortly afterwards they caught up with the locomotive and plough, idling in a deep snow cutting and Dave asked if they could hitch a lift. When he was told they could not they clambered up the bank to the A9 while the plough drove forward into the next drift, only to come – *whoof* – to an abrupt halt.

Six more kilometres took them past Slochd summit and a jam of abandoned vehicles. Where cars had been able to go no further, drivers and passengers had been rescued and given shelter at Slochd

Cottages. The owner had been quite a hero, ignoring his own safety to guide people to his home, organising food and hot drinks. Dave led Spey between cars, between a bread van and a van advertising Hunter's Crisps.

Legends have grown around those few days. It is said that some of the children taken into the Cottages raided the bread van's loaves to fend off starvation. There should have been fishes. A Volvo dealer from Inverness had delivered a new car and was driving the old one back when he got stuck. The car had been cleaned out by its previous owner so there was no blanket and very little petrol to keep the engine turning and the heater going. When he was rescued he was semi-conscious and hypothermic. A sales rep was trapped elsewhere and used his samples to keep warm, giving new meaning to his job description, 'traveller in women's tights'.

Just before they turned off the A9 for Carrbridge, Spey became suddenly very alert. A search and rescue trained dog, his master knew he had better investigate. Spey put his head down and moved forward intently. Dave followed and, in the silence that only deep snow and low temperatures can bring, heard a voice, two voices – no, more than two voices. Beneath the snow an eerie orange glow gave away the presence of an abandoned snow plough, the same plough we had heard about on our car radios. It had been left with its radio on and the voices he heard were those of the emergency services as they co-ordinated their rescue efforts.

At this time the A9 was being widened, a years-long project that would change it from a series of village connectors into the road it is today, something rather less than the motorway that is actually required. In Carrbridge they met the first mobile vehicle of the walk, a Land Rover from the construction company, Tarmac. The driver was heading for Aviemore and happy to give them a lift. They drove on a bed of hard packed snow, with walls of snow only a few inches away on either side. At one point, they had to reverse for what seemed like half a mile to let another vehicle pass. Site work had been postponed and, over the next week or so, Tarmac's earth moving vehicles would play a major part in reopening the road.

Dave and Spey still had 3km of difficult walking to the cottage in Rothiemurchus where his wife, Laura, was waiting. He was exhausted by now, but the Water Department would not give him much time to rest.

Back in Inverness we had decided that the day was taking its own course and there was no controlling it. With the Chief Inspector we hitched a lift from our turnip field in a police car. We got back to Raigmore where helicopters were still going in and out at regular intervals. Undaunted we piled into an RAF Puma. It was a more cramped aircraft than the Sea King and I was obliged to stand between the two pilots as we flew over the Monadhliath mountains to Kingussie.

The day was one of dazzling clarity and the sight of the hills and lochs, the wide horizon, took my breath away. Innumerable stories were being played out, of valour, endurance and luck, some good, some bad. As we discovered after we made contact with our families Dave's had been good, although not so good as ours. He got home 15 minutes after we did.

I looked into the shop to make sure all was well and spoke again to the Chief Inspector. He had already been in touch with Mollie and we had been assigned our duties.

All across the Highlands the important work that people carried out from day to day was left in abeyance and mine was no different. The pharmacy in Newtonmore dispensed a controlled pain-relieving drug to a patient who lived close by. The shop had its own pharmacist, but drugs were supplied by us in Kingussie. As the pharmacist who should have been on duty there, I was unfortunately delayed and the road between the two towns was still blocked. The Newtonmore patient's need was extreme. Anne understood all this and knew she somehow had to get the drug, controlled or not, to the patient. The question was how?

With this on her mind she made her way into Kingussie with the package to look for some means of getting it along the road. The first thing she noticed was that the air was rich with the smell of fresh baking. Our local baker had struggled in through the weather to make sure the people of Strathspey and Badenoch had their bread. It was the sort of story that was being repeated all over the Highlands where people were pulling together as seldom before.

A Land Rover might do the job, she thought, although a construction vehicle would be better. Maybe a dump truck? Failing that... Suddenly she heard the sound of boots tramping on snow. A platoon of 30 or so squaddies and one officer were marching down the High Street – but, what's this? They were carrying something on their heads.

Breadboards!

They were carrying new baked loaves on their heads for the hungry population of our neighbouring town, Newtonmore. Brave lads, they would fight their way through the drifts. Anne held up her hand.

'Halt!' cried the captain. The squaddies crashed their boots to the ground in unison.

'Ma'am?'

The upshot of this was that the officer took the medication to our shop and the patient was saved from excruciating pain that might have gone on for days. The rules, even the drug control laws, had been bent slightly but the needs of the moment had sensibly prevailed.

The next day Martin and I turned out with avalanche probes to be airlifted back to Slochd and its jam of abandoned cars. As far as was known everyone had been rescued. Many had been taken to Carrbridge. Under the circumstances it was impossible to account fully for everyone, so we were asked to walk the road, checking cars where we found them. Where the snow was deep we were to probe and ensure that no one and nothing had been missed.

The helicopter could not linger. Elsewhere in the Highlands there was a pressing need to drop food parcels to isolated people, feed packages for beasts, here and there medical supplies. Stories would come out later of parcels being dropped down chimneys, stories that would seem hardly credible.

We started by checking the vehicles for anyone who might have been missed, who might have passed out or even died. Continuing south along the road we probed the deeper drifts as we went, eventually reaching the abandoned snow plough. When we arrived one of the contractor's excavators was sitting on the snow at roughly the level of the plough's top, digging with its long, prehensile arm and its bucket. The enormous bulk of the two machines together was staggering. The plough itself was as big as a small bungalow and the excavator working above it almost as big.

In this area the snow was more or less undisturbed. We went to work again with the probes, aluminium poles 2.5m in length that were light enough to be carried but strong enough to be pushed deep into the snow. We went over the area thoroughly but found no more vehicles and no casualties.

These conditions prevailed for a week, the emergency services tested almost to the limit but not found wanting. After checking all the vehicles and probing all areas of deep snow we had little to do beyond awaiting first, the next call, and after that, the thaw. The thaw arrived first.

Our weekend at Peanmeanach had extended into quite an adventure, with a wide array of anxieties, not least when Dave set out on his long walk. The helicopter ride across the Monadhliaths would have enlivened anyone's life. The painstaking job of checking vehicles and probing snowdrifts was, in itself, dull, but we completed it assiduously and without complaint. Team spirit was strengthened, as were relations with the police, army, navy and air force.

Dave's fears were well founded. Deep snow and freezing conditions blocked the Strathspey water intake so the Council had to transfer to the new supply more quickly than planned. Dave played his part, and what would have been a complex and difficult operation even in the best of weathers was carried through without mishap.

Here and there harm was done, but the people of the Highlands experienced the sort of togetherness that only comes when a shared danger is met full on and overcome. If they had been unsure before, they now knew that their emergency services were ready and capable. We reopened our pharmacies and went back to the necessary business of dispensing medicines. Tarmac resumed their work that would further extend and drive the northern economy. Chief Inspector MacLean stood his officers down warily when the A9 reopened. Mollie Porter viewed what she had made of her Team with quiet satisfaction.

SIX

'There was indignation along the Cairngorm Valley yesterday about the Scottish Office decision to demolish the three high-level bothies on the Cairngorms. In November 1971, a party of six perished in a blizzard near the Curran Bothy, one of those due to be demolished.

'Following the enquiry into the tragedy, the Scottish Secretary asked the Scottish Sports Council to gather opinions on the bothies. Although the majority of those consulted were in favour of demolition, the Cairngorm Mountain Rescue Association were not. They maintained the bothies had saved lives.'

The above is an extract from an article in *The Press and Journal* dated 17th May 1973. Rightly it should have referred to 'unlocked shelters' rather than bothies. Rudimentary in the extreme, a bothy would seem luxurious beside these cramped, unheated windbreaks. Peanmeanach was like the Ritz in comparison.

The Cairngorm Plateau Disaster fired much discussion and many disputes. The party of eight, of whom six died, had been attempting to reach Corrour Bothy in the Lairig Ghru by traversing the Cairngorm Plateau. Defeated by the conditions they attempted to reach the Curran Shelter beside Lochan Buidhe. Not achieving this they made a forced bivouac beside the Feith Buidhe, the stream that flows from Lochan Buidhe into Loch Avon. At the same time a companion party attempted to reach Corrour by a more ambitious route but, in the same horrendous conditions, found the Curran and took refuge. Eventually they dug their way out to return to

Lagganlia, assuming they would find their friends there. Not finding them at Lagganlia they raised the alarm.

There were two other small, high-level shelters. St Valery and El Alamein, named after two famous World War II battles, one the famous last stand by the 51st Highland Division which bought the necessary time for the evacuation at Dunkirk, the other a tide-turning victory in North Africa. Their names not only point to the generation of men who created them but to the degree of emotion invested.

My feeling at the time of the dispute, as a novice mountaineer well aware of his own limitations, was that the shelters could not be held responsible for the deaths. The passage of over 30 years has not changed this view, nor has experience gained through many hundreds of rescues. The deaths were caused by bad decision-making, itself the product of poor leadership. The circle of responsibility closes on an education system that had, at that time, neither fully appreciated the hazards of the mountain environment nor itemised or quantified the skills and knowledge they demanded.

The number of climbers to take refuge within the shelters over the years could not be so much as guessed at. Their presence may well have saved lives, but many of us used them for the simple expedient of getting out of the wind for a flask of coffee. Inanimate objects, the high-level shelters had neither lured any walker, nor offered a certain safe haven, as would later be alleged.

The Curran had been erected years before, at a time when cross-country skiing was coming to be seen as a recreational activity for which the Cairngorms were particularly suited. If encouraged this could mean increased visitor numbers and a beneficial impact on the local economy, and it was at this level that pre-construction discussion was mostly carried out. As a result the shelters were built as stopping points, or refuges, on the plateau, the work carried out by naval apprentices stationed with HMS *Caledonia*. Ownership and responsibility was always something of a muddle.

Warnings had been sounded almost from the time of construction by some distinguished mountaineers who felt their worst fears had been tragically fulfilled. Other, equally distinguished mountaineers were as strongly positioned on the preservation side of the debate. When the inquiry that was eventually held in Banff recommended, 'In the matter of the high-level bothies, advice as to their removal or otherwise should be left to the experts', there was no shortage of experts on either side with the police obliged to take the lead role in actioning the demolition.

The Cairngorm Mountain Rescue Association led the resistance to the removal of the Curran with Mollie Porter writing many long and erudite letters. Feelings ran high and I find this following statement, a response to the police, among her correspondence. It references earlier letters and might be thought typical.

'This Association in turn respects the sincerely held opinions of those persons holding different attitudes to our own: it does not consider that to differ strongly from them, publicly or privately, is either anarchic or defiant. The saving of lives is the paramount concern of all of us involved in mountain rescue and we should not need to stress that this is our motive in disagreeing with the plan to demolish the shelters. That we have been troubled by the manner in which the decision to demolish was reached and the unworthy imputations of a personal nature aimed at both the Association and individuals is of secondary importance.'

Reading through the correspondence I can almost feel the vibrations of emotion from both sides. Mountaineering is a small world and mountain rescue a village. Strong personalities demand their own way. Hard-won reputations cannot be compromised. Sides are taken and things said which later give cause for regret, or should. The high-level, unlocked shelters dispute acted as a lightning rod for many differences that pale into insignificance beside the loss of six young lives.

More than one Mountain Rescue Team takes an interest in the Cairngorms. Both the Braemar Team and the Grampian Police Team are based to the south of the plateaux. The RAF Kinloss Mountain Rescue Team is on the Moray coast. At that time the police force for the area south of the plateaux was known as the Scottish North Eastern Counties Constabulary. Of the four Teams involved only the police had a territory with a prescribed, formal boundary but the practicalities of access meant they could not have sole or even primary responsibility on their side of that invisible line. Geography and the ski road into the Northern Corries meant the Cairngorm Team could be on the scene in two hours where a southern approach could take four, or even six.

Local planning at that time was in the hands of County Councils operating under the Secretary of State for Scotland. Taking responsibility for such weighty matters as oil-related developments and inward investment, they were also obliged to assess the value and risk of a lonely gathering of stones piled on a metal box in the middle of nowhere. The Cairngorm Mountain Rescue Association claimed ownership but, by a cat's whisker or two, the Curran Shelter was located within the County of Banffshire, as was St Valery. Who then, had authority? Lobbying was undertaken intensely, meetings were convened, and an article written and circulated privately. Letters were exchanged.

'I am informed that the Cairngorm Mountain Rescue Team claims ownership of the Curran Bothy and refuses to co-operate in the removal of the structure,' thundered the Chief Constable of Scottish North Eastern Counties Constabulary.

'We still have expert evidence to consider,' Mollie replied, in a neat reversal of roles.

The planning inquiry held in Banff reached no definite conclusion. The Chief Constables of Inverness-shire and North-Eastern Counties produced a plan for demolition, deferred while the Scottish Sports Council was consulted. The Mountaineering Council of Scotland sought its members' views. The Mountain Rescue Committee of Scotland decided on demolition. A local MP described the decision as 'lunatic'. The plan was postponed after much lobbying. The MP changed his mind. Letters in the newspapers generated more articles and still more correspondence. The police Team withdrew from the Mountain Rescue Committee of Scotland and later rejoined.

Unknown to me at the time Mollie was to a great extent arguing against the grain of her own convictions. She and Jo were already keenly aware of the sensitivity of the mountain environment. Like many others, they felt that increased visitor numbers would deprive the environment of its atmosphere of isolation and 'apartness', the irreplaceable 'wild land qualities' they loved with all their hearts. At the time I, along with other rescuers, did not share this view, as most of us would probably do now. Mollie's adherence to the Cairngorm Mountain Rescue Association's line and her articulacy in its pursuit speaks volumes for her commitment to the Team and its development. In later years her environmental beliefs would take her to a point of compromise she could not, in conscience, pass – but that was for the future.

In the end both the Curran and St Valery shelters were taken down. The apprentices of HMS *Caledonia* assisted with demolition as an earlier generation had with construction. Already located in the most obscure of locations El Alamein survived the cull. Close to the rim of the cliffs above Strath Nethy it was possibly the most hazardous of the three to approach.

How many lives were lost because of the shelters is a matter much thrashed in debate. I would say, none. Responsibility lies with competence and leadership. How many they saved is also debatable. What was unmistakably exposed throughout the whole affair was the singular determination of mountain rescuers, the same stubborn determination that repeatedly takes us onto the hills to preserve the lives of others. It is to be hoped that petty jealousies, territorial disputes and statements of identity have never put lives at hazard. I do not believe they yet have. In fact, I would say that the only real loss in the whole affair is the relief the shelters gave tired walkers from the wind.

The 1975 reorganisation of local government in Scotland created the giant authorities of Highland and Grampian Regional Councils, and the second tier of District Councils they contained. The invisible boundary across the plateaux did not change but instead gained a greater hindrance potential from the increased mass of authority ranged on either side. Clearly it was best ignored.

Not least among the changes that followed was to Martin Robertson who became Director of Finance with Badenoch and Strathspey District Council. Martin continued in mountain rescue and, in fact, chaired the Association for three years. In those years Anne and I grew the business still more, taking on another shop in Aberdeen. Paradoxically our business success freed more of my time for mountain rescue and all that attended it. When Martin stepped down from the Chair I took over for the following three years that included the departure of Mollie Porter.

Possibly the most important thing she wrote in her mighty correspondence over the shelters was this: 'The saving of lives is the paramount concern of all of us involved in mountain rescue and we should not need to stress that this is our motive in disagreeing…'

She understood the ramifications of these words very well. Implicit in them is the Cairngorm Mountain Rescue Association's indifference to politics that are not directly related to rescue and safety, as the shelters dispute had been. Team Members, of course, would hold their many views and retain their freedom of expression. The Team Leader though, had an authority that could compromise a passionately held conviction. Six years later it would with Mollie.

The saving, or preservation, of lives was indeed the primary motivation of all concerned in the unlocked shelters dispute, but another matter surfaced at just about every juncture and meeting of minds. That matter was development and the mountain environment. It is sometimes claimed that there are no wilderness environments left below a level of 700 (or so) metres. Everywhere else in these islands has been ploughed, built on, driven across, excavated, bored into and extracted from, and in every way turned over. This puts an additional premium of value on the mountain environment. In more than one sense there is nowhere else to turn.

Stand on the rim of Coire na Ciste in summer and look down. What you see is a sort of devastation around the old ski tow and beside the road. Metal rods are bolted into rock, concrete blocks stand incongruously among the heather. There is the same sense of abandonment here as in similar ski developments elsewhere in the world.

This is not so much the case around the new funicular railway in Coire Cas. The funicular itself is neat and tidy. It does not look like 'part of the mountain', or to put it another way 'natural', but thought has been given to its appearance and environmental impact. It terminates at an underground station with a restaurant and viewpoint above. Passengers are not allowed to get out and roam around the hill.

The Cairngorm Mountain Rescue Team and Cairngorm Mountain PLC have always got on well. A sound working relationship was founded during the consultation process and continues to the extent that we will sometimes use the train to transport rescuers and casualties off and on the hill. This might be disconcerting for other passengers, but no one has ever complained.

The railway attracted a good deal of controversy when it was mooted but, by that time, there had been a steady gathering of experience in relation to matters of the mountain environment and anything that might be considered a 'threat'. Skiing and the commercial development of Aviemore proceeded almost without comment at a time when the Highlands were starved of investment, and an influx of people followed of which Anne and I and the children were four latecomers. Soon people began to look more closely at what, exactly, was going on. Developers and environmentalists established rival camps.

In the course of the debate planning difficulties became apparent, that is to say difficulties of balance between conservation of the environment and economic development. Investors in outdoor tourism were faced with the paradox that the more they supported economic development the more they damaged the very environment the tourists and skiers came to enjoy. They were trading with seed corn.

Environmentalists were faced with the paradox that the more they promoted wild land in books, television and lectures, the more people they attracted who would, in turn, erode the low-level footpaths with their boots, cut up the meagre topsoil of the plateaux and demand more and better facilities everywhere. Birds would be frightened and deer disturbed by people who shared their values and sought only to emulate their mentors. They were consuming the seed corn.

Throughout this infinitely varied, never-ending debate the Cairngorm Mountain Rescue Team kept in mind the principle that Mollie Porter had articulated and that is worth repeating, 'The saving of lives is the paramount concern of all of us involved in mountain rescue and we should not need to stress that this is our motive in disagreeing…'

Otherwise the Association and the Team had no opinion.

It was in my time as Chair of the Association that a radical extension of the ski facilities in the Northern Corries was proposed, this time in Lurcher's Gully. The westernmost of the Northern Corries, it is located between Coire an Lochain and the Lairig Ghru where it is overlooked by Lurcher's Crag. The gully has, in fact, been used by cross-country skiers since mountaineers first arrived. It has excellent slopes and would have been developed earlier except that the natural line for the access road leads into Coire Cas.

Lurcher's Crag is among the less visited peaks of the Cairngorms but all the more prized for that. It gives fine views through the pass and across to Braeriach, as well as across Rothiemurchus and Strathspey. Constructing ski tows would destroy its privacy and plant life but those were not the only issues. To allow vehicle access the road would have to be extended from the high, Coire Cas, car park. Running across the face of the major corries, Coire Cas, Coire an t-Sneachda, and Coire an Lochain, it would destroy their wilderness qualities forever.

The vehicles that used it would emit exhaust and create noise. Arguably, the people who used it would have little appreciation of what was lost. They would bring bright-coloured, expensive ski outfits and attitudes at odds with an environmental lobby which has always included a pro-poverty, or at least anti-wealth, element.

Highly committed and informed environmentalists, Mollie and Jo felt very strongly about this development. After a long acquaintance with the Coire Cas area they, like many others, had a feeling of 'enough is enough'. Of course, this is an essential quandary in 'development and the mountain environment', not just when to call 'enough' but how.

Mollie called a Team Meeting to discuss the proposals with a view to the Association forming a position in the light of a coming Inquiry by the Secretary of State. We discussed it in the round, balancing the local economy against environmental erosion. To the surprise of many I, as a local businessman who would benefit from increased numbers of visitors, was not enamoured of the development. I very much took to heart the points that Mollie and Jo made. A halt had to be made somewhere, or there would eventually be no wild land left.

This was not a unanimous view though, and there was an obvious danger of division in both Association and Team. By this time Mollie's Depute was the experienced mountaineer and author Pete Cliff, who ran an Outdoor Centre nearby. He pointed out that the mountain safety element in this debate was tenuous. It could be argued that the proposed road would put more people in the Lairig Ghru, and more people on the hill generally, but that was not an essential mountain rescue issue. These points were accepted but Mollie and Jo were committed to giving their personal views to the Inquiry. Both resigned from the Team and, in time, Mollie made an articulate, informed submission on the basis of her own reputation and record. On 24th December 1982 the *Strathspey and Badenoch Herald* reported as follows.

'The long wait is over for the verdict on one of the biggest issues to split skiing and conservation factions in the Spey Valley and else-where. Scottish Secretary Mr George Younger has come down on the side of the conservationists in the highly controversial proposal to extend downhill skiing facilities into three northern corries of Cairngorm.'

Walk today from that position on the rim of Coire Cas to the head of Lurcher's Gully. The quiet of the area is preserved, the ptarmigan still chuckle in the heather and if you are lucky you might see an eagle, but there is no snow – at least, not enough to make commercial skiing practical. Climate change has done its work here as everywhere. If the proposal had gone ahead it seems likely that we would have lost everything, environment and investment both. Instead, Lurcher's Gully is preserved and we have at least a working principle of limitation: there should be no commercial development on the plateaux, or widening of the damage to the Northern Corries.

Mollie played her part in reaching the correct decision, but her principled stance cost us our most respected Leader. On her departure her Depute and the Team's most obvious successor, Pete Cliff, took over.

Beside his many outdoor accomplishments Pete was also a lawyer. Now he brought his widely informed and deeply incisive mind to the job of leadership, nourished as it was by a long involvement in climbing, hillwalking, and mountain rescue. He had different ways from Mollie but pointed in the same direction and, if anything, increased the level of professionalism. Training was intensified, including rock climbing. We went on week-long trips to the Lake District and Wales. He was a great ski mountaineer, a great technician in every field. He was also a fine yachtsman. All of these skills he honed and taught at his Outdoor Centre, and the Team reaped the benefits.

He also carried on the tradition of fundraising, and, when he decided the Team could use a van to work beside its Land Rover, wrote a letter to the Ford Motor Company that might be summed up as follows: Any spare transits? He was as surprised as anyone when a positive reply came back from the company's Hamburg office. Our van would have four-wheel drive with double wheels at the back, an aid to traction in difficult terrain, and be big enough to carry both equipment and rescuers. We were chuffed to bits.

The only qualification was that it was a loan not a gift. Still pretty good, we thought.

In addition the company wanted to use it in an advert. Free publicity for the Team is also good, we agreed.

Could they use some of the Team as extras? It was the least we could do.

Of course, they would be paid!

Team Members leaped at the chance and, in the end, we bought the vehicle for a tiny fraction of its market value. Ford's generosity was exceptional and I still remember it with warmth.

'One more thing,' they said. 'Don't let anyone know.'

Time passed and I duly stood down from the Chair. In 1986 I became Pete's Depute and in 1989 became Team Leader myself. Deciding on this level of commitment was remarkably easy after the many years I had spent in service, one way or another. Thanks to the great transitional work that had been carried out by Mollie, and later Pete, I inherited a Team that was honed into an efficient body of dedicated, trained and equipped rescuers. Many of us were about the same age and we would travel together as a generation. Anne and the children were fully supportive, already aware of the sacrifice of time that must be made, aware also of the inroads into family commitments that would be necessary. It seemed a natural transition.

Among other things, it meant I was present when the Team was consulted on the funicular railway proposal. Along with its increasing professionalism the Team was now aware of the limits to its interest. We played no part in the environmental debate, only in the safety aspects. I met with fire officers and senior police officers to talk it through.

What would happen in the event of a fire? I asked.

There would be full-scale emergency procedures from the Aviemore Station, the fire chiefs said. If that should be insufficient there would be support from Inverness.

That would mean several tenders, I noted, but there is limited width to the access road. In addition, it is exceptionally steep and has many hairpin bends.

The fire officers asked how long it would take the Team to get to the incident.

One to two hours, I told them, assuming we did not have to negotiate our way round a stranded fire tender.

If the train caught fire halfway up, I asked, how would you get to it?

On foot was the answer. The fire officers would be required to carry their equipment uphill, across rough ground, while dressed in full equipment. Obviously the Team could be major players in assisting in any evacuation of a train, or indeed of the restaurant. Protocols and procedures would have to be varied as the occasion demanded.

There was no point in saying that such accidents were unlikely. That was true but unlikely things happen all the time in the mountains. I pointed out, to some scepticism, that a plane might crash into the Ptarmigan Restaurant. Only a few months earlier a plane had flown through cables that supported a cable car in the Italian Alps and sent it down into the valley. That hadn't been expected. In addition, in 2001, the Team was involved in the search for two USAF F15 Eagle jets which had crashed into the summit of Ben MacDhui. My words proved prescient. In April 2008, shortly after my retirement, a private plane flying in blizzard conditions crash-landed only 1km from the restaurant, taking the life of the pilot but, by great good fortune, no one else's.

Everyone involved, the police, the fire service and Cairngorm Mountain Company, was reluctant to accept that absolute safety could not be assured but, in the end, the realities had to be faced. Absolute safety on the mountain is not achievable.

Today the railway generates most of the Cairngorm tourist industry's income. Skiing now accounts for only a small part. Weddings and other functions are held in the restaurant at the head of the line. People who could never manage the walk for reasons of health or age can now absorb at least some of the big views. Older walkers, like Corky Morrison, can recharge their memories. Passengers are not allowed to get out and wander but few are daunted by that.

Huge numbers enter Strathspey by road and travel up Cairngorm every year. It has become very much a part of the Highland tour that includes Skye, Loch Ness and many other beauty spots. It provides employment directly and feeds into many local businesses to provide still more employment, and its contribution to our local economy is tremendous.

On the long return from Lurcher's Gully you might pause on the lip of Coire Cas to watch that little blue box travelling up and down. It is filled with happy passengers. I am glad they are there and welcome them to the Highlands. Almost certainly their experience will be entirely positive and they will return safe and sound to valley level. For all that, they should know what competent mountaineers accept, what the rescuers observe all too frequently, and what everyone with children in their charge should hold constantly at the forefront of their minds. To venture outwards and upwards is to accept an element of risk that can be reduced by knowledge, skill, and planning, but never eliminated.

SEVEN

'Love is patient, love is kind. It does not envy, it does not boast, it is not proud. It is not rude, it is not self-seeking, it is not easily angered. It keeps no record of wrongs.'

Those beautiful words are from First Corinthians, in the New International Version of the Bible. They, or words like them, were spoken over my head when I attended the church at Anniesland with my parents. Church of Scotland ministers tended to have their favourite passages, and beauty compels return. I cannot say I had much reason to recall them in many of my years among the Cairngorms but 1987 was one.

In early March spring was coming in, crocuses and daffodils beginning to appear, and the high snowfields were becoming less stable, when a couple checked into a hotel close to the station in Kingussie. The man, whom I will call Mr Black, was in his fifties, and the woman, Ms White, in her forties. They had travelled from the south intending to climb some of the seven Munros that lie on either side of the Drumochter Pass.

Drumochter is one of the highest passes in Britain and the highest to carry a major road. In certain conditions the pass is impassable and, in the years when winters were colder, it was frequently blocked by snow. To prevent over-ambitious travellers attempting the impossible it has snow gates at either end. Anyone travelling north who finds their way blocked but has to reach, for example, Inverness is obliged to retreat all the way to Perth and reroute along the much longer coast road through Angus, Aberdeen and Moray. Access to six of the Munros is taken from car parks located between the gates.

The couple set off in the morning having booked dinner for 19.30. By 22.00 they had not returned and the proprietor called the police. The snow gates at Drumochter had been closed in the course of the previous night which meant that, of the seven Drumochter Munros only Meall Chuaich would have been accessible to them. Generally approached from an A9 pull-in, a walk along approximately 5km of Land Rover track allows a not-too-difficult, direct ascent to the summit.

A speedy check by the police established their car was not there so it followed they had made a more radical revision of their plans. They had not discussed any other hills in the proprietor's hearing but the make and colour of their car was known. They had seemed intent on bagging a Munro and there is a limited, although plentiful, number in the Kingussie area, all with their recognised start points.

At that time Pete Cliff was Team Leader and I was Depute. We understood the urgency of the situation but until the couple's car was located it remained a police problem. Some detective work was called for.

Both the Great Moss and the Cairngorm Plateau would have been tempting as targets, especially since a high start was possible from the Coire Cas car park. Conditions at those heights though, would have been horrendous. The Monadhliath range on the west of Strathspey contains four Munros. Approximately 300m lower than the Cairngorms conditions are generally easier although they can still be extreme. In present conditions they would have a deep coating of fresh, unstable snow.

The police went round the start points and car parks and at 01.00 the next morning, located the vehicle beside the Spey Dam on the Laggan Road. This is the usual starting point for Geal Charn, the 926m, westernmost Munro. From here a Land Rover track runs north along Glen Markie for about 4km where it reduces to a narrow footpath and is the obvious, and most used, route of ascent.

Using their discretion to enter the vehicle they found a copy of the Scottish Mountaineering Club book, *The Munros*, lying open at the page on Geal Charn. Many other pages in the book had been ticked but this one had not. There was quite a bit of other, normal hillwalking gear in the car, dry clothing and flasks of tea to come back to, but no rucksacks. It seemed very likely, almost to the point of certainty, that they had tackled this hill and so the police once again called the Team.

By now it was after 02.00 and, with low cloud cover, the night was starless and dark. There was a lot of snow lying and we knew that Geal Charn was prone to avalanches, particularly at the back of the corrie we would be entering. Weighing everything up we decided a first light search was in order, summoned as many Team Members as possible to meet at Spey Dam at 07.00, requested additional searchers from the RAF Team and called the Aeronautical Rescue Coordination Centre (ARCC) at Kinloss to request the assistance of a helicopter. To meet at this time the rescuers would have to be up at 05.00. Given the late hour at which these decisions were made not much time would be lost.

All went according to plan with the helicopter waiting when we arrived. I looked forward to a quick aerial reconnaissance of the corrie but mechanical failure, for once, defeated us. The helicopter could not take off. We radioed in another request and set off along the Glen Markie track in Land Rovers.

If the couple had merely misplaced themselves, it was likely they would survive. Walkers who are well equipped rarely lose their lives simply by being lost. More worryingly they may have been avalanched and, if so, locating them might take quite some time. Probes would be required, possibly dogs. If they had been engulfed the bodies might not turn up before the thaw.

Parking at the end of the track we piled out and continued along the path until we were opposite the mouth of the corrie. Breaking into three teams of 12 we crossed the Markie Burn and spread out across the hill. Two streams run out of the corrie. One rises from springs on the northern slopes. The other is known as the Piper's

Burn and spills from the lochan in the heart of the corrie. At the top of the cliffs and close to the edge is the mountain's summit cairn and beyond that a low-angled descent onto moorland and bog.

The three groups formed a line with mine on the south side of Piper's Burn. Each in sight of the other we entered the corrie in a mile-long horseshoe that loosened and stretched as we advanced. The other parties swept towards the northern shoulder that would lead around the cliffs to the summit and a view across the moors that might, possibly, reveal a coloured cagoule or a waving figure, while mine searched around and below the cliffs.

Up ahead I could see a low, ruined wall. Little more than a rickle of stones it was a moss-covered relic of times gone past when the Highlands were populated by a native society that would eventually disperse, or be dispersed, across the face of the globe. It would have been part of a sheep fank in those days, or a shieling, and behind it we found Ms White's body curled into itself and still. We examined her for vital signs and found none but noted a visible head injury. Soon we heard shouts from above. The others had found Mr Black's body among avalanche debris at the foot of the cliffs. He had suffered broken bones and was in a seated position with a flask beside him. Traces of blood led from the scene in the direction of the wall.

Their story was not difficult to put together. The couple had altered their plans of necessity, but without informing anyone, planned their new adventure as they went and tackled the hill by its usual route. It must have seemed like a sane and relatively safe retrieval of the day. In unstable snow conditions they had been avalanched and Mr Black was too severely injured to help himself. Ms White was also severely injured, but still mobile. Between them they will have made Mr Black as comfortable as possible before she retreated from the corrie, possibly remembering the wall they had passed on their way in, probably haemorrhaging internally. Here she reached the limit of her endurance, huddling behind the wall for shelter and eventually giving up her life.

It was a sad but typical tragedy of a sort we were well used to.

They had died together, doing what they wanted to do. Presumably they understood the risks, but that would provide very little comfort for those left behind.

By now we had been on the hill for some hours after a broken night. We were hungry and cold, and rescuers are as prone to hypothermia as the people they search for. It may seem callous, although I hope it will be understood, but we had our lunch there. We ate our sandwiches and drank our coffee and after that packaged the bodies and took them down.

The weather had by this time worsened and the second helicopter could not enter the corrie. Thirty-six people is the right number to stretcher one body on a long carry but with two to carry we had only 18 to each. Thankfully our route was entirely downhill and most of the remaining journey would be by Land Rover. An ambulance was waiting at Spey Dam and the bodies were taken to the mortuary in Kingussie. This meant our job was almost complete and I could stand the Team down.

Only one thing remained and that was to drive the couple's car back to town. Chris Barley was a local dentist with whom I had formed a friendship that was destined to deepen through years of adventures in both Scotland and the Alps. He had followed my three years as Chairman of the Association with three of his own and was the logical person to accompany me. It was only on that return journey that any kind of emotional contact occurred between either of us and the couple. *The Munros* book was still open on the back seat with their dry clothing lying beside it. Their spare flasks were still warm. The previous morning they had gone out to spend a day in beautiful surroundings and to enjoy each other's company. Now they were gone.

The contrast between our feelings in the actual presence of the couple's bodies on the hill, and here in the car with only a few suggestions of their lives was profound. In dealing with human remains, concentration on the job is very much to the point. So is the survival and well-being of the rescuers themselves but, then again, there may be more human presence in a turned page and a warm pullover than in the cold flesh and bones of a dead body.

There matters rested. Spring passed and the calendar's pages were torn off one by one. A good, long summer sent its warmth down on the Scottish hills and the people who take their recreation there. Around the time that leaves were turning gold Anne heard footsteps on the gravel outside our house and a knock on the door. She answered to an attractive, well-dressed woman of about 50.

'May I speak with Mr Allen?' she asked. Anne called me to the door.

'Can I help you?'

'I understand you were part of a search party on Geal Charn in March.'

'Yes, I was.'

'I wonder if you could show me where my husband's body was found.'

My face must have betrayed me.

She put her hand on my arm and said, 'It's all right, I know.'

We invited her in and spread the map across a table where I was able to pinpoint the spot where Mr Black was found. The easiest route was to ascend beside the Piper's Burn to the ruined wall and take a compass bearing from there. I told her all these things as kindly as was possible in the circumstances, patiently going over the details until I was sure she would recognise the spot when she reached it.

Her request was not that unusual in itself. People who have lost loved ones often venerate the location where they died and sometimes approach us to help them. As well as being a superb mountaineer our Team Member, Heather Morning, is also a ranger with Cairngorm Mountain. When she was asked to light a candle at a particular spot on Cairngorm she took time away from guiding school groups and skiers, from monitoring the hill's flora and fauna, from teaching and other duties, and went out of her way to do so. Not only that, she took and sent back a photograph. Heather says it is a privilege to be entrusted in this way, to carry someone else's light.

Mrs Black was with friends who remained in town while she

visited me. No doubt they would accompany her into the corrie to her rendezvous with the past. She left us armed with precise details of how to travel. It was as much as we could do. My abiding impression is of a polite woman whose dignity was intact, who had released the memory of being wronged, if she had been wronged, to retain such memories as were good and all the love that was worth holding onto.

EIGHT

It is no unusual experience for people wandering past the restaurants and bars of Aviemore to have a Sea King fly over them. The Air-Sea Rescue helicopters have been doubling as mountain rescue craft for decades. Their essential task is the carriage of troops to and from the battlefield but the greatest part of their activities over the same period has been in the civilian field. They were used in the Falklands in 1982 and in every major conflict that British forces have participated in since. It is the same craft that are in operation now, although much subject to repair and replacement. Ask the crew and they will tell you the Sea King is like 'my grandfather's axe'.

This is my grandfather's axe. My father replaced the head and I replaced the shaft. This is my grandfather's axe.

They carry a crew of four, pilot and co-pilot, navigator and winchman, but can accommodate 15 passengers when conditions are right. 'Conditions' include not only such variables as wind conditions and load but also distance and fuel requirements. The sheer weight of fuel in the tanks at any time is an important factor, reaching beyond any straightforward fuel/distance ratio. It is not unusual for the Sea King's load to be limited to only the crew on its way to a distant location, but to carry a full complement of passengers on the return journey thanks to the reduction in fuel weight. This careful calculation is frequently a significant factor in rescue operations. The aircraft has two tanks and the crew can transfer fuel from one to the other in the air, ensuring an even distribution of weight.

On news bulletins they can regularly be seen hovering over damaged fishing vessels, lowering a rescuer down to attach himself to a casualty so that both can be winched back up. An indication of the power generated by the rotor is given by the surface of the water as it whips and rises as a sort of inverted rainstorm. They are less often filmed at the crux of a mountain rescue. The 'rescue at sea' and the 'rescue in the mountains' are very different. At sea there are likely to be strong winds but, chances are, they will be more or less steady. In the mountains the cliffs and passes create an unpredictable turbulence that makes hovering close to the rock faces a particularly dangerous enterprise.

Pilots and crew are extraordinarily brave, but never foolhardy. As mountain rescuers we understand that when they have pushed forward, close to a cragfast casualty, retreated and tried again, and finally said they have no choice but to depart the scene – this is reality and has to be accepted. In these circumstances we will have to do it the hard way, almost certainly culminating in carrying the casualty out over rough terrain for several hours. If the casualty is seriously injured, as is likely, this will extend the period of discomfort and possibly worsen his or her injuries.

The importance of these aircraft to mountain rescue is difficult to overestimate. That they have saved lives is obvious, but they have also salvaged the quality of many future lives by minimising trauma. Also, a reduction in rescue duration means the Team's resources become available again more quickly. This is doubly important when you realise that bad weather, heavy hill usage at given times such as holiday weekends, and group activities mean that accidents tend to happen in clusters.

Should either of the Sea King's massive Rolls-Royce engines break down, the workload can be transferred to its companion. Of necessity though, the aircraft have only one gearbox. If it breaks down the rotors will keep turning and an emergency, controlled descent can be effected, as I experienced during the blizzards of 1978 when we made a controlled descent into a turnip field from a relatively low elevation and not, thankfully, from the aircraft's ceiling of 3,000m.

The rotors have a span of 18.9m, just short of the aircraft's total length of 22.15m. Slightly tilted forward they give the aircraft its forward drive. The small rotor on the tail, operating in the vertical plane, turns the craft and, between them, an extraordinary manoeuvrability is achieved. The Sea King has a range of around a hundred miles and 30 minutes of winching time. Its time in the air is limited to five and a half hours.

An early experience with helicopters came after a Glenmore Lodge group walking in Coire Laogh Mor witnessed another party being avalanched. They radioed Fred Harper at the Lodge itself to report two casualties, one of whom had suffered severe leg injuries. These injuries were causing such considerable pain the Lodge party requested that morphine be supplied. Fred called for an ambulance to attend at the Coire na Ciste car park and set out for the scene of the accident with a local GP who happened to be present, driving as high as possible before ascending into the corrie on foot. In the days before Sea King helicopters were less available than they were later, thankfully, to become.

When the avalanche struck it swept the two climbers off the face and down the hill. On a winter climb both were naturally using ice axes. An ice axe has a shaft of about 50cm in length. Its head has a flattened blade, an adze, at one side for cutting steps in the ice, a pick at the other. This point, when used correctly, being turned into the ice as the climber slips, will act as a brake. The other end of the shaft also comes to a point, called the spike, this time to make a secure connection to the ice when the axe is used as a walking stick.

When they arrived the doctor examined both casualties. One had, indeed, suffered an extremely painful leg injury. He was voluble and had been for some time. His companion lay on the ground, looking on in silence. The doctor examined the man with the most obvious injuries first and then turned to his silent companion whose abdomen he found to be quite rigid. This suggested internal bleeding and was sufficient prompting for him to investigate further under the casualty's clothing. There he discovered that, during the fall, the pick of his ice axe had pierced and entered the casualty's abdomen. Although he was the less obviously injured of the two, his plight was by far the greater and it was vital that he be taken to hospital quickly and with as little additional trauma as possible. As so often, speed was of the essence.

Fred radioed RAF Kinloss to request a helicopter and, much to the casualty's good fortune, a Wessex from 202 Squadron was available. It arrived promptly and the Glenmore Lodge party carried the casualty aboard. The doctor travelled with him to Raigmore Hospital where, slightly more than an hour after his accident, he was given a transfusion that amounted to 11 pints of blood. On the hill his companion's pain was deadened and the Glenmore Lodge party carried him out on a stretcher.

I listened to proceedings on the radio with the other Team Members who had turned out, perfectly happy not to have to go on the hill. My respect for the medical profession had increased dramatically though, and I was left to ponder not only the distinction between the urgent and the critical, but also how long the first casualty would have survived if we had been obliged to carry him out.

Three great lessons were reinforced that day. The first was that it is not always the casualty making the most noise who is in most need of attention.

The second was the Golden Hour that the emergency services refer to often, the quickly passing first hour after an incident when correct diagnosis and treatment are most likely to be effective.

The third was an underlining of the value of helicopters in a mountain environment.

Crew entry to the Sea King is from the port side, just behind the pilot and co-pilot. Winching is carried out on the starboard side using a hydraulically operated hoist operated through a broad sliding door located behind the rotor and pontoons. The pontoons contain retractable double wheels so that, between them and a much smaller wheel at the back the aircraft can come down on either land or water. Tucked between the port side pontoon and the fuselage, these days, is a video/infrared detection pod, a recent addition.

To see more you have to climb the ladder and duck your head to enter. When you straighten again you find yourself facing shelves with medical supplies and other essentials. Among the essentials is a flexible aluminium pipe with an open tube at one end, big enough to hold a big, fat Cuban cigar and if the winchman is showing you round, as is likely, he will tell you it is the pee-tube. Evidently the RAF has not yet caught up with gender equality.

Pilot and co-pilot sit behind a wide control console where everything is doubled against the sudden incapacity of one human. Among the many switches and dials are satellite navigation, multi-band homing systems, radios, and search radar. Here and elsewhere are electrical connections to the aircraft's many batteries and generators, mostly suitable for powering sophisticated medical equipment that include incubators for the newborn, including those children who might be born in-flight.

Travelling towards the back you will come across a small cubby hole with a computer screen and chair. The navigator sits here, subject to a constant flow of information including pictures from the infrared detection pod. This screen will show the heat of a cigarette at a distance of several miles and he can direct his pilot in to such a range as the night-vision goggles they also carry can come into play.

The body of the aircraft is where the winchman sits, taking charge of the hydraulic hoist and its electrically powered, emergency substitute, various straps, ropes, flotation jackets and much else. The winchman is the crew member who will strap himself in and go over the side when required. In addition to all this he will normally be a fully trained, paramedic qualified to administer morphine and other drugs. In what can be desperate circumstances he will supply immediate first aid, often life-saving. Like the others he will not consider himself to be heroic.

This is the 'what-it's-all-about' area. This is where the troops wait to tumble out onto the battlefield, and the mountain rescuers to jump down onto the plateau. It is also where the casualty lies on the way to, usually, Raigmore Hospital. None of the crew speaks much because the engines and rotors make such a tremendous racket. To transfer information it is necessary to don communication helmets that shut off all external sounds and are connected by radio.

The Team Leader, in charge of the rescue operation, is likely to understand the terrain better than the crew, having walked across it often. Many times I have stood between pilot and co-pilot as they made their final approach, letting them know about the bumps and gnarls of the ground, or of a cliff face, to a degree of detail that even their instruments were not sensitive to. Frequently it takes them into positions close to the extent of their skills, where it is necessary to stand the aircraft on its tail or tilt it delicately above the corrie's rim or turn it in its own length with uncompromising rocky cliffs on three sides.

At Glenmore Lodge, and in more recent years at the Mountain Rescue Centre at Inverdruie, you will often find a helicopter landed. The crew might be having their lunch or just drinking tea. Again, they might be assisting in training new Team Members, giving them the feel of what it is to stand under a hovering aircraft, or winching them up and down. As a familiarising exercise they might take them out to the Northern Corries and lower them onto the rocks to make their own way back.

Aircraft and crew are controlled by the Aeronautical Rescue Control Centre (ARCC) at RAF Kinloss. ARCC's whole purpose is to assist in the saving of life through 'the efficient coordination of information and assets', to quote its own website. In addition to the Mountain Rescue Teams it works with the police, coastguard and ambulance authorities.

Mountain rescuers and professional flyers rarely meet off the job but generally get on well. In the air communication is by helmet microphone, and only the Leader is likely to make much contact. The same helmets disguise appearance and create a sort of anonymity. I find rescuers and crew enjoy much the same things, such as sport and the occasional pint of beer, and all of us like to laugh. We share the same exhilaration when a rescue comes off, the same heartache when it does not.

NINE

On 14th August 1989 at about 10.00 a group of three walkers left Linn of Dee at Claybokie. Their intention was to walk alongside the Lui Water to Derry Lodge, continuing over Luibeg Bridge, around Carn a'Mhaim and into the Lairig Ghru, eventually finishing at Coire Cas car park. The leader of the group was a Mr Volker Mallinson, a 44-year-old accountant from Göttingen. The others were his two children, 11-year-old Peter, and daughter, Helen, aged eight. In total length this walk was about 26km with an ascent of 500m, long and challenging enough for most adults.

The group was dropped at Linn of Dee by Mr Mallinson's wife, Juliette, who then drove the long route to Strathspey and up into the skiing areas to meet them. When they set out it was a lovely day so, by the time they arrived at Coire Cas they would be a tired but happy group.

When Mr Mallinson reached Derry Lodge he decided to alter his route, turning north to enter Glen Derry, which is at the south end of the Lairig an Laoigh. There is no mystery attending his decision. On a wonderful morning such as this the call of the heights is strong. The additional ascent would be accompanied by a reduction in distance travelled which might also mean a reduction in duration.

The diversion took the group into the forest around the lower reaches of the River Derry, which is a joy to walk through in almost any conditions. Close to the summit of the pass they turned into Coire Etchachan and climbed to Loch Etchachan at a height of about 920m onto high, wild land. Continuing their ascent onto the Cairngorm Plateau they reached the summit of Ben MacDhui, the second-highest mountain in Britain, at about 13.00.

So far all was well but, unknown to Mr Mallinson, a mighty storm was blowing in from the north. At the summit cairn the group was overtaken by torrential rain and powerful winds with visibility reduced to only a few metres. They wore summer clothing only and their waterproofs were limited. Mr Mallinson carried a map but no compass. Presumably he had anticipated clear views for the whole day and believed his map-reading ability would be sufficient even without a compass to determine north.

He took out the map but it was not protected by a plastic cover and very soon was pulped by wind-driven rain. The group had been walking and climbing for over three hours and now discovered how quickly conditions on the plateau can turn from warm, clear and idyllic to something horrendous, even, if we are to ascribe them human characteristics, savage.

With no way of knowing which way was which, Mr Mallinson gathered the children to him and set out on what must have been a random course. There are rough tracks running in several directions from the MacDhui cairn and they may have followed one of these. In fact, they did indeed set out north, the correct direction, but it was an error of judgement founded on inexperience of the area.

When Mr Mallinson considered the alternatives of retracing his steps or continuing he must have realised that by retracing he and his children would be faced with a longer distance than by continuing. In addition, there would be no vehicle waiting for them and no way of getting word to his wife. To someone inexperienced in this particular landscape and its weathers the logical decision would have been to continue, albeit into the teeth of the gale. However, this plateau is the widest and most exposed in Scotland and affords absolutely no shelter. Their route took them in the direction of the car park, but they would have done better to turn back and descend as quickly as possible out of the wind.

Mrs Mallinson reached the car park around 18.00 and began

what proved to be a long wait. At some point she decided to report her husband and children as possibly missing and, as the new Leader of the Cairngorm Mountain Rescue Team, I received a call from the police at 22.00. Had the call been about adults I would have thought twice about calling out the Team at this early stage. Children were involved though, and that changes everything since their stamina levels are so much lower. I made a general call-out and 18 of us turned out.

Mrs Mallinson had been taken to Glenmore Lodge and we met her there, learning first-hand of the group's plans for the day. From the information given the Lairig Ghru was the obvious focus for the search and our course of action seemed clear. People do not normally get lost in this pass since it is steep-sided and has few possible turns from the track. It could be that one child had become injured or exhausted and slowed all three down; again, they might have turned back.

I decided that a group including a dog and handler should be sent through the Chalamain Gap into the pass, to turn south and meet them, provided they had neither turned back nor, by now, proceeded through. Against this last possibility another two parties would enter Rothiemurchus Forest from the road and walk south towards the Gap.

As is normal with dogs and their handlers Sgt Kenny Lindsay and his 18-month-old German shepherd, Sasha, went on ahead to avoid the confusion of smells and sounds that are likely to accompany any large rescue group. They did not get beyond the car park before they met with Mr Mallinson on his own. It was just after midnight.

He was hypothermic and disoriented but managed to communicate in what was little more than a mumble. He had left the children on the hill. They were in a bad way but not far to the west of the car park, not more than 15 or 20 minutes away.

Armed with this new information we abandoned our earlier plans and 17 of us set off at high speed for the mouth of Coire an t-Sneachda. One of our senior members, Dave Craig, was suffering from toothache and decided to remain at Glenmore Lodge where he could look after Mr Mallinson, the first casualty, get him warm and dry and hot food into him. He would also attend to the radio, communicating with me as I organised from the front line, and linking with the other emergency services.

No one thought for a moment that Mr Mallinson was wrong in leaving the children when he did. His decision to go as speedily for help when he was sure of his location was exactly the right thing to do, but the prospect of endangered children only 15 minutes away energised the whole Rescue Party. We made our way quickly but in ragged order along the path, and it is true to say we were less organised than I would have wished. All of us were physically fit but some were fitter than others and took to the front, stringing the Rescue Party out along the path.

We reached the burn that flows out of the corrie with still no sign of the children. It was evident that Mr Mallinson, in his disoriented condition, had been mistaken about distance. That being so he might also have been mistaken about direction. I called the Team together and arranged a line search across the hill as we advanced towards Lurcher's Gully. Each rescuer remained within sight of the next and I radioed back to Glenmore Lodge to keep Dave informed.

Separate from the main group Kenny forged ahead so that Sasha would not have to concentrate through a confusion of scents and sounds. Not too long after, he called me on the radio to say, simply, 'I've got them.' A calm individual always, his voice breaking with emotion left me in no doubt that things were bad. It was now 02.20 and the children had been on their own for more than two hours.

Helicopters can only be requested by a police officer of at least sergeant's rank, although over the years that rule would prove to be as elastic as circumstances demanded. Now with exact knowledge of the children's location I radioed Dave at Glenmore Lodge and gave the grid reference, asking him to call Aviemore Police Station to ask the duty sergeant to call ARCC and request the services of a helicopter. High winds still prevailed and visibility was low so there was a real doubt about this being possible.

When I reached Kenny, Sasha sat close by, her job done, leaving her master free to attend the casualties. Young Peter was in a much reduced condition, but conscious and responsive. 'Where is your sister?' I asked, as gently as I could.

He pointed over his shoulder and said, 'I think she's dead.'

At that point John Lyall had been a Team Member for six years and to some extent I had taken him under my wing. Still in his twenties he was working for the Forestry Commission but had a natural aptitude in all the mountain skills and had already surpassed me as a climber. In time he would become an accomplished mountain guide. I left him and some others with Kenny, helping Peter into warm, dry clothes and a sleeping bag and assisting him in any way they could.

Helen lay behind a boulder where it appeared she had taken shelter. A tiny, delightful, elfin creature, at first sight she looked very much alive. Her eyes were clear and blue and still bright. Her skin was soft to touch but closer examination revealed no vital signs. We were aware her father had left her under the impression she was well. Her decline may well have been sudden and may not yet have been complete. Only a doctor can diagnose death and we understood that hypothermia can reduce the body's vital functions while the spark of life still shines.

Wes Sterrit was a key member of the Scottish Avalanche Information Service and Roger Wild an ex-marine and policeman, later a professional mountaineer. Paul Grey was a physical training instructor with the RAF. All were supremely competent hill men. Stepping out from the others they joined me beside Helen and we discussed the merits of attempting cardiopulmonary resuscitation. Once begun, we knew, we would have to keep going until Helen reached a centre of medical excellence where her life, if she was truly still alive, could be supported by machines. To reduce the possibility of brain damage we would have to start as quickly as possible, but we also knew CPR had its own, inherent, dangers. All of us were fathers and felt intensely about her plight.

In the course of these few hours on the hill I had realised and accepted that the front line of an operation like this was not the place to co-ordinate from, as the Leader should. It was impossible to step back and take an overview. Once again I called Dave Craig. Fully confident of his abilities I asked for all messages to be transferred through base, so delegating this aspect of leadership to him. At the same time I learned that Dr Marjory Langmuir, a general practitioner in Aviemore, was present at Control. Keenly aware of the urgency of the situation we were anxious to make a start. Assessing the situation as best she could under difficult circumstances Dr Langmuir told me she had no objection to our proceeding.

Helen was lying in a hollow and we were concerned that we might simply push her down into it during the CPR process. To give a firm base, and to make her as comfortable as possible, at the same time helping to retain her body's warmth, Roger lay flat on the cold ground so we could lay her out on top of him. Wes began the process of pressing down rhythmically on her diaphragm with Paul administering mouth-to-mouth resuscitation, tilting back her head, pinching her nose and inflating her lungs with his own breath. The system would not have worked with anyone heavier than Helen but seemed to be successful on this occasion. After a short while Paul and Wes exchanged roles and continued in this back-and-forth fashion for a seemingly endless two hours.

On the Moray Coast the crew of Rescue 137 were already out of their beds. Given the conditions they had doubts about taking the Sea King so close to the cliffs of Coire an t-Sneachda but, when they heard that children were at risk, brought themselves to a state of readiness and waited impatiently for a break in the weather. Now it was my job to keep Dave informed at Glenmore Lodge and look out for the helicopter as it approached. In fact it would be 03.40 before they arrived, so unremitting was the storm. What went through Mr and Mrs Mallinson's heads in those hours, the emotional turmoil, how desperately they must have wished to be present, can only be guessed.

In the early morning conditions abated enough for the pilot to make his attempt. I remember looking down on the lights of

Aviemore when suddenly other lights appeared among them, closing the distance between us rapidly. My radio crackled and I heard my own call sign. 'Cairngorm John this is Rescue 137 – three minutes from your location – over.'

The pilot made no attempt at landing in winds gusting with such force. Instead he brought 137 in as close as he dared and sent down a winch.

Our challenge on the ground was to withstand the battering from the downdraft while keeping Helen's CPR going for as long as possible, securing her in the harness and getting her aloft with Paul and Wes. They had to restart as quickly as possible in the aircraft. Young Peter was winched up in the winchman's arms and dropped at Glenmore Lodge where his parents were waiting. At 04.10 the children were properly off the hill.

To save Helen's life, should that be possible, reaching a centre of excellence was of the first order of importance. We knew that Foresterhill Hospital in Aberdeen was closer to the North Sea oil industry and felt it was more likely to be equipped for such cases and suitably experienced. In fact we were wrong in this and Raigmore Hospital in Inverness would have been equally suitable.

At our request, the pilot set out in the direction of Aberdeen. Wes and Paul continued CPR on the floor of the aircraft and, other than the short period of the hoist, never stalled or gave up hope. From a point shortly after they began working on her Helen's colour remained rosy and healthy-looking until they handed her over to the doctors at Foresterhill. Optimism and hope proved to be ill-founded. At 05.07, after a thorough examination, Helen Mallinson was pronounced dead on arrival.

This news was devastating to all the rescuers.

Rescue 137 flew Wes and Paul back to Lossiemouth through the breaking of another day and a sympathetic duty officer drove them the rest of the way home. It was a journey of many hours in which to contemplate the events of the night. Roger and I were perhaps more fortunate; then again, perhaps not. We sat at my kitchen table for hours going over all the 'might have beens' and 'what ifs'. Our sense of identification and emotional involvement was much higher than normal, and how much they impacted on decision-making would always be a debatable point. The Team's hasty advance into the corrie was something for me to ponder at length. Anne supplied us with endless cups of tea until Roger left and kept me going until exhaustion overcame even the adrenaline and grief. Through the daylight hours while I slept she fended off call after call.

We learned later that Mr Mallinson had carried Helen until they dropped below the cloud base and could see the lights of Aviemore. Knowing more or less where they were he made his decision. Leaving the children to get help was the right thing to do but, tragically, hypothermia had already set in.

We took it hard that we had failed to save Helen's life. In time my expectations of what might be achieved in such conditions would be modified greatly downwards. In the immediate aftermath though, we wondered if we could have done more or better. In addition, we were upset that she had been taken into such a situation in the first place, and that the dangers of the Cairngorms had been so underestimated.

The point of high debate, in the press and within the medical profession, was the use of cardiopulmonary resuscitation. This was the aspect the press picked up on after the initial shock of the death. The following day, in my absence, it was to Kenny Lindsay they turned for comment. He answered their questions fully but with sensitivity and I look back on that with gratitude. In time I would learn how to deal with reporters and, in fact, establish good relations with many. For now though, his closing comment is probably worth repeating.

'Whatever the rights and wrongs of it, the parents are suffering acutely and I am not going to say anything that will add to their distress.'

Remembering our own feelings, and the example that had been handed to me by Mollie and Peter, I kept this in mind through all the years, and the many rescues, that lay ahead.

TEN

The wide fin of rock that separates Coire Cas from Coire an t-Sneachda is known as the Fiacaill Ridge. One of Cairngorm's easier climbs it presents a fair amount of exposure on both sides that demands a cool head. In good conditions though, it can be ascended without use of the hands. Hard winter conditions make for a different story, as we were reminded late in 1993.

The big corries to the west contain some of the most demanding climbing routes in Britain. First ascenders have the right to name them and some of the names they choose, such as 'fellatio' and 'strapadickonmi', both on the cliffs of Creag Dubh near Newtonmore, will leave you in no doubt that extreme climbers tend to be very young men packed with vigour. Not all though, there are many fine women climbers of whom Jane Thomas was one.

In the fortnight before Christmas a party of three made their way into Coire an t-Sneachda, to the area known collectively as The Mess of Potage, intent on a route known as The Message. All three were experienced technical climbers, with high general fitness levels and wide knowledge of the hills. Robert Thomas was an outdoor training instructor based in Cumbria and his wife, Jane, maintained similarly high standards. On this trip they were accompanied by their friend George MacEwan. Their ages ranged between 28 and 33.

The weather was fine when they set out but the forecast was for a general worsening in the course of the day. When they reached the foot of The Message Robert felt unwell and thought better of making the attempt. He had assisted in carrying the ropes and other technical gear but was now concerned that he might slow the party's progress. Jane also did not feel at her best but decided to continue. Robert returned to their car and waited, looking on with some concern as the weather changed. Wind speeds rose to around 100mph and gusted even higher. By the expected time of 19.00 George and Jane had not returned. Robert waited until 21.00 and then called the police. They in turn called the Cairngorm Mountain Rescue Team.

The Message tops out on the Cairngorm Plateau at around 1,000m above sea level with no cover and nothing to break the wind. I knew the two climbers were very experienced and would understand the necessity of getting off the hill quickly in the prevailing conditions. Putting myself in their shoes I felt it was likely they had aborted the climb part of the way up, and abseiled back down.

At 22.00 two climbers who, by chance, had spent the day in the area met Robert in the car park. They had seen ropes near the top of the route which looked like they were not in use, which is to say they were not under tension. When they mentioned the colour of the ropes Robert, by now anxious, confirmed that, yes, these would belong to George and Jane. This increased my feeling of concern because if they had topped out they would have carried the ropes with them and if they had abseiled down they would have drawn them after. Possibly they had abseiled down in extreme conditions and abandoned the ropes, but I felt this was unlikely. Again, they may have become stuck on the route and still be up there. At least we had an indication that they were still in the area.

At 22.30 Chris Barley interviewed the two climbers at Aviemore Police Station and afterwards we decided to turn the Rescue Team out. When we assembled at Achintoul at 23.45 the weather at low level was so ferocious we decided to put on harnesses and extra gear before even leaving Aviemore. At 00.30 we left the base and set out for the plateau to look for the top of the topmost rope, and so get an indication of the highest point reached. I led a party of ten up the Fiacaill

Ridge while Chris, who was then our Depute Leader, remained at the Lodge to listen on the radio and co-ordinate the rescue.

In harsh winter conditions the Fiacaill was by no means the pleasant saunter it can be in summer. Instead it was covered in snow and entirely exposed to a hurricane wind that drove us onto our hands and knees and obliged us to dig in with our ice axes. Recognising the dangers inherent in winds of such force Donnie Williamson, the largest and probably strongest of the rescuers, deployed to the back to act as a 'catcher'. More than once he had to take hold of someone who had been dislodged and help them back on their way. We were over two hours on the ascent but saw no sign of the climbers.

Sometime after 03.00 we reached Point 1141, at the top of the ridge and an important location marker on the plateau, and after some rest set off into the wind along the corrie rim in search of the ropes. I was always aware, and hopeful, that a technical rescue might not be required because these two accomplished climbers had managed to get out of trouble under their own steam. I felt that if the ropes were gone it would mean they had somehow coped. At the limits of reasonable hope it might still work out for the best.

Around 03.30 we reached the top of the route – but there was no sign of any ropes. It seemed now that they had either abseiled back down into the corrie where they would be met by one of our parties walking in, or that they were still on the plateau either lost or taking shelter if that was possible. Our party decided to search the high ground around the corrie rim with our head torches piercing the blackness. We continued to do this until we received a radio call from Chris at Glenmore Lodge.

George MacEwan had called from the public phone at the Coire Cas car park at 04.00. After a long and dramatic struggle he was safe but on his own. Having done all he could for Jane he had eventually left her in Coire Raibeirt to make one last desperate attempt to get help. Somehow, he had found the ski area and stumbled against a ski tow. Now understanding where he was he found his way to the public phone.

Chris went on to say that he would go up to the car park to collect George and that the RAF Team was on its way to take over or assist as required. On the plateau, enduring terrible winter conditions ourselves, we weighed up the position. We were fatigued but the RAF would have to ascend to our height before they could take over and that would take time. In present conditions there was no question of a helicopter flying in. The Cairngorm Team was still best placed to search for Jane.

If what George said was correct it was evident they had taken an extreme wrong turning. Coire Raibeirt was on the south side of Cairngorm, on the opposite side of the mountain from the road and safety. A path down into the glen ran beside its stream and, on a good day, afforded wonderful views of the loch, the Shelter Stone and, on the other side, Beinn Mheadheanach. If they found themselves there it meant they had incorrectly turned south instead of north. We regrouped, took a bearing from Point 1141 and set out across the top, into Coire Raibeirt, the wind still blowing hard but reducing in strength. As we walked I had time to muse on what Chris had reported.

George MacEwan was a serious and competent mountaineer. I had known him, rather vaguely, before and was to get to know him better in future. He was already well respected and, in time, his reputation would grow still further. For him to have made such a wrong turning it was apparent that he must have been in an extreme condition. In fact, Chris reported that his face was a 'mask of ice' and that he was hypothermic. By this time I was becoming hypothermic myself and had some concern about the safety of the Team.

We reached Coire Raibeirt and searched for Jane but found no sign. As dawn broke I radioed this news back to Chris. Intent on covering all possibilities he sent an RAF Team up to our location to relieve us. In addition, he sent PC Jimmy Simpson and his rescue dog, Cobra, into Coire Cas accompanied by some of the RAF Team. Cobra was a big, strong German shepherd who had been involved in search and rescue for four years.

It was not until around midday that Cobra discovered Jane's body. She was in Coire Cas, on the other side of the mountain from where our main party was searching. Jimmy reported that there were no signs of life and that her airways were blocked with snow. George, in his hypothermic condition, had become confused and sent us in the wrong direction. Another party made its way quickly into Coire Cas to get Jane onto a stretcher and rush her off the hill as quickly as possible.

By this time we had returned to Glenmore Lodge and I recognised that I was slightly hypothermic. The media was also present, there and around the lower car park, and the place was a hive of activity. Realising that Jane was almost certainly dead I asked that the returning stretcher bearers make their way to the Ski Patrol hut and that other members of the RAF Team, some of whom were fresh from a training course on emergency medical practices, make their way there with the local doctor. In fact the RAF Team brought Jane's body directly down to the lower areas and the waiting media scrum.

The RAF Team was armed with a new device called a pulsoximeter that was designed to fit over a finger. A pulsoximeter determines the percentage oxygen saturation of the haemoglobin in the blood. It is of no value in determining whether or not a victim of hypothermia can be resuscitated, but using it was part of their procedures. Placing it on her finger they were able to take a reading. Apparently in the mistaken belief that this indicated the presence of a pulse, and again in pursuance of their procedures, they began CPR.

Recovering in the warmth of Glenmore Lodge we received radio reports on all this. I felt quite strongly that these dramatic efforts were pointless and possibly extending the suffering of the survivors. Jane had been outside in horrendous conditions for many hours. Her time simply lying in the snow had been lengthy. Almost certainly she was already dead when she was found as her nose and mouth were filled with snow to such a degree that breathing was impossible.

To maximise any chance of revival she had to be taken to a centre of excellence as quickly as possible. By initiating a process of revival procedures, contrary to the policy and accumulated experience of the Cairngorm Mountain Rescue Team, time had been wasted.

Eventually her body was delivered to Raigmore Hospital where she was pronounced dead on arrival. I was in no doubt that exposure and hypothermia had taken her life long before she was found. Disabled by advanced hypothermia she had simply frozen to death. The RAF Team's attempts were well meant in the stress and fatigue of the situation. Their commitment speaks well of their character, but sometimes the best and bravest thing to do in first aid is nothing.

As a consequence much of the press reporting would claim she had been minutes from death when she had been found. *The Express* headlined, 'Rescue Came Minutes Late' and *The Glasgow Herald*, 'Woman Climber Dies after Surviving Night on Mountain'. All of this would later provoke a passionate correspondence in the national press but, for the present, we were tidying up and determining exactly what had happened. George MacEwan gave a lucid and professional account of the personal courage displayed by both climbers in conditions that would eventually prove hopeless.

They had taken quite a hammering from the weather in the course of their climb of The Message. Jane's condition, less than ideal at the start, had worsened as they ascended until she eventually required assistance from George. At the top they ate some chocolate and roped up to ensure they would not become separated. In swirling snow and high winds the beams of their head torches penetrated only a few metres and wind chill took the temperature down below minus 20 degrees. Their faces and outer clothing were covered with ice and, no doubt, hypothermia was by now well established in their systems.

As they made their way slowly across the plateau George came to believe that the ground was sloping the wrong way and asked Jane to check his compass bearing independently. They corrected their direction but then Jane tired suddenly and asked to sit down. Both were by now exhausted and, without doubt, hypothermic.

George recognised this as a significant point in their decline and tried to keep them both going. Eventually the conditions became too much for Jane and they attempted to dig an emergency snow hole, but the snow was soft and drifting and it filled as quickly as they could dig. When they started again Jane made such progress as she could on her hands and knees. When she could go no further George grasped her jacket and dragged her backwards through the snow almost like a sledge. Soon she began falling in and out of consciousness. He scraped a shallow indentation in the snow and arranged her body so her rucksack shielded her from the wind as much as possible.

Jane could do little or nothing to help herself so George lay with her, sharing his body heat as best he could. He kept talking until she lost consciousness, not responding to shouts or even pinched cheeks, and then was faced with the most difficult of decisions any climber may have to make, however apparent the logic may be. He untied the rope and left his companion, his friend, and set off in hope of saving them both. Navigating through blunted concentration and continuing low visibility he found his way, at last, to the ski road and followed it down to the car park and the public phone. Although George had been in Coire Cas with Jane, in his condition he believed he had left her in Coire Raibeirt

Jane Thomas and George MacEwan were a strong and experienced climbing pair and her death serves to underline the element of risk that is inherent in all hill activities. With hindsight it seems apparent they should have turned back when Robert decided to do so and Jane also felt less than fully fit. There was much less discussion afterwards about the rights and wrongs of their decisions, or any mistakes they might have made, than about the attempts to revive her; indeed, of what it is possible to achieve when a casualty's condition has dropped to the level that Jane's had when George was obliged to leave her.

ELEVEN

Much has been written and said on the subject of hypothermia by people who have good cause to be regarded as experts. Sometimes though, professional expertise is a field for disagreements as much as for specialist knowledge and shared experience. The tragic case of Jane Thomas and the misleading headlines that followed sparked a public debate among doctors which *The Glasgow Herald* hosted in its letters column, and at least one article.

Only days after the events on The Message and across the Cairngorm Plateau a former Medical Officer with the Scottish Mountain Rescue Committee, Dr Alastair MacGregor, was reported as calling for a 'heightened awareness in methods of resuscitation for victims of severe hypothermia', in light of 'recent experiences in Alpine countries where hypothermia cases previously confirmed as "not saveable" were now surviving'. He added that his comments 'were not a criticism of the management involved in the rescue of Mrs Thomas'.

In the same article Mr Mark Janssens, a senior doctor in Accident and Emergency at Raigmore Hospital, Inverness, was reported as believing that 'Mr MacGregor had clearly implied the hospital did not know how to deal with cases of severe hypothermia', and was reported as being disappointed that Mr MacGregor had chosen to comment so soon after Mrs Thomas's death without knowing 'all the facts'. A third comment in the same article, from Dr Gavin Brown, a consultant at the Belford Hospital in Fort William, weighed in on behalf of his Raigmore colleagues. 'I don't think any hospital in Britain,' he said, 'regularly dealing with cases of hypothermia, would fall into the trap of pronouncing people dead when they were not.'

The undertones of anger and restraint were detectable by all with even a measure of sensitivity. Like Mr Janssens I believed this was not the time for such a public debate and felt deeply for the survivors who might not only be reading these comments but would perhaps be obliged to answer questions, if not from the press then from friends and concerned relatives.

The debate having been entered though, I felt a point had to be made on behalf of the Team. The death of Helen Mallinson in 1989 had been sufficient to prompt a consideration of how such cases should be treated on the hill. Much discussion within the Team had followed as well as reading and consultation. Dr David Snadden, who was our Medical Officer between 1985 and 1992, had gone so far as to publish a paper titled 'The Field Management of Hypothermic Casualties Arising from Scottish Mountain Accidents' in the *Scottish Medical Journal*. By the time of Jane Thomas's tragic death our policy was so well established we felt obliged not so much to defend it as to share it. With Dr Peter Grant, who had become Medical Officer of the Cairngorm Mountain Rescue Team in succession to David, I signed a carefully worded letter that confirmed the Team's policy and procedures in all cases of hypothermia.

This is the essential part of what we wrote:

'…it is NOT the policy of the Cairngorm Mountain Rescue Team to commence cardiopulmonary resuscitation on hill casualties with severe hypothermia.

'Our policy is to transport such casualties to Raigmore Hospital in Inverness without delay and with no interference other than insulation from further heat loss. We have every confidence that the decision to proceed or not with rewarming will be appropriately made at Raigmore by a senior clinician.

'This policy has been agreed by doctors who are active participants in mountain rescue and in the light of a recent review of the world literature on profound hypothermia including the Swiss experience.'

Mountain hypothermia is different from most others in that the casualty is almost invariably obliged to endure wind and low temperatures for a considerable period of time. Someone who falls in a river, or even in the sea, can hope to be taken out in a reasonably short time. They may well be in a position to save themselves. Their drop in temperature is likely to be sudden and, in most cases, brief where the mountaineer's is likely to be sustained. In the course of many rescues we came to believe, indeed had no doubt, that to do as little as possible by way of resuscitation is the best course of action, and that speed of evacuation is of the essence.

Efforts to maintain oxygenation of the body by cardiopulmonary resuscitation are only of value if they can be sustained until a proper circulation of the blood can be restored by medical means. To commence CPR on a hypothermic casualty on the mountain is worse than futile. In addition to being impossible to perform effectively it is likely to delay evacuation of the casualty, possibly for hours.

All who go on the hill, whether they be competent individuals venturing alone, or groups of adults, or groups of young people led by teachers, should be continuously aware that hypothermia can and does happen. The condition comes in two classes, or stages, mild and severe. 'Mild' hypothermia left unattended will develop into 'severe' but can be recognised in its early stages and action taken.

As often as not it sets in when people are unfit. They may, over the course of a long and demanding day, become unable to continue to keep warm by means of exercise. The human body generates heat as a by-product of muscular activity and unfit muscles are less able to continue for lengthy periods. At whatever standard of fitness, all muscle needs fuel and once the fuel provided by food has been burned off, and reserves in the form of glycogen in the liver have become depleted, the body becomes exhausted and can no longer generate heat. Like a house without heating its temperature will then drop unless really well insulated. Wind chill will exacerbate these processes.

When I give talks I like to illustrate this in a couple of ways. I say, 'If you want to understand what the wind can do imagine this – you take off all your clothes, give yourself a cold shower but do not dry off, and climb onto the roof. It won't be long before you start to shiver.' This imagined example usually serves, so I continue. 'Now, think how much worse this will be high in the mountains in blizzard conditions.'

Wind chill can easily take ambient temperature down as far as minus 18 degrees or even lower, and often does. This is optimum running temperature of a domestic freezer.

'Now, imagine a piece of meat, a piece of venison or beef – how hard it goes. This is much the same material as we humans are made of. Any notion of being "tough enough" to withstand it, or shake it off, should be discarded. No one is that tough.'

Hypothermia develops from exposure as the body draws blood away from its extremities to protect the vital organs. The right clothing should be carried and put on BEFORE conditions worsen. Adequate shell clothing should be worn from the outset in winter and carried in summer conditions. Many people who carry overtrousers in their rucksacks seem reluctant to stop and put them on, even as the rain sweeps over them.

People should not go out hungry and should be sure to eat as they go. It is all too easy in the course of a long day to forget about food but having that energy inside, and wearing the right clothing as insulation, is imperative not only for survival, in extreme cases, but for comfort and enjoyment.

Adequate clothing, physical fitness, food, recognising the effects of wetness and wind, these are the essential require-ments for preventing hypothermia. They can be enough even in extreme conditions and, indeed, it is possible to survive over-night by simply getting out of the wind, by taking advantage of whatever natural barriers, boulders or hollows in the ground the landscape might offer and huddling there with your back to the wind.

Some professionals and advanced amateurs will dig snow holes of considerable size and take shelter there. In the Cairngorms these caverns can remain intact for some time and may be used by quite a number of climbers as part of a planned exercise. Indeed, sometimes they are dug side by side and linked together by tunnels. Advanced mountaineers are trained in this and accomplish it as a matter of course, as I often have. I also make the point though, and repeat it here in this context, that the walker or climber who is in trouble on the Cairngorms, whether on the plateaux or the surrounding mountain ranges, is better to make his or her way down even assuming possession of the correct digging tools. Such is the time and energy required it would be better spent in reaching a safer, lower place.

Mild hypothermia can be difficult to recognise as its symptoms tend to appear gradually. Leaders should be alert to any group member who begins to slow down or becomes quiet. They may stumble or just seem mentally slow and, as the body attempts to generate heat, there may be shivering. At this stage the condition is treatable and the great thing is to get the casualty off the hill and warmed up. The casualty will almost certainly recover quickly. If no action is taken the condition will worsen and confusion will follow. Eventually the shiver reflex will disappear and 'mild' will deteriorate into 'severe'.

The disappearance of this reflex is an important indicator of severe hypothermia but it is also possible for a casualty to become severely hypothermic without passing through a state of shivering. Shivering is a muscular activity switched on by the body in an attempt to generate heat. If the body's temperature drops because it has used up all its body fuel it does not shiver.

For all cases of severe hypothermia it is imperative to get the victim off the hill and to an appropriate medical centre such as Raigmore Hospital in Inverness. The body's systems are shutting down, drawing blood rapidly into its core to surround and protect the vital organs of brain, liver, lungs, most of all and finally the heart. Soon the victim will lose consciousness and have to be carried off the hill.

For mountain rescuers the sequence of decision-making at the site can be summarised as follows. Is the casualty shivering? If yes, the condition is mild. Rewarm by giving a warm drink and food to fuel the body's own natural heat generation. Insulate against further heat loss. If the casualty is capable of walking, and has been refuelled and insulated, evacuation on foot is preferable to a stretcher. It is quicker and it promotes the natural generation of body heat by means of muscular activity. Try to avoid over-treating semi-conscious casualties.

If the casualty's shiver reflex has stopped and/or he or she is non-responsive the condition is severe. That being so, is the casualty conscious? If yes, insulate from further heat loss and evacuate to hospital. If the answer is no, are there signs of life, vital signs? If yes, insulate from heat loss and evacuate to hospital. If not, the important point is made in our instructions to rescuers, DO NOT START CPR. Instead, insulate and evacuate as before.

All this may seem complicated and difficult and an unreasonable level of responsibility to place on the shoulders of volunteers with no medical qualifications. In practice though, in rescues over many years, it has never been difficult to distinguish between those casualties who will be capable of walking given food, drink and insulation, and more serious cases.

All this circles round to our letter in *The Glasgow Herald* and the deaths of Helen Mallinson, Jane Thomas and many others. The condition 'severe hypothermia' can be stabilised but not reversed on the hill. As mentioned earlier, cardiopulmonary resuscitation is futile in these circumstances. Misguided attempts in a case of apparent cardiac arrest can convert a slow, undetectable circulation into ventricular fibrillation and true cardiac arrest.

Faced with the condition of Helen Mallinson now, even allowing for the emotional impact that comes with an endangered child, we would do no more than place her in a zipped survival bag and get her off the hill and to hospital as quickly as possible. In the case of her brother, Peter, who was exhausted and cold, but responsive, we would put him in a warm bag such as a sleeping bag, provide him with warm drink and food and, again, get him off the hill. There was nothing to be achieved in beginning CPR on Jane Thomas when she was eventually found.

Sometimes the Team can be called out before the condition descends from mild to severe, as we were in June 2004 to a group of schoolchildren from Vale of Leven School, on an expedition over Bynack More. In more recent times people have carried mobile phones on the hill and their teacher called in to report that some of his young charges could not continue. The Team attended this call immediately and very quickly realised that the pupils were suffering from no more than early, mild hypothermia. Their teacher had, correctly, stopped the party, put a tent up and got the casualties inside. Hot drinks and warm clothing did the rest, but the youngsters were rather dispirited and felt they should be carried out.

The idea of stretchering them out unnecessarily was not an attractive one. It would also give them a sense of failure and turn a positive early experience of our sport into a negative one. Instead we had them change into the dry clothing they were carrying in their rucksacks. We got some food into them and a hot drink. Banter with the rescuers lifted their spirits. Once out in the open air again we invited them to walk 'just a bit further so we would have less carrying to do'. With their own muscles fuelled by food and drink their dry clothing provided the insulation necessary to retain this heat. When they got properly going again they found they were able to continue and finished their walk independently.

It was no miracle, only the body responding to sensible treatment, but it may have seemed like one. The right action had been taken before anything like a critical point had been reached. Conditions, of course, had been nowhere near as severe as they had for the Mallinson family or for George MacEwan and Jane Thomas.

Our Team Doctor, Peter Grant, tells me it is a well-established medical fact that not all unresponsive casualties are beyond recovery and that resuscitation can sometimes be achieved in the controlled conditions of the hospital after an experienced clinician has made the decision on whether to proceed. That is why he is reluctant to diagnose death on the hill, and why our policy is to insulate cold and unresponsive casualties with minimum disturbance, and deliver them to an appropriate medical centre as quickly as circumstances allow.

Another fact though, is that in all of my time with the Cairngorm Mountain Rescue Team we have never taken anyone rendered unresponsive by hypothermia off the hill who has then survived. Climbers and hillwalkers facing the decision on whether to continue or retreat, particularly those leading children and young adults, will decide which fact is the more salient.

TWELVE

Climbers, walkers, travellers, adventurers of every kind come to the Cairngorms from all across the world. They bring their talents and skills and take away mementoes that might be as simple a thing as a stone from a mountain stream or a seed cone from a Scots Pine. The force of attraction, even after daunting experiences, can be remarkable. In London there is a medical photographer who might have used his skills to picture the metalwork that holds his right leg together except he has no need of *aides-memoire*. His experiences are burned deeply into his memory and, besides, he comes back every year, still in love with the hills.

The 28th March 1991, the Easter Weekend, gave mostly bright, high-pressure days ideally suited to mountaineering. Mel Walker and his friend Paul Hyett had called the Ben Alder Estate Office from London and been given permission by the Head Stalker to drive along the track from Dalwhinnie to Ben Alder Lodge. The sun shone on snow-covered hills and crystal clear streams as they walked from there deep into the Ben Alder area. The long walk allowed for a valuable stretching of the muscles and time for a mental adjustment away from the pressures and bustles of city life into the slower pulse of wild land.

To leave the road at the gothic Ben Alder Lodge is to enter a different kind of terrain where broad expanses of level ground are bounded by mountains and water, herds of deer graze and dotterel and grouse lay their eggs among the moorlands. At Loch Pattack the path turns south-west, below a long range of four Munros

.with many sub-tops and spurs. Of these, Geal Charn is the highest summit. Beside one of its spurs the path runs over a narrow pass known as the Bealach Dubh, the Black Pass, on the other side of which lies another pair of Munros, the closest being the area's crowning glory, Ben Alder.

For most of the remainder of their approach this mountain and its eastern companion, Beinn Bheoil, loomed directly in front of the two. On the other side of the pass the range terminates above Loch Ossian with, beyond that, Glen Nevis and the path to Fort William. It is tremendous country and the paths from Dalwhinnie to Fort William afford one of the great Highland foot journeys.

Before you reach the Bealach Dubh, still within the broad flat-lands but tucked into the embrace of the hills, lies Culra Bothy. Here the two spent the night, rising early on Good Friday with the two mountains that had filled their imaginations on the walk in still on their minds. As they made the approach to Beinn Bheoil their attention could not but have been arrested by Ben Alder with its round, snow-covered top distinctly outlined against the blue sky. More experienced climbers would have known that, in these cold spring nights and bright sunny days, the condition of the high snowfields can alter rapidly.

At the time Mel was an experienced walker and climber, not so Paul, but on this occasion neither carried ice axes or crampons, absolute necessities for walking on Scotland's winter hills. It being March they might have thought in terms of spring weather in London, but on the high tops of Inverness-shire winter conditions still prevailed. At least both wore good-quality outdoor clothing which would play an important part in the next day's events.

The Scottish Mountaineering Club guidebook, *Central Highlands* by Peter Hodgkiss, has this to say about the mountain: 'Ben Alder shares with the deeper recesses of the Cairngorms a quality of genuine remoteness. When winter storms blow there, and they seem as fierce in the long glens as on the top, the strongest party will be taxed.'

It began to snow about the time they reached Ben Alder summit. Paul was elated at having completed his first two Munros and privately swore to complete many more, but it looked as if the weather was worsening. To get down more speedily they attempted to glissade for part of the way. This is to say they used their waterproofs to form a slip plane with the snow and slid down on their bottoms. To control such a descent it is usual to use the ice axe, holding it in both hands, turning the head into the snow so the pick acts as a brake, pressing down with the upper body.

This simple method means the rate of descent can be controlled by turning the pick more deeply into the snow and is the recognised method for arresting a slide. It is the usual technique that is taught and practised by mountain guides throughout the world. If the walker should find himself slipping head first, perhaps after a fall, he can turn himself upright again by simply jamming the pick in and holding on.

Without ice axes they attempted to control their descent by digging in the heels of their boots. This is not an acceptable practice, but their primary error was being on the hill without proper equipment.

Unknown to either of them they were glissading over the route of a hill burn that eventually reached a vertical fall of at least 50m, interrupted, part of the way down, by a small ledge. Water pooled and swirled on the ledge before spilling over to fall the rest of the way onto the rocky floor of the glen. Entirely covered by snow it was out of both sight and sound, and the condition of the covering snow was such that it gave no indication of the burn until a hole appeared just above the drop.

Paul was glissading joyously but in an uncontrolled fashion behind Mel when he noticed they were being funnelled into a much steeper gully. With a feeling of uncertainty he stopped and stood up. Below him the gully grew narrower and icier with, clearly visible below, a metre-wide hole that Mel was cautiously negotiating his way around. Deciding discretion was the better part of valour Paul remained upright and moved to the left where he eventually encountered rocks and a sheer drop onto more snow. He had no alternative but to retrace his steps.

By now Mel was safely on the other side. Attempting to join him, Paul slipped. 'Dig your heels in!' Mel shouted, but it was too late.

With his heels scraping the ice in front of him Paul slid uncontrollably down 15m of icy slope and dropped into the hole. He fell for a further 10m and, when he came to rest, found he was on a narrow ledge surrounded on all sides by walls of either frozen snow or icy rock. Centimetres to his left the water took a sharp 90-degree turn to continue its fall, still under the snow, into the glen. He had chipped his left ankle and broken his right femur in two places. Although he was unaware of it at the time his broken right leg was slewed in front of him to become trapped against the cliff by his raised left foot. It was this arrangement that arrested his momentum and prevented him continuing over the edge to his death.

The femur, or thigh bone, is the largest bone in the body and its fracture means immense internal blood loss and shock. Fortunately, the wound had not opened to make infection more likely; even so, this injury alone was life-threatening. He also found himself unable to move, up to his waist in a pool of cold water, as cold as it is possible for water to be, water that did not freeze only because gravity obliged it to move, being constantly drenched by more water cascading from above. He had lost his glasses, but it was almost lightless down there anyway. All he could see was the hole in the snow he had fallen through and the still darker patch to his left where the burn spilled over. It was about 17.30.

Mel scrambled up to the hole. 'Paul,' he called down. 'Are you all right?'

'I've broken my leg!'

'I'm coming down.'

Mel bravely climbed through the narrow gap in the snow and descended into the darkness. Weighing the situation up quickly, his first great fear was that Paul might drown. He suggested that he carry his friend out of the hole on his shoulders, but Paul decided

against. Another fall could see them both badly injured on the
ledge, or over the edge to their deaths. There was no choice but for
Mel to return to Culra and seek help.

In fact he did not have to go all the way back. He met a number
of walkers in the glen who raced to Culra where they passed the
message to a group of mountain bikers who, in turn, sped off to
Dalwhinnie to sound the alarm. Details are sketchy but it seems
there was also a honeymoon couple just moved into the bothy.

Here I pause to invite the reader into a moment's contempla-
tion. Paris more readily comes to mind as a romantic honeymoon
destination than Culra – but, could the bustle of city streets match
the sound of the river through the bothy window – could the bright
lights of Montmartre match the stars above Ben Alder – could
celebrated French cuisine match pre-cooked mince reheated on
a gas stove? All this to be shared with whatever passer-by might
happen along? These are the irresistible attractions of the Scottish
Highlands that any prospective bride should weigh up carefully
before calling the whole thing off.

When Mel left him Paul knew he had a long wait ahead and it
was only now he realised how badly he was injured. His right leg
was so badly broken it was completely disconnected from the hip
and his left ankle was chipped which led to severe swelling within
his boot.

Mel returned, followed by the male honeymooner remembered
only as 'David'. David brought a sleeping bag with him, as well as
a survival bag and a small stove and on the ledge the three of them
assessed the situation. Deciding that Paul would be best moved out
of the water David suggested using an ice axe as a splint.

'A broken leg is one thing,' Paul replied, 'and a vasectomy is
another.'

A small area beside the pool was relatively dry. David and Mel
moved Paul onto it, with Paul's assistance, as far as was practical.
They put him first into the sleeping bag and then the survival bag to
insulate him and then, thanks to David's presence of mind and the
stove, had tea and chicken soup. After this David had done all he

could and returned to his, no doubt impatient, bride and Wedding Night plus One.

A message can alter quite considerably as it moves from mouth to ear and on, especially when it is fired by urgency. The alarm was finally raised at 19.30 but the message I received was that a climber had been trapped in a 'snow hole' with a broken leg. This was a puzzle because every winter mountaineer knows that a snow hole is a hole dug by the climbers themselves for the purposes of shelter and is not a place where a broken leg is likely to be sustained.

Rescue 137 picked three of our rescuers up from the football pitch in Kingussie, Wes Sterrit, Roger Wild and Tony Burley, and flew them as close to the scene as was possible. By this time conditions had changed for the worse and visibility was much reduced. The pilot decided he would park the aircraft at Culra and wait while the three rescuers climbed the hill to investigate.

Shortly afterwards I arrived with the rest of the Team in a convoy of Land Rovers. Immediately I asked two fit members, Sarah Atkinson and Willie Anderson, to proceed directly up the hill. Both were strong and committed rescuers. After checking with the pilot I asked Chris Barley and the other Team Members to follow with the stretcher and set off up the hill myself. Sarah and Willie were already with our first party when I arrived.

'Where is he?' I asked.

'You've just walked over him.'

The temperature had dropped and the snow now had the appearance of being reliable. The breach Paul had fallen through was not particularly wide though, and we were wary of enlarging it since there was no way of telling what area of snow was unsupported by ground. As in all first aid situations our primary duty was to ensure we did not become the next casualties. The sound of cascading water came up through the breach.

Since we were unwilling to meddle with the breach it would take a smaller man to get through and down. Wes, Willie and I all qualified quite comfortably as 'not too large', but it was Wes who stepped forward first. We lowered him down and a cursory examination determined that Paul's injuries were much worse than we had been led to expect and his pain was very great. By this time he was hypothermic, his blood pressure was low and although he never lost consciousness he was very tired.

Among our first aid supplies we carried a canister of Entonox, an analgesic gas most often used by midwives. An effective painkiller it would have the virtue of keeping Paul in possession of his senses when used cautiously. When he reached the ledge Wes said, 'I'm with the Mountain Rescue Team', the most welcome words Paul had ever heard, and showed him how to use the gas. He also pushed a heat bag inside the sleeping bag. The canvas bag contained chemicals that generated heat when wet, not only countering the danger of hypothermia but heightening the casualty's morale.

Willie Anderson followed and assisted Mel to climb back into the cold night air where it became clear that he was chilled, shocked and almost hypothermic. Our situation was wide open to the elements so Sarah led him downhill to a more sheltered area and got him insulated and hot liquids into him. Our colleagues had by now arrived with the stretcher.

Eric Pirie was lowered to assist Wes with first aid and, when they had done all that was possible, Willie and I lowered the stretcher, holding it against the force of falling water that tossed and scraped it from side to side against the rock face. Paul must have viewed its descent with some fear that it might be suddenly tugged from our hands and down onto his injured leg. When Eric and Wes finally caught it and lowered it the final metre or so, Willie and I followed and together we got Paul aboard and secure.

The space was cramped and severely confined with no room to avoid the water crashing from above. On three sides we were surrounded by hard packed snow that glittered and sparkled in the light of our head torches. In Willie Anderson's words, it was like the diamond cave in Walt Disney's *Snow White.* On the other side was bare rock, which was what we leaned against as the water pooled and swirled around our gaiters before dropping over the ledge into nothingness. This alarming sight at least gave us some idea of how far from the casualty we might venture. In the course of our work my radio slipped out of its pocket, over the edge and down, never to be seen again.

Paul remained conscious throughout, talkative and as cheerful as possible but, in these conditions, the minutes must have seemed like hours. He held the Entonox mask to his face but, unknown to me, his breathing was so weak it was not operating the valve.

It was apparent that he would have to go through the hole in a vertical orientation, that even in the vertical we might struggle to get stretcher and casualty through. Fortunately, our colleagues had anticipated this and harnessed it accordingly, so we did not have to adjust it in our cramped location. Wes, Willie, Eric and I between us got Paul onto the stretcher and strapped into place with its mesh basket fixed over his head to protect him from falling debris. He was brave, talkative and positive throughout, but now came a phase that would try anyone's courage. Knowing he was unable to assist himself he understood he had to be hoisted upwards over a drop that might be hundreds of metres deep. The others went topside leaving me to offer moral support and take care of the rear. A shout went up and the lift was made, delivering a surge of pain to Paul that made him draw in his breath. The drawn breath brought a charge of Entonox with it and Paul thought, 'Ah, so that's how it works!'

As feared, when he was hoisted to the breach the combination of stretcher and body width was too great to get through the narrow gap. There was no question of lowering him again. The others took the strain from above while I climbed up and cut away at the snow with my axe, showering Paul with chunks of ice. Normally I am a man who moderates his language even in difficult circumstances, but Paul later assured me it was choice during this process.

Back in the cold night air we felt we could allow ourselves a reasonable confidence that he would survive. I radioed the pilot at Culra to let him know what was required and we formed ourselves into a stretcher party. Eric shouted the words that have since become immortal, 'Let's kick ass!', and we carried both stretcher and Paul down to the Bealach Dubh where the pass was most narrow. When, on the way, one of the rescuers mentioned how cold it was Paul offered the heat bag from within the sleeping bag, which was politely declined.

We could only hope the pilot would manage in, but if he could not we would at least be well placed to carry Paul down the path to Culra. In fact, the pilot gave a demonstration of flying skill that would have graced an air show. From our position in the pass we heard the engine start and the rotors begin to turn. Soon the aircraft came into sight, rising slowly as it advanced between the narrowing crags. When the pilot reached us he set down on only one wheel, tilting the helicopter to allow us to advance under the rotors in safety and get Paul aboard. With a wave he was gone and before Paul knew it he was in Raigmore Hospital.

As far as the Team was concerned the rescue was now complete, but we did not achieve a full sense of closure until we reached Culra where Chris presented David and his new wife with a large, red, furry survival bag to snuggle up in. Memorable honeymoons are not rare but theirs was a standout.

Paul had lain injured for 11 hours and the blood loss and shock he suffered in that time might have cost him his life. In his case though, low temperatures conspired to work to his benefit. The cold water on his wounds acted as an ice pack works on a muscle strain for an athlete. With a temperature around zero degrees it slowed down the flow of blood around the breaks and reduced loss to a minimum. It also numbed the pain, at least to some degree.

Now a great friend of Cairngorm Mountain Rescue Team, Paul no longer refers to 29th March as Good Friday but as 'Kick Ass Day'. His recovery went well and he continually expresses his gratitude to the rescuers who saved his life. He completed our sponsored walk two years later using walking poles, raising a considerable sum, as he has done every walk but one since. If anyone in London should speak highly of the Cairngorm Mountain Rescue Team there is every chance it is Paul or one of his friends. He felt a close bond with me which was and remains a humbling privilege.

1. *The Curran Shelter in summer (Ch 6). Note the chimney.*

2. *The Curran Shelter location in winter (Ch 6). Note the chimney top.*

3. *Snow probing near the A9 after the blizzard of 1978 (Ch 5).*

4. *Advancing into a storm.*

5. *Denise Barley's Search and Rescue dogs Bob and Bess in the Lairig Ghru (Ch 32).*

6. *Backpacking the McInnes stretcher.*

7. The Chalamain Gap in winter (Chs 9, 13, 26, 27 and 29).

8. *The Lairig Ghru looking south from near the Pools of Dee*
   (Foreword, 4, 5, 6, 9, 14, 17, 23, 26, 28, 29 and 30).

9. *Shelter Stone Crag and Carn Etchachan in summer*
   (Chs 3, 4, 10, 13, 17, 27, and 31).

10. *Climbers on Savage Slit, Coire an Lochain, in summer (Ch 13).*

11. Fording Loch Pattack (Ch 12).

12. Ben Alder in winter (Chs 3, 12, 13, 17, 19 and 20).

13. *Rescue 137 coming in on a smoke flare (Ch 8).*

14. *Inside Rescue 137 (Ch 8).*

15. *Rescue 137 lifting stretcher and winchman.*

16. *Allen Fyffe climbing The Cascades, Stag Rocks, in winter (Ch 18).*

17. Heather Morning and Millie.

18. Line searching across high ground.

19. '... the kilted warriors who leaped out of the heather and chased them the last few metres' (Ch 26).

20. 'All they needed to survive they had walked away from.' (Ch 21).

21. Rescue 137 stranded in Coire an t-Sneachda (Ch 31).

22. *Stretcher and casualty being lowered down a cliff face (Chs 28 and 30).*

23. *Jas Hepburn about to go over the edge of Hell's Lum on the* Touching the Void *rescue.*

24. Stretchering a casualty to Rescue 137.

*25. The Rescue Centre at Inverdruie
(Chs 8, 19, 20, 21, 22, 23, 26, 28, 29 and 31).*

For all the closeness of his shave with death, and for all the pain and anxiety he suffered, there has been no diminution of his love of the Highlands. With a 10cm-long dynamic hip screw in place, and a 30cm plate curved around the length of his femur and attached by a further ten screws, he returned to Ben Alder as quickly as was practical. Where he might have developed an aversion, he in fact became highly enamoured of the whole area, so much so he proposed to his fiancée at the summit of the very mountain where he almost met his end. They invited the Team to attend the wedding in London but distance was too much of a barrier. Instead we sent the happy couple a painting of their, or at least his, favourite mountain with our best wishes and the following brief message.

'This is one hole we won't be able to get you out of.'

THIRTEEN

The Scottish Highlands have many associations with the supernatural. Ben Alder Cottage on the shores of Loch Ericht is supposedly haunted and Tulloch Castle near Dingwall has its famous Green Lady. Second sight, in the sense of seeing the future, is understood to be an inherited attribute and the Brahan Seer who forecast the doom of the Seaforth line is possibly the most famous psychic in world history. Readers will afford these legends such credibility as they feel is deserved.

The Cairngorms' main contribution to this hidden history is Am Fear Liath Mòr, the Great Grey Man of Ben MacDhui, who is supposed to inhabit the Cairngorm Plateau. As distinguished a climber and scientist as the late Norman Collie reported he had been scared out of his wits by a 'crunch, and then another crunch as if someone was walking after me but taking steps three or four times the length of my own' while walking alone through a dense mist in 1891. Seized by terror he took to his heels, not stopping until he had dashed four or five miles and had a full field of vision all around.

Since he made his famous utterance, at a Scottish Mountaineering Club dinner 35 years later, many climbers, some distinguished, some less so, have made similar claims. By now a sort of identikit image has been formed of a 3m tall, long-limbed, naked wild man covered in thick grey hair. I would not care to oppose such reliable witnesses but have to report that in many hundreds, probably thousands, of hours on the Cairngorms I have seen neither droppings nor footprint, and have no idea how one such creature, never mind a colony, could remain so elusive nor what they would eat.

However, to harbour a healthy scepticism is not to deny the inexplicable or the possibility of a world not seen, still less is it to reject direct experience.

At the close of each rescue the Team Leader is required to complete a report form. In recent times the job has been transferred to computer, but this was not always so. A plain A4 sheet with boxes to fill and numbers to be supplied, it might have been a surveyor's report, a mechanic's or a nurse's. The forms were issued by the Mountain Rescue Committee of Scotland, to whom they were returned, to be processed into statistics, costs, new thinking if possible. Statements with no room for emotions or speculation, it is to the world of facts and objective reasoning they belong.

The form I am looking at now is dated January 1984 and was completed by Pete Cliff, Team Leader at that time. It confirms my memory that our attempt to rescue two soldiers lost on the Cairngorm Plateau was made over two days. I also see that 20 rescuers were turned out by our Team, an unknown number by Glenmore Lodge, and between 50 and 60 from RAF Leuchars and RAF Kinloss. Three helicopters and six search and rescue dogs were utilised. In all, 1990 person hours were expended.

Under *Nature of Incident* the word 'mountain' is underlined where it might have been 'Coastal Search' or 'Aircraft Crash' or any of several other headings. There are lists of causes, what equipment the casualties carried or did not carry, as well as their activities and degrees of experience.

Name of Mountain is given as 'Feidh Bhuidhe'. This is not, in fact, a mountain but the burn on the Cairngorm Plateau, between Cairngorm and Ben MacDhui, where six young lives had been lost 13 years earlier. Under *Names* two are given, Paul Rogers and Bill Scott. Under *Operation* the word DEAD is circled.

The weekend began innocuously enough one Friday when Willie Anderson and I decided we were unlikely to be called out and that we would have a quiet day on the hills. A big fall of snow landed on the Cairngorms the next day, Saturday 21st January, blocking all the passes to make a sort of low-lying island of Strathspey. So severe was it that the southbound train from Inverness could not get through Drumochter Pass and many cars were trapped on the A9. It was also very local; Chris Barley's wife, Denise, who at that time was a search and rescue dog handler, spent the day in the Monadhliath mountains on the west side of Strathspey on a photo shoot, setting up 'avalanche and desperate situation' pictures, and knew nothing of it until that evening.

By then our Team Leader, Pete Cliff, had spent the day assisting the police to locate vehicles buried, or semi-buried, in deep snow in Drumochter Pass and escorting the occupants to safety. In the course of their operations the Road Department's snow plough, whose driver had by every account done an amazing job, finally got stuck. Before long the windows blew in so the driver and his mate joined two rescuers and eight rescued drivers in the Team's transit van for the night. Since it was going to be necessary to keep the engine going Pete knew he was bound to run out of fuel. Soon Chris Barley arrived with two others and a supply. It was a very crowded transit they all slept in that night.

Willie and I, our hillwalking plans abandoned, had a relatively easy time. The stranded train had been carrying a prisoner to the jail at Perth and we were tasked to escort him, with Jimmy Simpson and his German shepherd, Rocky, to the police station at Kingussie. We were all given food for thought that night when Fred Harper let us know that 32 people were missing on or around the Cairngorms. Not only that but he had decided that conditions were so severe he could not sanction any rescue attempts that night.

On Sunday morning Pete and the rescuers dug about 150 drivers and passengers out of the snow and walked them to Drumochter Lodge above Dalwhinnie. Since no one was prepared for (now) 300 guests, food and hot drinks had to be organised. While this was going on the police borrowed a train which was stuck at Dalwhinnie and went up to Drumochter Lodge to fetch the stranded people. In due course Willie and I also arrived with a fleet of Council snow ploughs and we worked as a Team steadily from the afternoon into the night with at least part of our collective mind on the 32 possible casualties in the mountains.

At one point, Pete received a radio message that four students from Heriot Watt University were in trouble in Coire an Lochain. They had gone into the corrie on the Friday, making for Jean's Hut, but weather conditions turned much more severe than they expected or were prepared for and visibility dropped to just a few metres. Failing to find the hut by nightfall they had been obliged to bivouac in terrible conditions of heavy snow and sub-zero temperatures exacerbated by severe wind chill.

On the Saturday morning the weather was not much better. Their physical condition was much reduced, but they had at least some visibility. They decided to attempt a return to the car park but three of the four were overwhelmed less than a mile from safety. The other eventually reached the ski road early on Sunday morning where he was found around 10.00. An alarm was raised and instructors from Glenmore Lodge went in to look for the remaining three but found that, at different locations between Jean's Hut and the ski road, they had lost their lives.

This was tragedy enough but, in the course of that Sunday, Pete received another notification. Two soldiers were also missing. They had gone onto the Cairngorm Plateau as part of a survival exercise on the same Friday night and now, with Sunday wearing on, had neither returned nor communicated. Temporarily stationed at the Joint Services Mountain Training Centre at Ballachullish both were accomplished mountaineers. One was an assessor, instructing his partner who was already highly experienced. The area they had entered was much higher than Jean's Hut and without any feature that might give shelter. This presented us with a different kind of concern. If they had not returned it was very likely that something was wrong and their exact location would be difficult to ascertain. Pete Cliff returned to Glenmore Lodge to talk matters over with Fred Harper and, between them, they decided on a first light search from the Lodge.

We finished in Drumochter Pass at about 21.00 and a dozen or so of us, including Jimmy Simpson and his dog, Rocky, made our way back to my house. Anne cooked for our small army of hungry rescuers who then drove to Glenmore Lodge to spend the night on the floor. Before first light we set out onto the Cairngorm Plateau in four parties, two from the RAF and two of our own. One of the RAF parties turned back fairly quickly, the other when it was avalanched off the Goat Track in Coire an t-Sneachda. We continued but the wind was so powerful on the plateau we were unable to do a line search and radio communication was almost impossible. Jimmy kept Rocky slightly separate, as is usual, and let him off the lead. They were advancing around the rim of Coire an t-Sneachda when the dog was lifted by a sudden gust and tossed over the edge, leaving Jimmy staring into space and billowing snow.

Unaware of the loss of Rocky, Pete pulled off a tremendous feat of navigation in almost zero visibility by getting us to Feidh Bhuidhe. We probed the area as thoroughly as possible but found nothing. The soldiers' intention had been to dig a snow hole and remain inside for the night. This is a survival practice that all of the Team were familiar with and all had carried out from time to time. Experience told us that snow holes can take hours to prepare, especially in conditions of drift, and in that time the mountaineers are exposed to the conditions with nothing to generate warmth but the effort of the dig. Once inside it is important to keep some kind of passageway clear for air to travel through and it is wise, and usual, to leave some sign of location marker outside, such as a ski pole. We found neither air hole nor any kind of indicator and were obliged to return disappointed.

Conditions were better when we returned next day, searching a wider area but again drawing a blank. There would have been no news, and certainly no good news, if Jimmy had not stubbornly believed that Rocky had survived. He and Malcolm Sclater patrolled along the corrie rim until they heard a *yip* from below. When they peered over they saw Rocky unhurt on a ledge where he at least had shelter from the wind. He was cold and hungry but alive. Malcolm threw down a sandwich which the dog gobbled instantly and between them, with Rocky's claws scrabbling on the cliff and the two men hauling on the scruff of his neck, they got him topside again. All of us were relieved but not so much that we abandoned our sense of humour. At Glenmore Lodge we serenaded Jimmy with 'How much is that doggie in the corrie'.

However, things looked increasingly bad for the soldiers.

By the following day the wind had dropped to a breeze and, under blue skies we gazed across miles of sparkling snow. In these superb conditions we made an even more thorough search but still found no sign of the two men. The RAF helicopters that were at last able to fly across the plateau also saw nothing. A new and harsh reality now presented itself. We had done all we could and to continue was simply to repeat ourselves. Whether by intention or otherwise it appeared that the two soldiers were buried somewhere. If so, they would surely by now have lost their lives. Peter discussed the situation with the police and the decision was made to stand down. The arrival of spring and snowmelt would reveal all.

On the Wednesday night Pete received a call from Chief Inspector Gordon Noble, who had taken over from John MacLean at Kingussie. Four army instructors from Ballachullish had asked if they could go on the hill in an attempt to locate their two colleagues and had asked if they could borrow our radios, which were tuned to the mountain rescue frequency. Pete, of course, agreed.

This wasn't all though. They told Pete a medium based in Devon had been in touch with the army and given some indication of where she believed the two men's bodies lay. Her name was Rita Rogers and she would later be described as 'Princess Diana's favourite mystic'. She had met Bill Scott a number of years before and told him he would become a great mountaineer, but at some point would be trapped by snow. They had formed, it seemed, a continuing link.

When an army general got in touch with her, she had asked to meet one of the relations and was introduced to Paul Rogers' father. She said she felt that Paul was still alive. She said she also felt Bill's presence although he was in spirit. Now she 'saw' Paul among mountains, trapped near the top of one of them. Below him were three or four trees and, further below, a lake.

If there was any truth in it the lake had to be Loch Morlich and, in fact, from this and other clues I had a good idea of where the location must be. In her autobiography, published much later, she would claim that she guided a helicopter in but deteriorating weather prevented a landing. In the course of the following night the words 'He's dead' entered her mind and she was burdened with feelings of depression and loss. She then supplied coordinates for rescuers on foot, the soldiers who asked to borrow our radios.

Next day I was working in the Kingussie pharmacy but around 10.00 broke my day to step across the road to the police station, to find out how the search was proceeding. I was beside the radio when the soldiers called in. They had found two bodies within a few steps of where Rita Rogers had said, on the lip of Coire an t-Sneachda. Our Rescue Party must have passed by them several times without seeing them.

The bodies were quite some distance from Feidh Bhuidhe and the likelihood is that they were either unable to dig their snow hole because of drift, or found conditions just too awful to withstand. Their condition must have deteriorated quickly and, when they finally made their dash across the plateau, were simply too weak to keep going. Loch Morlich was in view of their final stopping place and there was no shortage of trees in Rothiemurchus Forest. However, there were also three or four stunted trees on the banks of the Chalamain stream and these must have been among the last things the two soldiers saw.

Later I discussed it with Anne who suggested that Rita Rogers seemed to have looked through the young soldier's eyes, almost like a window. Then again, she may have had a more passive role, acting only as a sort of receptor for a message that was somehow 'sent'. I make no comment and draw no conclusion. The division between natural and supernatural is not the business of either mountain rescue or pharmacy.

By March 1995 all this had receded into the collective memory of the Cairngorm Mountain Rescue Team when, as Team Leader, I was approached by BBC television to take part in a programme called *999*. This particular episode was about a rescue the Pattadale Team had carried out in the Lake District. Unfortunately for Pattadale there was not enough snow to make the shoot on home territory and the producers wanted to know if the Cairngorm Team would step in if the programme was made in our area, where there was more than enough snow. A fee was agreed, and we signed with the condition that any live rescue would take precedence over programme making. We did the shoot from the Coire na Ciste car park where there was both shelter and power for lights since the Pattadale rescue had occurred at night-time.

We were working with the crew when we received a call from the police. There had been an avalanche in Coire Laogh Mor and a number of people required assistance. I instigated a full-scale call-out, asking all who could make themselves available to join those of us who were already on the hill. This seemed to us like a golden opportunity to film a real rescue but the Director wasn't interested. She wanted her Lake District rescue and nothing else would do.

It had been a busy day in the Northern Corries, so busy we had to call in Glenmore Lodge and the Avalanche Information Service to help. Eight were injured in the avalanche, four of whom had to be removed on stretchers and taken to hospital. Among the injured was John Lyall, now a professional mountain guide who had been teaching the group winter skills in preparation for a trip he would later lead in Nepal. Others managed to ski or walk the final stretch to the road. With at least half an hour's walking between the site and the road, all in all the rescue took quite a while.

Crisis over, so we thought, we returned to the film crew and pretended to be Pattadale, trudging the snow in line, pushing in avalanche probes every few metres. It was then the police called for a second time, this time reporting two people missing, a couple from Fife. The crew carried on filming with the rest of the Team while I began an investigation. The question was where to begin? There was some detective work to be done.

It was now about 22.00 and quite clear, a pleasant winter's night, as we drove the ski road looking for their car. Finding it, we thought, would give us at least some idea of their route into the hills. After searching thoroughly and drawing a blank I radioed Glenmore Lodge to say that we had not found the car and therefore could do nothing. Simply striking out into the hills without a clue where to look would be a waste of time so we returned to filming and this time got the job done.

Next day, a Sunday, the Fifers turned up in Braemar. However, the police were now concerned about two young men who had been reported missing. No one knew for sure where they had gone, far less what climb or walk they intended. It was possible they were not even on the hill. As the sun went down their car was located in the Coire na Ciste car park and we agreed things looked bad.

That night was spent in more detective work, asking everyone they had spent time with what climbs they talked about, even what mountains. Through their parents in England we contacted friends and asked whether they had discussed particular routes. In fact they had discussed many routes on both Cairngorm and Ben MacDhui.

One of the drivers of the shuttle buses that ferry skiers between the lower car parks and the chairlift thought he remembered them. He seemed to recall they had left at about 10.00 on the Saturday. The days were still short at that time of year so the two men could not have gone all that far. For example, they would not have had sufficient time to reach the Shelter Stone, make their climb and return. It was likely they were in either Coire an t-Sneachda or Coire an Lochain.

Now we had at least some idea of where they might be I called out the Team. Armed with information from their friends in the south I felt the route known as Savage Slit, in Coire an Lochain, was the prime suspect. The Team went in but found only massive avalanche debris which was too dense, physically hard, to probe.

Noting this daunting hardness Donnie Williamson said to me, 'You'd need a JCB to probe this.' The dogs picked up no scents and found nothing. Over the next few days the Team continued to search while Malcolm Sclater and I overflew the wider area in a RAF helicopter looking for more avalanche signs. We continued in this way for some days until it became apparent that we were wasting our time. The area where the two bodies *might* be lying was just too great and the indications we had were too vague.

The families were in contact and it was my duty to tell them I had to stand the Team down. This was painful, although necessary. Chris Barley, who was my Depute Leader at this time, and I had many conversations with them and it was obvious they were good people deeply anxious about the fate of their sons. As often happens on a long, drawn-out search a rapport grew between the rescuers and the family and we came to feel almost that we knew the two missing lads, their personalities and ambitions.

We remained alert as spring approached and the snow retreated upwards, waiting to see what the thaw would reveal. Otherwise I put them to the back of my mind until the last Tuesday in May when I was wakened at 05.00 by an unexpected call. Rubbing the sleep from my eyes I listened to Chris Barley, the most sane, both-feet-firmly-on-the-ground, practical dentist you could wish to probe your gums, also the most well-balanced and trustworthy mountaineer, say this: 'I know where they are! They're in Coire an Lochain exactly where we first thought.'

'Okay, how do you know?'

'I saw them in a dream, high in the corrie, to the west of Savage Slit, near a ledge above the Twin Burns, with rocks all around. The ground rises slowly from the foot of the corrie and then gets suddenly steeper. You know the place? We've been there often.'

'I know exactly that point.' In fact, the Twin Burns area is extremely prone to avalanches. Indeed, in 1997, two climbers would have an almost miraculous escape there, a self-rescue that is still discussed and will find its place elsewhere in this book.

'Can you go?'

I had to say I was too busy, and as it turned out so was Chris, but it played on my mind. As a result, I called Chris's wife, Denise, on the Thursday to let her know I was going out on my own with the radio.

I went directly to a ledge just beside Savage Slit. The climb is a pleasant one in summer, more demanding in winter but by no means lethal. Although it was by now the end of May there had been a fresh fall of snow, but it was no more than a dusting. A cold breeze and low clouds that brushed the edge of the plateau completed the picture. Climbing above the loch I found the ledge and sat down. Possibly because of Chris's certainty, possibly because of the strong empathy we had formed with the parents, I was convinced the two bodies would be here. When I did not find them I was surprisingly upset and sat looking down across the frozen loch, its ice bleakly reflecting the snow clouds. In that mood I radioed Denise and asked her to tell Chris that we had drawn another blank.

Two days later a party of students from Jordanhill College who were walking in Coire an Lochain noticed a brightly coloured object sticking out of the ice in the loch. Wisely, they did not venture close to investigate but later reported it looked like a foot. The police called me and I called Chris. Surely, we thought, this must be them. Between 14.00 and 15.00 we arrived with the Team and a number of police detectives who were obliged to view such a scene as that of a possible crime.

It was indeed a foot, complete with boot and gaiter. A closer examination than the students had allowed themselves revealed the face of one of the dead casualties apparently staring up out of the ice. It was a tragic discovery that left none of us unmoved, so tragic we did not notice the direction and significance of that steady gaze.

At last we had discovered the whereabouts of the two young men although we could not be exactly sure how they arrived here. The likelihood is that, having completed the climb, they were avalanched as they made their way down, carried onto the ice and entombed one above the other. Possibly they lost their lives on impact. If not, pressure and low temperatures would quickly finish them. The avalanche as it travelled will have changed its form several times, breaking down into lumps, the flow dividing on rocks, possibly reforming again. If the lochan was frozen all the way to the bottom when it struck it is possible that the snow was compacted hard, instantly, by the force of arrested momentum. Frozen together the ice absorbed the two bodies under fresh falls of snow and defied our search techniques.

It fell to the Team to cut the bodies free and this we did with ice axes, chipping resolutely at the frozen loch in turns, taking care to treat the two men with full respect and not damage their bodies. The job took some time and in the course of the day the rising temperature loosened the slab of ice from the shore so that it bobbled on the water. It was not dangerous but the unsteadiness obliged us to secure it using ice axes and ropes. This done we continued until, at last, we carved sufficient space around the bodies to lift them from the ice.

I stood at the loch's edge behind Chris while he stationed himself by the head of the lower man, steadying it with his hands while others took the arms and legs and lifted. My gaze rose with them and continued to rise until it came to the ledge, boulders and broken ground I had looked down from only two days before. The dead man's eyes must have been fixed on the area from the moment his body came to rest. How his last sight might have lingered so long in the half world between life and death is anyone's guess, but this was the vision that Chris eventually received in the form of a dream to send me on my solitary search.

FOURTEEN

Anyone's financial good fortune might put ideas in someone else's head. Money is the root, if not of all evil, at least of copycat actions, and sometimes suspicion.

These were the last things on my mind, or anyone else's, when I received a call from our colleagues in the Braemar Mountain Rescue Team one Sunday in February 1994. A woman named Jacqueline Greaves, later described as 'a 53-year-old grandmother', had been reported missing on Derry Cairngorm by two male hillwalking companions. The party was said to be an experienced one but nonetheless had been carrying only one map.

Snow that extends out from the rim of a corrie is termed a 'cornice'. They were descending the hill in blizzard conditions when the two men apparently walked too far out on one. It gave way beneath them and they dropped out of Mrs Greaves's sight, falling, for all she knew, to their deaths. In fact, not only had they come to no harm but they had also walked out and raised the alarm.

Derry Cairngorm is located towards the south end of the Cairngorm Plateau, overlooking the Lairig an Laoigh and the delightful pine forest of lower Glen Derry. As such it is outside the Cairngorm Team's call-out area, so much so that, in discussion, we decided it was extremely unlikely that Mrs Greaves could have wandered into our area. Given the strong likelihood that our resources would be required for some other rescue we decided that the Braemar and RAF Kinloss Teams could handle the situation without us. We would keep an ear to the airwaves and if an extended, widened search proved necessary would turn out as required. Over the next two days the blizzards continued so fiercely that helicopters were unable to participate in the search.

Mrs Greaves was eventually found by a group from RAF Kinloss at 09.15 on the Tuesday, having been on the hill for two nights and the intervening day. Hopes for her survival had been fading, but she was clearly a redoubtable and strong-willed woman who was well equipped other than being without a map. Cpl Alan Sylvester, who led the Rescue Party, is reported as saying, 'When she saw us she stopped walking, sat down and there were tears of pure relief and emotion.' Well there might have been: she had quite a story to tell.

It seems that, at some point, she lost her ice axe in a fall. Realising her predicament she put on all the spare clothes she was carrying, intent on preserving as much heat as possible. She was also carrying an orange survival bag and used it on the first night to rest behind a snow bank. The wind was so great that sleep was out of the question and the survival bag was torn to shreds. To survive the second night she dug a snow hole with her gloved hands, and it seemed she spent the intervening day wandering in circles in low visibility.

Her food supply ran out on the first day, so by the time she was found she was very hungry indeed. The rescuers gave her hot drinks, Mars bars and other high-energy food, but not before she uttered the immortal words, 'I am looking forward to a pint of Guinness.' These were the words that ran through the media, what we might call the 'money quote'. Not only did she survive her ordeal but she did so almost completely unharmed.

It was a great story with an articulate protagonist, and the media fell on it with a will, especially the aspect of how long she had survived. Her 40 or so hours were presented as a record but, of course, they were no such thing. Many competent people venture onto the mountains in winter and deliberately stay out for longer.

Mrs Greaves appeared on a television show to describe a series of visions she claimed to have experienced on the hill, visions that might have been sent by someone, or something watching over her, some guardian angel, or might have been hallucinations with their origins in hunger and cold, or just a tale that might be interpreted more cynically. It seemed barriers had dropped in front of her to prevent her wandering over an edge, and when two converging ridges were illuminated with a brilliant light, like a giant letter 'V', she felt it was pointing her way off the mountain. One tabloid paid her a large sum for her story of heroic, even miraculous, survival, a sum rumoured in rescue circles at between £20,000 and £40,000.

In justice, I felt at least part of such a sum should have gone back into mountain rescue. Rewarding the incompetent, or even the unlucky, seemed wrong. I remained silent but felt that the smell of money might have an unsettling effect on some people, that some future casualties might be bogus. It was clear that suspicion had entered the world of mountain rescue.

It was also clear that a long search increased the level of publicity and, it might follow, a bidding war for the story. A number of lengthy rescues around Scotland followed the events on Derry Cairngorm when, typically, the press would appear on the second day to observe and question. Often their numbers would be high and their questioning urgent. No doubt the public had a genuine interest which had to be served, but the effect was an increase in pressure on the rescuers and an occasional pondering on whether the whole thing had been set up.

A year later a story was published with certain similarities to the Derry Cairngorm rescue. A male skier lost his way in the Glenshee area and became lost in a blizzard. I never met him but his photograph in the papers suggests that he was a fit man. He also seems to have had a good knowledge of winter hill craft since he was able to dig himself a snow hole and take refuge as light faded and the temperature dropped. Here he waited through two days and nights of atrocious conditions for a rescue that did not come. As light faded towards the end of the second day he decided he could not survive another night and, as *The Scotsman*'s front page report was to put it, 'risked everything in the early hours of yesterday by setting out on a perilous trek to safety'. He was spotted from the air by a Sea King in a condition that was described as 'close to the edge of survival'.

The echoes from Jacqueline Greaves's rescue were unmistakable. The casualty had survived for 67 hours, described as 'longer than any other person in the history of Scottish winter mountain rescues'. On first contact he asked for a drink of Irn Bru, a product as much associated with Scotland as Mrs Greaves's favoured Guinness is with Ireland. Even the supernatural element was present, although her mysterious barriers and guiding lights were replaced by his wife's feeling that, 'Last night I just knew he was alive. Don't ask me why. I just knew.'

When he was examined by paramedics at Glenshee he was unable to stand, but by the time he arrived at Ninewells Hospital in Dundee doctors could say he was in remarkably good health. No doubt this is testimony to his rescuers' competence in getting him insulated, and warm food and drink into him, as quickly as possible. There was never any suggestion that money changed hands for the story, so the echoes may have appeared simply from the key note struck a year before. As far as I was concerned it all added to the atmosphere of suspicion.

In particular the idea of long survival periods was becoming wearing. It is not difficult to survive for such a period when you have good equipment, especially if you can stay dry and get out of the wind. I joked at the time that I, or any competent mountaineer, could easily break these imaginary records, gasping out to my rescuers through a dry throat, 'Oh, how I would enjoy a Ferrari and a case of Macallan'.

That winter passed and summer of 1995 followed until, in November in our own area, we were faced with a rescue in the hills above my favourite Glen Feshie.

The Munro Sgor Gaoith and its subsidiary tops, Sgoran Dubh Mor and Sgoran Dubh Beag overlook the deep cleft of Loch Einich and, in clear conditions, offer fine views eastwards across the Great Moss to Braeriach and southwards to Mullach Clach a'Bhlair and Cairn Toul which, in turn, overlooks Corrour Bothy and the Lairig Ghru. From Glen Feshie they are relatively easily ascended from a pull-in at Achlean which accommodates perhaps half a dozen cars.

Delightful as the Sgorans are, a fall into Glen Einich from any of them would be almost impossible to survive.

At 01.30 on Sunday the 19th an experienced hillwalker with over 100 Munros under his belt left his home in Falkirk with the intention of soloing the Sgorans and Mullach Clach a'Bhlair. He did not return at his expected time, nor at all that day. By the following morning he had still not made contact, and his wife sounded the alarm. I called her and went through my usual list of questions, a list I still have in my records. The first four points have ticks beside them.

1. Fit
2. Navigation
3. Whistle
4. Goes out in winter
5. Medical history – occasional trouble w disc/back
6. 100 Munros
7. ROUTE Mullach then Sgor Gaoith
8. Map – unknown which one
9. Normally goes on his own
10. Has been late before
11. His occupation

We gathered what I believed would be sufficient resource and at midday began the search with 19 Rescue Team Members, two dogs and a rescue helicopter. The weather was fair with reasonable visibility, and the likely area is a particularly open one. Assuming he was unharmed, I anticipated no great difficulty in locating the casualty, but we found no trace. The story made the television news that night, word went round the press community and reporters turned up in numbers, among them Paul Hunter of *The Press and Journal* whom I knew from his time with our local paper.

The following day was wetter and visibility was reduced. We established a rescue control point in the lower reaches of the glen where there is a gliding club, providing a good landing site for the helicopters. Given the unexpected blank we had drawn the previous day I decided to make a considerable increase in resource. Locating the casualty, assuming he was alive and well and on his feet, should have been easy. Since he remained unfound it seemed likely that he was lying somewhere, possibly injured. He might even be unconscious and curled up behind a boulder and, in these circumstances, even the most assiduous of rescuers could pass closely without seeing him. I assembled 19 of our own Team Members, with seven dogs and their handlers, 19 rescuers from RAF Leuchars, four from RAF Kinloss, and 21 from Braemar of whom nine were police officers. The helicopter took them onto the plateau in several lifts.

That morning Paul approached me at the rescue control vehicle and asked, 'How's it going?'

I had to admit that my concern for the lost walker was touched by a measure of cynicism. 'There was no reason *not* to find him yesterday. The area isn't all that big and resource was sufficient by any reasonable standard. Listen, if he turns up uninjured, safe and well, and tries to sell you his story, let me know.'

We did not have to wait long. The casualty did indeed turn up, safe and well, at Coylumbridge road end. From there he called to reassure his wife and then called the police. The police in turn called me. Paul Hunter reached him almost immediately on his arrival at Rescue Control and afterwards approached me.

'You were right,' he said. 'He's looking for money for his story, at least £1,000. What will I do?'

'Give him the money if that is your judgement, but if you do I will give you another interview and say that navigational skills such as his make him unfit to go out alone.' Since the press is well aware that Team Leaders are normally extremely careful, even reserved, in their comments on casualties this was a strong position for me to take.

When a police officer and I finally got the casualty to interview it was, first of all, apparent that he was uninjured. We learned that he had slept for a few hours in his car on arrival in Glen Feshie. On waking he had ascended the hill and on trying to take a compass bearing had become lost. Apparently he had been taken aback by the mist and snow conditions but had sufficient food and drink to last more than one day, as is sensible and advisable. That night he made a bivouac at the head of Glen Einich and on Monday made his way eastwards and into the Lairig Ghru, although at what point he entered he was unsure. Wherever it was he again made a bivouac for the night. Unusually for any walker he was carrying flares in his rucksack. He told us that on one occasion he had been surprised by the sudden appearance of the helicopter over a ridge and not managed to set them off. On another occasion, he failed to attract the crew's attention with his torch.

No payment was made. He went home and there the matter ended except for Paul's story in *The Press and Journal* with my own broad-brush comments on the necessity of sound navigational skills. I have that report before me now along with a photograph of the man apparently well prepared for his venture onto the hills. He wears a good-quality fleece jacket and has an equally good, tightly packed rucksack thrown insouciantly over one shoulder. An ice axe is strapped on, and at least one walking pole.

I still wonder about that rescue. The possibility of money being paid to casualties, of reward for failure, whether through incompetence or ill luck, and the notion of record durations for survival, brings suspicion into the benevolent equation that has always existed between rescuer and rescued. I wish it were not so.

I have no accusation to make against any of the casualties mentioned in this chapter. Everything that happened can be explained within an assumption of honesty and goodwill; the reader will judge from the base of his or her own experience but will almost certainly not be sure. This is the nature of suspicion; once it has entered any system it is difficult to eradicate. Such suspicions might be without foundation, but I will be happy if any climber or walker whose mind has been crossed by the thought of engineering an unnecessary rescue, understands that Team Leaders are alert to them.

FIFTEEN

The call I received one night in February 1993 from Aviemore Police Station was prompted by a call from Loch Morlich Youth Hostel. Three walkers had checked in that morning to ensure they would have beds if they required them when they came off the hill. The party was described as experienced but by 23.00 they had not returned and the warden felt sufficient concern to call the police.

Duty Constable Woodburn on calling a relative of the three men learned that at least one of them had recently returned from the Alps. No one was worried at that time and it was felt likely that the party had decided to remain out of doors overnight. It seemed they were sufficiently competent and well enough equipped to do this in safety.

Dr Chris Mayo was 45 years old and had driven north with his 15-year-old son, Matthew, from their home in Preston, Lancashire. In Edinburgh they had picked up Chris's brother, Michael, and made their way to the Northern Cairngorms. All were physically fit, able people. To add to this impression of competence Dr Chris Mayo was also a member of one of the Pennine Rescue Teams. Accepting these points of ability and fitness, and that the families had no particular concerns, we decided to do nothing in the meantime.

We were in a winter period when all too many lives were being lost in the hills, but when warnings are unspecific there is little to do but wait. Under these circumstances most people walk out themselves in time, sometimes cold and frightened, sometimes tired and even slightly injured. The alternative, with so little to go on, would be to commit sufficient resources to search all of the Cairngorms, an impossible task even if restricted to the area of the three plateaux.

The three had still not appeared by morning when Malcolm Sclater came on duty at 08.00. Concerned, he drove up to the Coire Cas car park where he located and entered their vehicle. A certain amount of climbing equipment was present but no note to describe the party's route or targets. In itself this was not alarming. There is no compulsion to leave such a note, and some people have concern that by doing so they give notice to a potential car thief that the owner is not nearby. On the other hand, search times can be much reduced when the Team Leader has at least a fair idea where to look.

Malcolm called me and we again called the family. There was still no great feeling of concern. Whatever the Mayo group's targets were, they were likely to be ambitious and take quite some time, perhaps longer than anticipated. If they were enjoying themselves they would feel no great hurry to return. As insurance we contacted Glenmore Lodge which would have instructors and students on the hill in various locations. All the instructors carried radios and were asked to keep their eyes open for the three, with descriptions given including names, ages, and colour of clothes.

At 11.15 Wes Sterrit and his party came across a body in Coire an Lochain. It was that of Dr Chris Mayo, whose injuries suggested he had suffered a fall. They looked around the immediate vicinity, but Dr Mayo's son and brother were not to be seen.

My earlier, tentative, theory was that, whatever else they had done the party had not gone climbing. The presence of climbing gear in their car supported that quite strongly. On the other hand the location of Dr Mayo's body, the nature of his injuries and the crampons he was wearing made a contradictory suggestion. Dr Mayo was wearing a compass looped around his neck, so it seemed likely that he had been walking on a bearing at some point in their outing. This suggested another possibility, which is that he had been navigating on the plateau when he walked over the edge, or perhaps a cornice had collapsed beneath him.

At this point, and with great concern for the other two climbers, I called out not only the Cairngorm Mountain Rescue Team but also requested additional searchers from the RAF and a helicopter. The two missing men were likely to be within Coire an Lochain, or possibly on the plateau above, but that general area was very large, and adequate numbers would be required for the search.

The rescuers were deployed all over the area in question with the helicopter looking down from above to no avail. We searched all day and when night fell came off the hill determined to resume in the morning. Events were now gathering momentum from a point of little or no concern to the certainty of at least one fatality and a serious search for survivors. The two wives drove to the scene and were made to feel as welcome and included as possible at Glenmore Lodge. One had already lost her husband and was in danger of losing her son. The other feared for her own husband and no doubt was conscious of their three children at home in Edinburgh.

The following day Malcolm, immersed in the rescue from its beginnings as a cautious warning, remained at Control with the two women. I went out onto the hill to participate directly as part of a party of four that included Roger Gaff, John Hall and Donnie Williamson. We went directly to the first body location and proceeded uphill from there.

Later we stopped for lunch just below the right-hand branch of Y Gully, a Grade 2 climb that I would have felt competent to solo in these conditions. It was a brilliant, high-pressure day, one which would have afforded the opportunity of a fine, enjoyable climb onto the plateau. We continued to the foot of Y Gully, the highest point we felt the party might have reached and here we discovered a gloved hand reaching out of the snow.

It was a traumatic event for all four of us in a way that will possibly be difficult to understand. All of us had looked at dead bodies, all had witnessed terrible injuries, but there was something suggestive of shared mortality in an open hand. It resembled a gesture of welcome or a signal for help, or despair. We dug down and found the body of 15-year-old Matthew Mayo. On examination we could detect no vital signs.

The likelihood was that he had been partly suffocated, partly frozen by the snow. We investigated further and discovered that Matthew had taken refuge in a dug hole, immediately prompting thoughts of the more experienced men with him and how concerned they must have felt for his safety when they found themselves in difficulty. It was also puzzling because the same competent, caring men would have understood that Y Gully, although far from the most demanding climb in the area, was not to be tackled without adequate climbing gear, particularly crampons which Matthew was neither wearing nor carrying.

Cautious of what I was saying, and conscious of the two women with Malcolm in Control, I radioed back to say that Matthew had been found with no vital signs and that he should be evacuated to Raigmore. In Control Malcolm correctly judged from the waver in my voice that we had come across the worst scenario possible for this one climber.

In the normal shorthand we use I had only said 'Raigmore' and not 'the mortuary at Raigmore' as I possibly should. People have hope beyond reason. They reach for it when loved ones are in danger. Not for the first time someone took hope where there was none, entertaining thoughts of 'rewarming' and 'life'. I had chosen my words as carefully as possible, but the message received was subtly transformed from the message given, or intended, by false hope. Malcolm took the brunt of this and dealt with it, I know, as gently as was humanly possible. It was the first of two occasions on this rescue where my words would be taken wrongly. On the second occasion I would have even more cause for regret, but that was ahead. For now we had to contend with our emotions and get on with the job.

The ground was decidedly steep so there was no question of carrying Matthew from this point. I asked for some of the searchers to be diverted in our direction while we lowered the body from our very high location to the floor of the corrie. Within this second party was our Team Doctor, Peter Grant, whose opinion was quite clear that the casualty should be flown as soon as possible to Raigmore Hospital in case there was some slight flicker of life that could not be detected on the hill, and where a more informed decision could be made on rewarming.

All in all it seemed likely that Michael Mayo was somewhere close by. We now made some logical assumptions. The two adults and Matthew had found themselves in difficulties on steep ground, inadequately equipped and unable to retreat. They dug a ledge into the snow and got Matthew into a survival bag. That done, Chris Mayo set out for help but came to grief on the way. Michael Mayo waited for a reasonable period of time, after which he must have realised that help was not on its way and he would have to seek it out himself.

The question now was what bearing would we take if we had been in his shoes? A secondary question was if he had fallen and slid on hard packed snow or ice where would he have stopped? Following this reasoning we set out, soon coming across an ice axe that was identified through radio contact with Glenmore Lodge as belonging to Michael Mayo. Continued searching revealed no more and, eventually, failing light once again halted operations.

Next day, and with RAF assistance, I put massive human resource onto the hill, arranging it in three successive line searches. A line can only be managed up to a length of 15 or 20 individuals. Longer than that and it tends to break, leaving areas of ground unsearched. By arranging our 70 searchers into three lines, with individuals filling, as it were, the gaps in front we ensured that every patch of ground was examined at least once, sometimes twice.

It was the RAF line that spotted a red patch in the snow that turned out to be part of Michael Mayo's cagoule. We dug down and found his body, like Matthew's without crampons but otherwise well equipped. Having succumbed to hypothermia he looked almost as if he had lain down and gone to sleep. The tragedy was now complete. At Control the two women had to contend with the loss of two, good men who were brothers, husbands, fathers, providers, contributors to society, and Matthew, a son and nephew. In all that followed they remained at the forefront of my mind, as they are now, and the minds of the other Team Members.

Like the others in my group of four I was deeply affected by the way we found young Matthew in particular. The memory of that beckoning, pleading hand will live with me always. The immense self-control that is required in these circumstances is understood only by those who have had to summon it.

My theory of what happened to the Mayos was as follows: when they left their car they had no intention of attempting any climb, serious or otherwise. This explains them leaving their climbing equipment in the car. It does not explain why one party member, the most experienced, took his crampons but the others did not. Most likely they were left to save weight, but in Cairngorms' winter conditions this would be a mistake.

This leads naturally to their target for the day. It must have been one which they could reasonably expect to achieve without ropes and slings and which they felt could be managed safely in boots. Near to Y Gully is the much easier Central Gully which, at Grade 1, and in benign conditions, can be completed as an easy climb. We believed that Dr Chris Mayo had been leading the group towards Central Gully on a bearing.

If we assume that he made a simple navigational error such as the most experienced can do, they could well have found themselves at the foot of Y Gully believing it was Central Gully. Continuing in that belief, if indeed they did, they would then find themselves ascending steep ground that eventually became more severe than they had expected. By cutting steps with their ice axes and kicking footholds in softer snow they eventually found themselves in a position where ascending meant facing serious technical difficulties for which they were not adequately equipped. At this point, if not before, they will have realised they were misplaced.

The decision to continue or retreat is often a difficult one with a case to be made for either side. However, descending in these circumstances would be hazardous, continuing next to impossible. They made the correct decision to secure the party while the best-equipped member went for assistance. The location of the dug ledge could have been better chosen, but choice may not have been a luxury they enjoyed. Snow tumbled from the plateau above and the two who remained must have had their work cut out to keep their platform from filling in. When Matthew was left alone it would not take too long for him to be buried and we must assume that Michael Mayo, in particular, included this in his calculations. The necessity for haste may well have led to his final fall.

That winter was a hard one in the mountains of Scotland and a large number of people had already lost their lives. Looked at as the press and politicians look, the Mayo group amounted to three more fatalities in a rising, unacceptable total. The press had been following the story almost from the outset, running with headlines such as 'Body found on peak and there may be more', 'Hunt goes on for two climbers as body is found' and 'Doctor and son die in climbing tragedy'.

In speaking with them afterwards I outlined our theory, emphasising that it remained a theory and, my great mistake, reminding them that when adults take children and older children, perhaps on the cusp of adulthood, onto the hills they are responsible.

This simple statement, which I will go to my grave proclaiming to be true, was misinterpreted and amplified into a statement of blame, a judgement on the two adults that was as far from my intention as could be imagined. The tone of the headlines altered into 'Climb family broke rules', 'Rescuer blames climbing deaths on footwear' and 'Climbers deaths were avoidable'.

I regret this change of direction now as I did then, and when I received a letter of complaint from Chris Mayo's Team Leader in the Pennines, pointing out that I should not make such judgements. I had some sympathy with his point of view, but he was not in possession of all the facts, so I sent him my report on the rescue, which contained both facts and theories regarding the accident. My choice of words when dealing with the press had been less cautious than usual and I had not taken cognisance of the emotional pitch that had risen in circles far beyond the Cairngorm Mountain Rescue Team and the immediate families.

When Chris and Michael Mayo took young Matthew into the Cairngorms it was to share their time through the processes of his growing up, to widen his experience and further introduce him to the pleasures of the outdoors. It was a good thing they were doing and if, as I believe, errors were made it is because they were only human – as I am. The consequences though, run into a future that is irrevocably altered and that must be lived with as we live with the knowledge of our shared mortality.

SIXTEEN

'The last thirty years have seen a huge increase in the popularity of mountaineering, hillwalking and climbing. Participation has been rising by 5 or 6% annually since the late 1960s. There have been increases in the number of accidents in the hills and considerable media attention has been devoted to such incidents. In the light of concerns raised about the cost of Mountain Rescue Services and the ability of Mountain Rescue Teams (MRTs) to cope with the increased pressure, the Scottish Affairs Committee decided to conduct a short inquiry into the operational and funding arrangements for mountain rescue. The findings of our inquiry are contained in this report.'

The above is the opening paragraph of the House of Commons' Scottish Affairs Committee Second Report on Mountain Rescue Services dated 5th June 1996. The Inquiry it reported on marked a crucial point in the history of mountain rescue and the narrow avoidance of a turning that would have taken the service into a very different culture than the present one of enlightened benevolence and charitable outlook.

By the early 1990s a notion had taken root in the minds of press and politicians, and all too many members of the public, that the cost of maintaining a Mountain Rescue Service in Scotland was exceptionally high.

This followed a period of rapid increase in the popularity of outdoor pursuits, many accidents where inexperience played a part, and when mountain rescue had achieved a degree of prominence. Simple – all too simple – calculations had been carried out. The cost of a Sea King helicopter, it was said, considering capital costs, maintenance, crew training and pay, fuel and all else that might be associated with a flight stacked up at about £5,000 an hour. The cost of a Nimrod surveillance aircraft, like the helicopters operating under the command of the Aeronautical Rescue Control Centre, weighed in at a whopping £25,000 an hour.

The Nimrod, in fact, is seldom utilised in mountain rescue, its search and rescue function being more appropriate for those lost at sea. Over the years the Sea King, in particular, has spent most of its air time on civilian rescue missions, but both aircraft find their ultimate roles wherever the RAF is operating in the world. The helicopters' primary function is the search and rescue of downed air crew while the Nimrod operates at a higher level still, acting as a flying control centre with unobstructed lines of communication.

Sharp tongues and pens pinned a good deal of blame on those unfortunate mountaineers who had walked or climbed into trouble. One letter in *The Glasgow Herald* read as follows: 'All using the privilege of access to the hills and countryside and who become involved in rescue operations should be liable for all expenses arising. If they were thus involved in Switzerland or Norway they would soon be faced with the bill.'

The Mountain Rescue Teams never took this approach. As a general rule the only element of judgement we may apply is when an adult knowingly takes children into hazardous conditions and brings them to grief. Even then critical comment is muted and given with great caution. However, it is true that most Rescue Teams in mainland Europe are fully professional. Their costs are paid through insurance claims on mountaineering policies bought by the climbers before they venture onto the Alps or the Dolomites or any of the other high ranges.

The idea was that a similar insurance scheme, or perhaps individual policies, be made compulsory for all recreational hill users in Britain. From this pool of 'private' money the costs of each rescue would be claimed by the Mountain Rescue Team involved. The rescuers themselves would be fully professional and their fees would be met as part of the claim. So would the costs of rescue equipment such as protective clothing, medical supplies and radios, and the flight and servicing time associated with the helicopters. Insurance and professional rescue make a pair and would provide massive savings, it was said, to the public purse.

The idea not only became fashionable but was soon associated with blanket assumptions about the casualties who were regarded as feckless and incompetent. In the course of the furore the Conservative MP for a Tayside constituency made it known that he was considering introducing a Private Member's Bill for mandatory rescue insurance.

The Mountaineering Council of Scotland spoke up for mountaineers by questioning the assumptions, and the debate went around in dizzying fashion. Eventually no one outside of mountain rescue and RAF circles could be sure which costs should be ascribed to whom. My view was absolute and clear and has not altered to this day. Only a limited element of RAF costs can be ascribed to mountain rescue, possibly some additional fuel and servicing costs.

The Sea Kings, Nimrods, their crews and ground support, as already stated, have a primary purpose which cannot be compromised and that is the defence of the nation at home and its interests abroad. This purpose would continue as a requirement even if mountain rescue, and indeed rescues at sea, were to terminate overnight.

In the interests of training, of communication skills, human sharpness and machine maintenance a certain number of hours must be flown each week, and challenge must be either manufactured or found. The RAF helicopters carry the responsibility of rescue when one of their aircraft goes down and this is the first, unquestioned part of those necessary flying hours. In these cases they carry additional responsibilities because national security is involved. Thankfully, such events are rare, but their very rareness creates an experience vacuum that is precisely filled by civilian mountain rescue.

Each rescue is a unique event that demands its own carefully thought out strategy and planning. Any of them might present problems of execution requiring the crews and Control to improvise and somehow 'come through'. This 'coming through' can be likened to tactical development on a battlefield, as liaison with the Rescue Teams can be likened to liaison with troops on the ground. When a casualty is hoisted into the aircraft the winchman may be required to utilise his paramedical skills – again as in a battle situation. Not only were the costs which were being ascribed to mountain rescue already committed and unavoidable but also 'real emergency' training, close to ultimate purpose, was being discounted.

The fact is if mountain rescue did not exist the Ministry of Defence would have to invent it.

In those pre-Devolution days the British Government was represented in Scotland by the Secretary of State for Scotland. As the pitch of argument and counter-argument arose he called a Public Inquiry. Proceedings were held with the eyes of Scottish, British and even world mountaineering on them. As was usual, the Committee was a cross-Party body. I have to say that, disregarding all notions of Party preference, they listened with care and arrived eventually at what I believe was the right conclusion.

The Committee met and listened to evidence in Glenmore Lodge over two days, 22nd and 23rd April 1996, under the Chairmanship of William McKelvey MP. I found it surprisingly laid-back, an enjoyable experience. We met upstairs in the bar with the MPs seated with their backs to the broad windows that look out onto the Northern Corries. Their audience of Chief Constables, representatives of the Mountaineering Council of Scotland, and Mountain Rescue Team Leaders, all of whom were also witnesses, sat facing them. I very clearly remember looking out over Mr McKelvey's shoulder at the mist that was swirling around the cliffs and reflecting how useful are the large numbers, 80 or so, we could bring to a rescue on a day such as this. A professionally structured Team would have many fewer, possibly only ten.

The usefulness of civilian mountain rescue to the armed forces, as outlined above, was established and accepted, as was the assignment of costs, and other areas of concern were noted, such as the skills gap identified by the Mountaineering Council of Scotland. Their view was that the number of participants in mountain activities was increasing at a greater rate than the provision of mountaineering education.

On 23rd April I was interviewed along with Donald Watt, Chairman of the Mountain Rescue Committee of Scotland, and Jim Fraser and Mike Dunlop of the Torridon Team. Mrs Ray Michie, MP for Argyll, articulated the concerns of many when she asked 'about "sensationalised" media coverage' and Donald agreed with her when he replied 'The media's treatment of mountaineering is not terribly good… all about "killer" mountains and all the rest of it.'

Questions to me mostly concerned training of the rescuers and safety, particularly getting the safety message across to the public when the media often seem intent on sensationalising, as Donald had noted. That said my own direct dealings with the press have been mostly positive and worked to the good. I was also asked about the small number of hoax calls we receive.

Questioning was as probing as it was friendly. Discussion of the funding side of mountain rescue led naturally to the possibility of litigation, particularly in the hypothetical case of a casualty being further injured in the course of a rescue. This type of insurance is covered through the police authority but it was identified as another area of concern.

No fewer than 152 memoranda were submitted for consideration, 19 of which were included in the final report. All of them were against change, particularly against the introduction of professional rescue, insurance and charging, with some Mountain Rescue Teams taking particularly strong lines. To take two examples, not quite at random, Isle of Skye Mountain Rescue Team began thus: 'After 20 years in mountain rescue as Team Leader it is even more evident that your committee misunderstands mountain rescue in Scotland. There is no need for change, or desire for change…' The Lomond

Team ended thus: '... as for us soldiers on the ground, we want no part of it – goodbye Scottish MR.'

Elsewhere, Highlands and Islands Enterprise as part of their economic summary noted that the financial impact of mountain activities in the Highlands and Islands in terms of 'total expenditure' (by visitors) in 1995 amounted to £164 million. Approximately one-third of this vast sum occurred between the months of January and March, the winter mountaineering months. This threw yet another light on the importance of mountain rescue. HIE closed significantly, 'We will watch with interest, therefore, your deliberations on the controversial issues of insurance cover and payments for mountain rescue services.'

It will be apparent to the reader that the overwhelming weight of opinion was against the introduction of compulsory insurance for walkers and climbers, and a professional, paid rescue service. The Cairngorm Mountain Rescue Team and its Committee were squarely and wholeheartedly of the same view and some people, outside the circle of mountain rescue, might wonder just why feelings ran so strongly. To further illuminate our attitude, and hopefully leaven what might be a rather dry subject, let me introduce the fictional couple Mr and Mrs Hill-Walker who live in the leafy suburbs of Aberdeen in a home they have scraped and saved for and invested in to their very limit.

First, the argument for any form of insurance is that it will *probably* not be required and many people, in all kinds of activities, take the risk of simply not bothering. If the youthful Mr Hill-Walker, who has not invested in insurance, has not returned from his day on the hill by, say, 22.00 his fearful partner when reaching for the phone might think of the bill she will be incurring, possibly unnecessarily. In these circumstances she might well retire to bed to endure a fitful, sleepless night. If in the morning her husband has still not called it might be too late and poor Mrs Hill-Walker, who loved him in spite of his harum-scarum ways, will be faced not only with early widowhood but the bill for transporting his body to the roadside.

In the second case the now middle-aged, fortunately employed and well-paid gentleman has, at last, taken out insurance. He has had a superb day on the hill, soloing top after top from the Coire Cas car park away out to the furthest reaches of Ben Avon. The day has gone past like a blur and he has barely noticed how fatigued he has become. On the way back he falls and breaks his arm. This is a very painful injury but it does not affect his legs and, in present circumstances, the likelihood is that he will walk out himself without question.

Most experienced hill people recognise this kind of risk as part of the hill experience. Insurance changes that. Such a walk will cost him time and discomfort so he calls his dear partner and lets her know his situation. Naturally concerned she asks him what his insurance is for anyway. Quite right, he thinks, and calls up a rescue. At enormous expense to the insurance company (and through them to other insured people) ten ace professionals from the reconstituted Cairngorm Mountain Rescue Team and a Sea King turn out. Back at home Mrs Hill-Walker puts her feet up and pours another G&T, congratulating herself and her husband on having tamed the hills – as indeed they have.

There is a third case that must be considered, although it poses a notion of character weakness in Team Leaders that I have never yet witnessed. Insurance brings with it the suggestion of bounty, the idea that the mountain rescuer will become a bounty hunter. In all rescues with any degree of seriousness the Team Leader is faced with choices such as how many Teams to turn out and whether or not to request an aircraft. Such decisions would have the effect of diluting the reward and the bounty hunter mentality will make its decision on the basis of profit. Such a decision would be impossible within the present mountain rescue culture, but insurance and direct reward would alter that culture and altered culture is exactly what we are talking about.

The rescuers' decision to go on the hill is untainted by money. That delightful young couple, the Hill-Walkers, who met through hillwalking and will continue to go out together at least until the kids arrive, need have no fear beyond the immediate effects of any accident. The Cairngorm Mountain Rescue Team will always do its best to get them safely back to the small first home they scrimped and saved to make a start in.

In Scotland all mountain rescue is carried out on a basis of goodwill. All interest remains with the casualty alone. Our obligations were, and remain, of a non-financial nature, and standards of professionalism are not dependent on payment. Indeed, many Team Members are already professional mountaineers. Fully qualified to British Mountaineering Council standards and above, they make their livings through guiding and training in Scotland, the Alps and elsewhere in the world.

Money still plays its part, of course. Equipment must be purchased, protective clothing, ropes, flares, transport – even within an amateur service the costs quickly mount up, and soon the new Mountain Rescue Centres would add considerable further expense. The British Government at that time annually donated through the police a certain amount that was 'down the queue' from other police needs and which, even at its maximum, did not cover capital costs. It was a bad arrangement that would later be addressed by the post-Devolution Scottish Government, although not before the Team Leaders had to some extent taken matters into their own hands – a story that is worth a chapter of its own.

The Scottish Affairs Committee in due course reported to the House of Commons and concluded with the following statement: 'Mountaineering is a risk activity and will always remain so. The challenge of the hills is what attracts so many people to the sport. Mountaineering has developed an ethos of self-reliance which has led to the evolution of a highly skilled Mountain Rescue Service consisting mainly of mountaineers. We believe that the current system of co-operation between volunteer teams, the police and the military provide a service, at little cost to the public purse that would be hard to improve. Regulation of mountaineering and hillwalking, or compulsory insurance for participants, would not enhance the current system or make it cheaper, and would probably have a detrimental effect due to the loss of voluntary Mountain

Rescue Teams. The costs of mountain rescue are far outweighed by the economic and social benefits derived from these services.'

So, after the media furore and the costly Inquiry, it was finally agreed that everyone's interests were best served by existing methods. On reflection the exercise was probably worthwhile in that it removed all doubt and brought much out into the open that had before been, if not hidden, at least unseen. Even so, not all costs could be directly accounted for then or now. The balance sheet never tells the whole truth. There is another group of contributors who must be recognised as essential to the country's mountain rescue effort and any chapter on this subject that left them unmentioned would be remiss indeed.

Most of the Team Members are either employees or are self-employed, and most have families. They have responsibilities to fulfil. Willie Anderson, my eventual successor, works as a teacher whose classes cannot simply be abandoned and left unattended. Chris Barley, a dentist, could not normally break his working day but was available at all other times. As a practising pharmacist I was unable to simply take off my white coat and walk out of the shop. Often I employed a locum to take my place, especially when involved in extended rescues.

Family support is also an important foundation and it would be inaccurate to say that families never suffer. In times of emergency Anne was never found wanting, to drive me when I was too tired, to cook for and look after other rescuers, to be a listener, to go the extra mile. All over the Highlands the rescuers have colleagues who cover for them at short notice, who are ready and willing to add to an already considerable workload and even give up their own time. Employers, again at short notice, have to bring in substitutes and reorganise.

These are the unsung heroes and heroines of mountain rescue without whom it would fail. As much as the rescuers themselves they contribute to the creation and maintenance of the most professional standards possible within an amateur ethos.

SEVENTEEN

'This river is known as the watermelon river. They grow under the water.'

The group of four young women looked at each other dubiously. We were at the Fords of Avon, the intersection of the Lairig an Laoigh and Glen Avon and a sort of crossroads at the heart of the Cairngorm massif, beside the tiny shelter identified on the map, rather grandly, as a Mountain Refuge Hut. The girls were in the middle of their Duke of Edinburgh Award expedition.

'We don't believe you,' one of them said.

'Oh, well, then…'

I rolled up my sleeves and guddled around at elbow depth. 'Here's one! Little blighter, it's trying to get away. Wait though… hup!', and I hauled out a large, round melon, cooled by the river since morning when Chris Barley left it there. Soon we had it sliced and shared around. There is nothing like melon for rehydrating the body and lifting the spirit when the sun is beating down and feet are sore.

The Award presents several challenges to senior pupils, one of which is a self-supported, summer expedition across wild land, a journey that demands preparation, training and teamwork. The young people are assessed by adults who should know what they are about, such as teachers, mountain leaders, and members of the Mountain Rescue Team. I served in this way from the mid-1970s through to the mid-1990s, as did many of the Team.

In our area we took the view that the certificate should be no give-away, that the young people who attempted the Duke of Edinburgh Award should be shown the respect of differentiation. Not all would succeed. The challenge had to be sufficiently great, as three or four days travelling through the Cairngorms certainly are. They would have to meet all the requirements, mastering navigation, pitching and sleeping in their tents, and carry all refuse back out with them. The words 'pass' and 'fail' were never used, but at the end their books would be signed, or not signed, by their assessor.

Now more than ever it is wonderful to introduce young people to the hills. Distractions today are insistent and trivial. Computer games, television, DVDs they watch in the privacy of their rooms. Football, which I have always loved, has become more than ever a spectator sport. Alcohol is more easily attainable, as are more dangerous substances. All this comes with a sense of fear among parents about the terrible things that sometimes happen to unattended children. In certain urban environments of course, these fears are well founded. Risk is ever present in the mountains but of a different nature that can be understood and, mostly, managed.

Often, somehow, word gets through to young people that there is more to life than can be found on a screen, and they escape to the outdoors on their own. Without an apprenticeship or a mentor they can easily get into difficulties, as the Rescue Team sees all too often. In winter especially they can experience distressing misadventures, often carrying good equipment without knowing how or when to use it. Hillwalking and climbing clubs are all keen to open their doors to the young. Dedicated practitioners of any sport want to see it flourish and continue. They are also protective of its reputation. For all of these reasons I view controlled school trips in the most positive of lights.

When our Depute Leader in 1973, Morton Fraser, found he was unable to continue as an assessor he suggested I take his place. I did and was immediately impressed by what the young people could do, by their spirit and optimism. They made decisions for themselves, read maps, navigated, camped, cooked, overcame problems, recognised and corrected their own errors, took responsibility, and worked together as a group.

At that time no qualifications were required to become an assessor and it tended to be loose and haphazard. I dedicated myself to the task, developed procedures and watched the experience become still more worthwhile for all involved. It was a short step now to join the panel of assessors whose area roughly coincided with that of the Cairngorm Mountain Rescue Team.

Other members of our Team also became enthusiastic and before long our panel was filled with mountain rescue experts. This meant the standard in our area was particularly high and, as a consequence, the youngsters received a more than usually exacting test. When they were not properly prepared, or did not complete the route as they should, we did not sign their books. Phone calls came in and letters arrived from the schools, but complaints gradually turned to appreciation. The idea took hold that if Cairngorm was one of the most difficult areas in which to gain the Award it was also scrupulously fair and, possibly, the most worthwhile.

We tested them with simple questions on such basics as magnetic variation in navigation. We did pre-expedition checks to ensure the pupils carried the required kit. If they did not we generally allowed them to go out anyway, because they were obliged to travel in fours and it would be unduly harsh if the others were not allowed to continue due to lack of numbers. We took great satisfaction when pupils who had – let me use the word 'failed' – returned the following year to enjoy the experience to the full and succeed.

We made a point of meeting with the pupils here and there on their trips without letting them know when we would appear. On one occasion, the first where we did not sign their books, a public school group was to spend the night beside Corrour Bothy, below the Devil's Point at the southern end of the Lairig Ghru. About 22.00 on what was a wonderfully clear, fine evening Jim Grant, also of the Cairngorm Team, and I took ourselves close to the summit cairn of Ben MacDhui where we could look down on the bothy. Six hundred metres below us the tents were pitched but had their entrances lying open. The pupils were nowhere in sight and the scene, quite simply, had a feeling of 'wrongness'. We decided to investigate.

When we got down we discovered the pupils sleeping inside the bothy. As assessors we had no objection to the group using the building, or any other facility, if they were soaking wet or likely to become so, or if one of them was injured. Using it as a response to necessity would be interpreted as intelligent use of resources. On this occasion though, on such a fine night, all was well and so the group, according to the rules, should have been sleeping in their tents. We did not feel we could sign their books and their headmaster later phoned for an explanation. To his great credit he accepted what he was told and improved the school's standards of preparation.

Paradoxically perhaps, our reputation grew positively among the schools, and some returned year after year. We developed superb working relationships with Harris Academy in Dundee, and Norwich Academy, who would send six or seven groups a year, all well prepared. All were good, some were actually great.

In the course of our assessments we were obliged to examine the pupils' logbooks, to read their expedition accounts and be privy to their thoughts. Time and again I was humbled by their lucid prose, command of detail, observation of bird and animal life, and the fineness of their sketches. Reading these accounts left me in no doubt that nature had already equipped them to face not only the outdoors, but their future lives. All either we or their teachers could do was keep the lines straight, impose nothing but standards, and point towards the hills.

In time head office asked us to take on the task of accrediting assessors, since some schools wished to use their teachers to assess their own pupils. Although we interviewed and walked with many aspirants, sadly none was successful. Although we were by no means elitist we could not find one we felt was up to the job, and the most usual point of failure was in having a sufficiently thorough knowledge of the area. Many were extremely familiar with the Cairngorm massif in both summer and winter, but our area is much wider than just that. Since some of the routes the pupils took meant crossing from one area to another they had to be sufficiently familiar with at least the more usual passes. None was. Sometimes, when we asked what maps they carried, they had no more than those which covered the plateau. In fact five were required, covering Ben Alder, Loch Ossian, Creag Meagaidh, Glen Tromie and more.

Eventually Award Head Office, wisely, decided on a national accreditation for assessors and everyone on our panel, all Cairngorm Mountain Rescue Team Members, went on the course. Times had moved on since the Awards' beginnings, even since we joined, and we were checked as to our suitability to work with children. All, of course, passed. In fact we were found to be well ahead in knowledge and techniques, as might be expected of mountain rescuers, but we also did more than was strictly required. Some assessors would leave their charges at the start of the expedition and meet them again at the end. We went into the mountains and checked them in their practices.

Chris Barley once went to the top of Meall a'Bhuachaille to rendezvous with a school group that never arrived, having taken the lazy option of a detour around the Green Lochan. When he finally spoke with them the pupils admitted they had opted out. He did not sign their books and their teacher later told him how glad she was the boys had been taken down a peg. They were fortunate in life, as well as clever and able, and tended to be arrogant and sarcastic. Some element of levelling, she felt, would be good for them.

In the mid-1990s head office reorganised the areas and ours was divided among its neighbours and sadly squeezed out of existence. It was a development that we, as a group, felt was at best mistaken. We felt we could not continue in the shadow of such a loss and our entire panel left the Duke of Edinburgh Award Scheme as one, albeit with our best wishes for the future of the wider movement.

All things pass. My memories of over 20 years' activity, of working with voluntary groups and schools, most of all with pupils, are almost uniformly positive. My life was enhanced as much as theirs. Through the experience I came to believe that outdoor education may now be compromised by an overzealous culture of safety, and a politically correct view of success and failure. It is not for me to say, and time will tell anyway, but I hope that pupils who took their Awards in the Cairngorms retain them as milestones in their lives, especially those who were challenged to raise their standards. I will leave the subject with a favourite memory.

In the mid-1980s I had to assess four girls from Harris Academy on a Silver expedition. The group was quite young, 15- and 16-year-olds, but were well prepared by their enthusiastic organiser, David Stibbles, who was the main force behind the school's deep involvement in outdoor activities. Their first day's route took them from Glenmore Lodge, along Strath Nethy, over The Saddle to Loch Avon and the Shelter Stone. From there they had to climb to Loch Etchachan and down in a loop to pitch beside the Hutchison Memorial Hut.

At the time I was in my early forties. My wife and I were deeply immersed in the business, our two adult children had their health, and my every aesthetic need was met by the outdoors. I went over the mountains at a run and at the Hutchison Hut met one of their teachers. It was now 18.00. The girls had not arrived and it was approaching time for her to go down the glen to Derry Lodge and phone for advice. It was such a beautiful evening I felt it unlikely that anything was seriously wrong. Perhaps a turned ankle had slowed them, or they had misplaced themselves on the hill. I told her I would return along their route and there was a good chance I would meet them. If so I would make all the necessary calls on my return to Aviemore.

I went back along the cliffs beside Loch Etchachan, moving easily and speedily and without any feeling of fatigue even after a long day. From there I looked down onto the Shelter Stone but saw no one. I made the long drop towards Loch Avon for a closer look and there was still no sign. From the head of the loch Coire Domhain presents an easy, but long and laborious, slope northwards back up onto Cairngorm. Back on top, around 20.00 I spotted a group of young women with map cases making their way across the hill.

Maybe those are my girls, I thought, but if so they should not be there, well off their route.

They called me over and asked if I could advise where they were. I decided not to reveal my identity at that moment. Chris Barley had carried out their pre-expedition checks and so there was no reason why they should recognise me. I could also be confident in their equipment and basic readiness.

'I'm not sure,' I said, 'and I don't have a map. Why not lay yours on the ground and we'll talk it through. Where do you think you are?' They pointed to exactly the right position.

'And where are you heading?' Again they pointed to the correct position.

'We think we took a wrong turning,' they said. 'Just there.' They pointed at Coire Domhain.

In fact they had made a simple 180-degree error at the head of Loch Avon and given themselves an unnecessary climb. I put them at their ease by telling them that I was, in fact, their assessor. They became slightly upset, but before any tears were shed I reassured them that they were doing well. The fact is, anyone can make such an error and, if they are truthful and wise, even the most accomplished will admit it has happened to them. Having made the error though, they had analysed the problem, assessed their own position and acted correctly. They would have concluded their day satisfactorily without me.

As it was now getting late I pointed down Coire Domhain to 'that little patch of green' beside the Shelter Stone and told them to pitch there for the night. It was short of their original target for the day but just as good a place to stop. I would call their teacher when I got back and explain. Tomorrow's walk would be that bit longer than otherwise, but they had done enough for today. The girls descended happily in fading light, leaving me alone among the enormous whaleback mountains and the silence. I felt like the last man on earth, never to be so fit again, or so complete, never with such feelings of wholeness and well-being.

EIGHTEEN

On 11ᵗʰ January 2003 a new Team Member, Duncan MacDonald, was canoeing with some friends on Loch Morlich. It was a Saturday and he was relaxing from his day job in deer management at which he was doing particularly well. At 28 he was already operating at a high level of responsibility and understood very well the importance of his work in terms of land management and conservation.

His life was in every way set fair for a prosperous and useful future but, for all that, he was not entirely happy. Some people have in their nature elements that prefer the adrenaline rush of immediacy to the anticipation of a distant future that may never arrive. Possibly that was why he joined the Cairngorm Mountain Rescue Team. Like all the rescuers he was qualified in first aid, but in addition Duncan had recently taken the Wilderness Emergency Medical Technician qualification through Glenmore Lodge. WEMT is growing in reputation as one of the leading medic training courses, specifically tailored for dealing with medical and trauma emergencies in real wilderness environments on land or sea. At that time though, he still had very little practical experience.

He was on the water when his pager sounded and so able to respond promptly to my request. He beached his canoe, collected his mountain equipment from Inverdruie and made his way directly to the Lodge where a helicopter was waiting. It must have been an exciting moment because, up to that time, he had never been ferried in to a rescue by helicopter.

The information telephoned to me was that a male climber had fallen from an ice route known as The Cascades in the Loch Avon basin. The Cascades is a very demanding Grade 5 climb near Stag Rocks, originally put up in the 1960s by legendary climber John Cunningham. From the Loch Avon shoreline the ground slopes steeply up to a ledge approximately 2m in width, and The Cascades rises vertically from there. At that time of year it would inevitably be covered in ice. The fallen climber would therefore have been front pointing with his crampons and digging in with an ice axe in each hand. As part of his basic technique he would try to ensure he had three points securely in the ice at all times.

After the fall another climber had ascended onto Cairngorm where he could receive a signal for his mobile phone. He had called the police and the information given to the duty constable suggested the casualty had suffered a broken femur. The constable correctly decided to call ARCC immediately to request a helicopter rather than, as was the agreed procedure, passing organisation of the rescue directly over to the Team. Only then did he call me.

Later it became clear how the accident occurred. The casualty was a hard rock climber based in Paisley. He and his companion walked over from the Coire Cas car park to descend into Coire Domhain Avon where they found the route was, as expected, covered in ice. They ascended to the ledge where they made a secure belay and there checked their ropes, karabiners and other equipment. Both men were well equipped with the leader wearing thin gloves and, over them, the oil impregnated mittens that have kept climbers' and walkers' hands warm in extreme conditions for generations. He looped his two axes to his wrists and made sure his crampons were secure on his boots before making a start.

The ice at the bottom of the route was thick and strong and had taken the belay screws without difficulty to their full depth. However, as the climber ascended the ice cover became thinner. Before he had climbed very far he found he could not put in security for further runners but continued without any kind of protection, other than his strength and skill, for almost the full length of the 50m rope. As he approached the top of the route and a slight overhang before its completion, he struck his right axe into the ice but was unable to make a deep penetration. It tore out again. With the left axe and both front points secure in the ice he would probably have been safe had his left hand not slipped out of his glove. Later this axe was retrieved by another climber who found the glove still dangling from its loop.

He dropped for the full 50m to land two-footed beside his partner on the ledge, breaking not one but both femurs. The force of the landing folded his legs behind his back from the fractures, as well as displacing three vertebrae. Even this did not fully absorb the momentum of the fall which drove him off the ledge and into a slide down the ice slope for another 50m until, eventually, the belayed rope arrested his descent.

Duncan started putting on his mountain equipment as he travelled to Glenmore Lodge and was still putting it on in the helicopter. Four other rescuers had responded and they discussed the situation as they flew over Cairngorm. Two had done no technical climbing and the others were newer to the Team than Duncan. Of the five only he had medical training beyond first aid. Since only one could go down with the winchman at a time it was evident it should be Duncan. As they approached the scene the two men strapped up and prepared to go over the side. Weather conditions were poor with low clouds and, as the day wore on, plummeting temperatures. The pilot, as Duncan later put it, 'did a superb job'.

Desperate as the casualty's condition was, from the moment his descent was finally arrested his luck turned. Quite a number of climbers had been in the area when the accident happened, among them an ambulance technician who got to him as quickly as possible and expertly put him into 'neutral alignment', which is to say he straightened his legs. This meant that nerves and blood vessels were able to function as well as possible given the tearing and twisting the broken femurs must have subjected them to. Most fortunate of all, the fractures had remained closed, reducing the possibility of infection.

While the technician carried out this difficult, specialist work the other volunteers used their axes to cut a ledge where the casualty could rest without worsening his condition still more. Rucksacks were packed around him, partly for insulation but also to wedge him into place.

Conscious of rotor downdraft the pilot moved his aircraft to hover over Loch Avon while he awaited an assessment from Duncan and the winchman. On the ground the severity of the casualty's injuries was obvious. One of his legs was visibly shorter than the other and he was in great pain. The winchman and pilot conferred by radio and the winchman went back up to collect a stretcher and a casualty bag.

By now it was apparent that Duncan's four colleagues would not be required. The pilot made a speedy return to Glenmore Lodge where he dropped them off and refuelled. Beside Loch Avon Duncan and the winchman had plenty to keep them occupied in moving the stretcher into position below the newly cut ledge and supporting it with rucksacks.

Duncan later noted that the casualty possessed a particularly hardy demeanour. At no point did he lose consciousness and he had complete recall of the accident. He remembered the climb and the loss first of his right axe, then the glove slipping out of the left, the fall and impact. The two of them had a detailed conversation about it while Duncan worked.

The level of pain must have been extreme but the casualty endured it stoically. What internal injuries he suffered could at that point only be guessed at, but the trauma that attends the break of even one femur is enormous both in the sense of loss of body fluids and shock. That he should be moved as little as possible was obvious but he had still, somehow, to be placed on the stretcher.

Duncan leant to his ear and told him, 'I know you have a lot of pain and moving you will give you a lot more. We have morphine in the helicopter but it will mean someone going up and getting it. Or we can just get you out of here as quickly as possible.'

'Out of here – now,' he replied.

There were eight present apart from the casualty himself. They tucked the stretcher in against the ledge and held it in position, arranging the casualty bag across it. Stationing themselves above and below the casualty they log-rolled him over and into position, taking as much care as possible with the fractures, anxious not to open a wound, all the time conscious that any head injury might not have manifested itself. The bag when tightened at once insulated and immobilised.

By now the helicopter had returned and was again hovering over the loch. At a word from the winchman the pilot moved into position. The stretcher was attached and lifted, the winchman travelling with it, one hand on the lifting cable, the other on the casualty's arm. At no point was he unattended. Duncan and the second climber were winched aboard afterwards and returned to Glenmore Lodge where the aircraft was refuelled before continuing to Raigmore Hospital.

Almost a year later we received a letter. The casualty was still enduring a lengthy recovery period and longed to be able to climb again. That he had survived at all came down to prompt expert treatment from the ambulance technician initially, then Duncan and the winchman with the assistance of several anonymous people who chose to help. His hardihood and spirit played no small part but most important of all was his speedy evacuation to Raigmore Hospital.

If not for the helicopter I would have been obliged to raise a much larger Rescue Party which would have taken more time, with still more time required for the walk in. The casualty would then have been carried out over rough ground on a journey that might have taken a further ten hours. Even with such an iron constitution the pain alone could have killed him. The fact is his chances of survival would have been close to zero.

When Duncan dropped by my office recently I asked him how he felt that day. 'Terrified,' he said, 'but it changed my life, that and other rescues.'

At the time he was the youngest Head Ranger working in deer management in Britain. He always had an interest in first aid but through mountain rescue he discovered his life's true direction and a real aptitude for emergency treatment. He left his job and joined the Scottish Ambulance Service and is now an ambulance technician working towards paramedic qualifications.

NINETEEN

In even the most exalted of medical circles disagreements occur about the best methods of treatment for different conditions and illnesses. Papers are written, lectures delivered, original work is carried out in labs and drugs are trialled. Fields such as stem cell research are opened up and, in Parliament, the ethics and morality of new methods are debated. The mystery and resilience of the human body remain.

So it is also in the narrower field of mountain rescue medical treatment. Long experience tells us that the essential task is to take the casualty as quickly as possible to hospital where more sophisticated and further reaching treatment can be administered. In all cases casualties from the Northern Cairngorms are taken to Raigmore Hospital in Inverness. Where spinal injuries are involved and more specialist care is required the patient will be stabilised and might be transferred to the spinal unit at the Southern General in Glasgow.

The mountain environment with its often next-to-impossible conditions demands an amendment of the normal aims of first aid, 'to preserve life and promote recovery', to the even more simple 'do no harm', with more than half an eye on the delightful acronym KISS, 'Keep It Simple, Stupid'.

Different Mountain Rescue Teams adopt different approaches and I hasten to emphasise that my experience is of the Cairngorm Mountain Rescue Team only. No criticism is implied where other Teams' methods vary, if only because different conditions may prevail. One area where they certainly do is in the carrying of drugs that are not specifically for the treatment of the injury sustained on the hill. Some Teams now carry ventolin inhalers for use where an asthmatic casualty has forgotten his or her own, as sometimes happens. Some carry insulin for diabetic casualties who may find themselves away from their normal supply for many hours longer than anticipated.

Our view on these necessary treatments is that responsibility for adequate supplies rests with the casualty. Experience elsewhere may well have suggested that stocking these additional treatments, which includes additional attention and management when drugs must be utilised within their use-by date, and additional expense, is justified. Some Teams, in more populated areas with less wild land, generally operate quite close to the roadside. In the Cairngorms, distances can be greater and wider areas often must be searched. The Cairngorm Team not only takes the view that the essential is sufficient, but also that the temptation to become more proactive and sophisticated is to be resisted. Effective, immediate action and speedy removal from hill to hospital are exactly to the point.

Bearing this in mind it is easy to see why there has been only limited change in 35 years. The McInnes stretcher has evolved through several versions in that time but carrying techniques remain exactly the same. The Sea King helicopter came on the scene almost three decades ago and remains our most brilliant and effective ally. Beside these it comes down to the rescuers themselves, and the human factor.

All members of the Cairngorm Mountain Rescue Team must hold a valid certificate in First Aid Mountain Treatment. The Team runs courses that include refreshers for more experienced members every three years, and the requirement to attend and achieve an adequate standard is absolute. In the course of an extensive search the Team may break down to Rescue Parties as low as three in number and each group must be strong enough to contend with the condition in which they find the casualty.

Beyond this basic qualification is the more advanced Wilderness

Emergency Medical Technician certificate, WEMT for short, which several of our members have attained, usually those who discover a natural bent for the subject. These Team Members tend to work closely with the Team Doctor and their skills only come into play on rare occasions.

It is probably worth noting that in practice only basic first-aid skills are normally required. Discussing this with present Team Leader Willie Anderson recently, he lifted his hand and displayed five fingers, the number of times more advanced first aid had been used in the year's 40 or so call-outs to that time. All the rescuers carry basic first-aid equipment such as crepe bandages, plasters and material for slings. The Rescue Parties are issued with first-aid group kits that contain other, more select equipment, analgesics, as well as still more bandages. A casualty reached by any Rescue Party is not likely to want for bandages and splints, or paracetamol for low-level pain (low level in comparison with the accident Duncan attended at Loch Avon), aspirin for heart conditions. All of these can assist the less seriously injured to walk out themselves or give them immediate treatment prior to being carried or flown out.

Some injuries are on an altogether higher scale of emergency and pain, broken limbs with severe distortions, shock and blood loss. Often the bravest thing to do in these circumstances, and the most effective, is nothing. Pain matters though, affecting as it does the processes of rescue when they are in particularly challenging surroundings, such as the snow cavern on Ben Alder where Paul Hyett was trapped. A carry of several hours over rough terrain to someone with a broken femur would be excruciating.

Often pain simply *must* be dealt with and to do this the Rescue Parties carry two major painkillers, Entonox, a gas, and cyclomorphine, administered by intramuscular injection. The second of these is a powerful drug with an anti-nausea additive. It not only kills pain but also induces a sensation of euphoria. It has addictive qualities and, as a consequence, is controlled by the Home Office.

In comparison Entonox is a relatively safe drug. In mountain rescue terms its main disadvantage is that in low temperatures its two components, nitrous oxide and oxygen (in a 50/50 mix), can separate. In these circumstances it is necessary to give the canister a thorough shake. Entonox is often administered by midwives during births and its advantages in those circumstances are equally of use on the hill. Entering the bloodstream and the brain through the lungs, its effects are almost immediate, and it can be self-administered, which means that, provided the casualty has use of his or her arms, the supply can exactly meet the demands of the pain.

This, in turn, means the rescuers are freed to concentrate on other tasks, such as securing the casualty or attending to the stretcher and lift. When we rescued Paul on Ben Alder it was Entonox we used and since his arms were uninjured he was able to participate. He later told us he had difficulty working the control until the stretcher was lifted into the vertical. With that the ends of his broken bones came into contact, raising his position on the Richter Scale of Pain to an excruciating magnitude, and he suddenly found he could not only make it work but also that he was gulping deep. On that rescue we used both of the bottles a Rescue Party normally carried.

For many years Entonox had a severe limitation in that it came in weighty canisters so bulky we limited our number to two. This was sufficient in most circumstances but a long carry can take 16 hours. Nowadays it comes in lighter canisters, and a greater number can be carried when required.

Where injuries are truly extreme the other, more powerful, drug comes into play. In contrast to the bulky canisters of Entonox, cyclomorphine comes in a package no larger than two matchboxes. In controlled conditions it might be administered intravenously to speedier effect, but in mountain rescue conditions this pushes on the envelope of practicality. In winter especially the casualty is likely to be well wrapped in Gore-tex and fleece which would have to be removed, possibly over already injured limbs. In these circumstances blood pressure will be lower and veins difficult to find, and an injection will require considerable expertise.

Chris Barley, a practising dentist who regularly administered intravenous injections in his surgery, once told me it was a difficult enough process even in controlled conditions and that he would not dream of making the attempt in any others. Nor would I, and would only countenance such an attempt by someone with a high degree of training and experience.

Intramuscular injection is in practical terms the only method in mountain rescue conditions in the Cairngorms. The target is the buttock and thigh area, the body's big muscles where the needle is unlikely to hit a bone. No attempt is made to remove the casualty's garments. Instead the needle is pushed through successive layers of Gore-tex overtrousers, trousers and underwear and the 10mg dose, possibly 15mg, injected. All that remains to be done is to rub the area with the heel of the hand to set the drug moving.

Low temperatures also mean the cyclomorphine's dispersal to blood and brain will be slower than anyone would wish, although it will do the job when it arrives. The rescuers are acutely aware that the temptation to administer a second dose when it seems the first has failed is to be resisted. Instead the casualty is placed in a survival bag and the rescue continued. The body's natural warming in the bag will aid the progress of the drug on its journey. A second dose *might* be administered four hours later if circumstances so demand. The hospital is always informed of the treatment and the attending doctors can reverse its effects if they so choose, by administering a second drug, narcan.

Doctors are divided on a host of issues and it is easy to see why opinions can differ. Cyclomorphine can have a depressing effect on the respiratory system and might impair the breathing of a chest injury casualty. Against that, when ribs are broken and muscles torn, breathing will certainly be impaired by pain. By relieving the pain, and inducing that feeling of euphoria, breathing can be eased on a long carry.

In mountain rescue, conditions are often extreme and if some means can be devised where the burden of decision can be removed from first-aid qualified volunteers of whatever depth of experience, and perfect accuracy assured, I would like to be informed.

Our Team Doctor, Peter Grant, and I have discussed this matter often and agree that the drug should be used where the judgement of the rescuers says it should. In Peter's own words, when dealing with the pain of multiple serious injuries there is no point in administering two paracetamol tablets. The drug used must be adequate to the task.

The near impossibility of locating veins means that Team Members do not carry plasma or blood substitutes, but they do carry another seldom-used item, normally found in the Rescue Party box. Plastic airways are sometimes used to keep the casualty's natural airway clear, but again considerable expertise is required in application. Within the neck the oesophagus divides into two ways, one leading into the stomach, the other into the lungs. If the airway should be placed wrongly any supply of air might inflate the stomach rather than the lungs. The danger is inherent even in normal conditions but, and this is to be emphasised, the extreme conditions of mountain rescue render the processes more difficult and hazardous than elsewhere.

The larger group will carry a vacuum mattress if it is understood its use will be beneficial. Air from the mattress can be pumped out so that it hardens around the casualty, acting as a full body splint and rendering him or her, including injuries, immobile. It is heavy though, a large, full rucksack in itself, and a heavy load for the rescuers on the walk in.

In all of these ways the Team endeavours to deliver the more serious casualties to hospital as quickly as possible without causing further harm, pain-deadened possibly, immobilised and wrapped almost certainly, sealed with a KISS.

TWENTY

Communication technology probably began with smoke signals, possibly reflectors, advancing through telegraph to radio. The portable radio with its whisker aerial I had carried so many years before to Stag Rocks to witness and assist in the retrieval of a body was much valued but clumsy and impractical in comparison with the mobile phones in common use by the end of the century. As a parallel technology a Global Positioning System (GPS), utilising between 24 and 32 satellites depending on position had been developed by the United States Defence Department. Devices came on the market that could inform walkers of their own location regardless of visibility.

Like the radios, but even more extensively, these developments altered the ways we communicate on the hill and navigate across it and widened the range of rescues that were possible. Provided a signal could be found it was possible to talk lost climbers down. Mobile phones also raised the horrifying possibility of being in touch with someone while helpless to assist. In his book on Everest, *Into Thin Air,* John Krakauer writes of how Rob Hall, when stormbound near the summit, was phoned by his wife in New Zealand, using satellite communication passed through Base Camp. He reassured her as best he could and told her to 'sleep well'. Shortly afterwards he died.

GPS devices, useful for location finding were less practical in navigating around hazards without recourse to a map. Mountain rescue had to learn about the usefulness and limitations of these technologies through experience. It was a continuously surprising process. Certainly, the young woman in Manchester who received a text message in January 2003 must have got quite a surprise, but not so much as I did when I heard.

In 2000 my circumstances within the Team had altered. I made the decision not to go on the hill with Rescue Parties but instead take the more sedentary role at the radio in the new Rescue Control Centre at Inverdruie. My reasons for coming to this decision had to do with a long-standing sports injury and will sit best in a dedicated chapter. Retiring was an option at that time but a strong wish to work in the new Rescue Centre, which we had worked towards for so long, and which also deserves its own chapter, kept me going.

The police called me at 20.00 on 4th January 2003. A young man had come into the station to report two of his climbing friends overdue. They had come north as a threesome but set out for different targets on the day, parting at 10.30 at Coire Cas car park. The two others, a 24-year-old man and his 20-year-old female companion, had gone into Coire an t-Sneachda to attempt Jacob's Ladder, a technical climb graded between levels 1 and 2. A secondary purpose was the young man coaching the young woman in her winter skills, mainly in the use of crampons and ice axe. The three agreed to meet again in the car park at 17.00.

The first man returned on time and waited for more than two hours, after which he decided to raise the alarm. He was able to give highly detailed information. The woman had shoulder-length red hair over which she wore a blue climbing helmet. The man wore a red Gore-tex cagoule. Neither used walking poles, as many climbers and walkers do nowadays.

All this would be of potential use the following day when, if we had still not located them, a helicopter would be deployed and would be better able to pick them out from other walkers. In addition, they each carried a torch and maps. It seemed they were a reasonably competent couple with every chance of walking to safety having overcome whatever navigational slip or minor injury had beset them. I decided to wait for a couple of hours to see how events might unfold, but at the same time called Chris Barley to give him a 'heads-up'. Visibility was too poor to deploy a helicopter to good effect.

At 20.40 the young woman in Manchester advanced everything by making a 999 call reporting a text message from two friends in the Cairngorms. Apparently, they had lost their bearings somewhere on the Cairngorm Plateau but were 'somewhere on the south side of the mountain'. One of the two had injured a leg and was unable to walk. Now we knew for certain there was a rescue to be carried out. Not only that, we had a reasonable notion of location, numbers and injury. At 20.45 the rescue began with my Depute Leader, Chris Barley, leading an advance party directly onto the hill and a stretcher party following about half an hour later.

We also learned that regular, real-time dialogue was not possible as the texter had to leave his injured companion unattended while he ascended 300m every time he sent a message.

At 22.30 the woman in Manchester received a second text message giving the map coordinates of the casualties. She relayed it to the police in Aviemore who passed it on to me at Inverdruie. I, in turn, radioed it to Chris and the Team on the hill. The male climber had a GPS device that gave him his position by locking into a satellite communication system. They were in Coire Raibeirt on the north side of Loch Avon.

By 01.00 visibility had improved and I requested the assistance of a helicopter. About the same time the advance party located the casualties halfway down the corrie, and noted their location was threatened by avalanche. To the good, it seemed the woman's injury was not as serious as had been feared. Apart from the avalanche danger all of this was encouraging indeed. Not only was the rescue running in textbook order but we had discovered something new and important.

Where a communication signal is too weak to carry a voice message a text message might still get through. It had become apparent we could use text messages to better effect than we had so far understood.

We were still left with the technical aspects of the rescue, in particular the threat of avalanche. The lesser extent of the casualty's injury suggested the stretcher might not be necessary in winching her aboard the helicopter. In a stretcher or not she could go up in the vertical. However, the downdraft from the rotors was likely to start the avalanche we feared. Both Rescue Parties were now together, the stretcher was abandoned, and a small group had begun the descent into Coire Raibeirt to assist her to a safer location on the loch shore.

Twenty-first-century technology continued to play its part in this rescue but continued also to find its limits. Helicopter navigators tend not to use the popular names of ground features, such as Coire Raibeirt or Loch Avon. Of unique value to them are the map coordinates. Supplied with these pilot and navigator can be safely left to do the rest.

All of our rescuers are these days supplied with GPS systems of their own. Both Chris Barley and Simon (aka Sumo) Steer were in Coire Raibeirt, illuminated by a descending flare. Chris was treating the casualty so I asked Simon for exact coordinates for the helicopter. He consulted his device and came back with a very precise 10-figure reference. I applied it to the map to discover he had given the summit of Beinn Mheadhoin, an obviously incorrect position.

I invited him to press the button again and this time he came back with the centre of Loch Avon. It was now apparent that the GPS signal was bouncing off the cliffs surrounding the Avon basin and giving wrong results. I called again in the following fashion.

'Cairngorm Control to Cairngorm Simon, we have an aircraft on the way. Can we go back to the days of pencils and rubbers and just read the numbers off the map.' There have been some suggestions that my language was less moderate than usual.

Simon consulted the map and returned a less precise but entirely accurate 6-figure reference that I could pass on to the aircrew and at 02.00 the helicopter arrived in the wider vicinity to find the weather had closed in again.

The pilot made several attempts, flying first along Glen Derry with a view towards negotiating the narrow gap between Beinn Mheadhoin and Beinn a'Chaorainn and turning westwards over the Fords of Avon. This proved impossible and a similar flight along Glen Feshie did not reveal the breach in the clouds we had hoped for. After an hour of futile attempts the pilot made a bold manoeuvre and the casualty was winched safely aboard.

At 03.55 she was landed safely at Glenmore Lodge and by 06.00 all Cairngorm Mountain Rescue Team personnel had returned to snatch such rest as was possible in the new bunk rooms at the Rescue Centre before getting up and going to their normal employment.

Later we learned that the two had taken rather longer to complete Jacob's Ladder than anticipated and, when they arrived on the plateau, discovered they had forgotten their compass. This led to them taking a wrong turning in low visibility and descending on the wrong side of the mountain. This basic error was a simple one that almost anyone might make. A rescue the following month, again involving text messages, speaks of a more troubling mistake that is all too common.

On 22nd February two 25-year-old engineers from the Bradford area had entered Coire an t-Sneachda to climb Aladdin's Couloir, a Grade I ascent they were quite capable of. By the time they reached the plateau night had fallen and the weather worsened. It was windy and cold and visibility was poor. They quickly lost their way and at 18.30 decided to call the police and ask for assistance.

I returned the call and went through our carefully developed procedures, ticking the form as I went. That done I told them they could not have wandered too far out of their way. They should use their compass to find north and walk in that direction until they reached the corrie's rim. Following the rim in a more or less north-easterly direction, to their right as they faced north, they would eventually pass Point 1141, descend into Coire Cas and so find safety.

To say they were reluctant would be an understatement. I engaged them in conversation about navigation and gradually came to appreciate that, although they were carrying both map and compass, and used a plastic bag to protect the map from the elements, they did not properly know how to use them. Using up the power of their mobile phone I went through the routines of finding north on the map, no more than deciding which way was 'up', placing the edge of the compass along the north–south line and aligning themselves with the magnetic needle which, above all things, could be relied on to do its job.

Time and again in mountain rescue we come across this particular form of ignorance. The fact is it is quite possible to make many visits to the hills with good and competent companions and never actually take a bearing. Many people either never learn or do not practise the skill, and evidently these two were among this group. They had good levels of general fitness, good-quality equipment and were capable of technical climbing. Even so, they had either bypassed or forgotten the most fundamental and important of all mountain skills.

Their personal energy levels were by now low and their confidence reducing rapidly. They conferred and decided not to move and, since they could not be persuaded out of this position, I got the Team going at 19.30. Fortunately, the two had a bivvy bag and when they found a suitable boulder took shelter behind it. They were now protected from the worst of the conditions but, in one of our last voice calls, reported that one of them had become unwell.

I controlled the operation from Inverdruie with Chris Barley beside me and Donnie Williamson leading on the hill. In the early hours of the morning, when the power level on their mobile phone ran low, we turned to communication by text. The Team was making as much noise as possible and firing off flares and, in the course of the night, expended 30 – as our local paper put it, '… worth £30 each'.

With typical thoroughness and accuracy Chris wrote down the casualty's text messages as we received them. The following examples should give a feel for what we were all, casualties and rescuers, going through and the frustration we felt at being so near but so far.

The times given are when the messages were received after midnight and are significant.

00.05: think we saw a flare lower down the slope but not sure tired now

00.22: flare lower down to our right as we face down

00.42: just seen it seemed to be to our right as we face down the hill couldn't be sure of exact direction just lit up that side of the hill

01.07: saw 2 then one came from behind us and the other was to the right

01.37: same direction as last time but closer

01.44: heard bang same dir as last time

02.01: that one lit up the whole area

04.37: we have not heard from you for ages are you still looking Matthew is in a bad way I have been flashing torch all nite please text back

This last message touched our hearts.

The Team on the hill continued to search but I was growing increasingly despondent. I was also concerned that the two young men seemed to be receiving our texts at best intermittently. A tremendous amount of resource had already been expended and at 05.30 I stood the rescuers down with a view to bringing fresh searchers onto the hill at 07.00.

Chris agreed to keep me company at Control while some of the rescuers caught some sleep upstairs, Donnie Williamson with his huge stamina among them, and together we made the long round of necessary phone calls. In addition to fresh searchers we called the RAF Kinloss Team to increase the numbers. Conditions were growing clearer so we contacted ARCC and requested a helicopter. The Search and Rescue Dog Association (SARDA) sent five dogs with their handlers. In the course of all this we received another text message from the missing two.

06.56: your close on our right as we faced south down the hill spirits still up just bloody cold

The searchers were by now off the hill and there could be no one close to them. It dawned on us what had happened. Unlike voice calls, text messages can be delayed at the server. We had not been conversing in real time.

At 07.00 Chris had to return home to prepare for another day at his dental surgery. I continued to co-ordinate the rescue and received one last, telling message before it all came to a satisfactory conclusion. I recorded the time with slightly less precision than Chris.

09.25: not a lot whiteout is it north wind compass seems ducked it has bubble and spins

A compass does indeed have a bubble and its pointer does indeed spin. These are its essential characteristics. Armed with just a little more knowledge and slightly more developed navigational skills they would have been off the hill much earlier and unaided.

With better visibility and the higher temperatures that came with dawn the two walked out to safety. They had been at the head of Coire Raibeirt, as suspected, and we must have come close to finding them several times in the course of the night. Instead they came hobbling down over Cairngorm's sub-top, Cnap Coire na Spreidhe, where the Team intercepted them and applied first aid. Otherwise they returned under their own, much reduced, power. Safe, thank goodness, and well.

TWENTY-ONE

A 48-year-old man from Inverness became lost in white-out conditions on the Cairngorm Plateau. Strong, gusting winds were prevalent and one of them plucked his map from his hands and blew it away. This is a very simple accident that can happen to anyone and escalate quickly into serious difficulty. What makes the story more interesting is the use of new technology as the principal means of his rescue.

He used his mobile phone to call the police who, in turn, called me. I called him on the hill and learned he did have a compass but, without the map that had blown away he was helpless. He needed both to take a bearing. He did have a GPS device and because of that could give me the map coordinates of his position.

This incident occurred in March 2006 when these devices were becoming more commonly used. From the Rescue Centre at Inverdruie I had already conducted several conversations with people in, more or less, these circumstances and devised a set of questions which I had laid out on a standard form. The questions ran: name, number of persons, mobile number and charge remaining in the batteries. With these simple questions answered I would know who I was talking to and have some idea of the scale of difficulties to be faced. Since walkers habitually venture out with their mobile phones turned on, battery reserves tend to be low, particularly in freezing temperatures. In a rescue situation I would advise them to turn the phone off. While the rescue was ongoing I would call at regular, agreed intervals.

In a second level of questioning I would ask the location of their car, its registration number and colour. With this information a simple check could be made that would ascertain whether the walker actually was on the hill. Hoax calls had happened, although not often. In addition, it is not unusual for a walker to walk almost accidentally to safety and drive away without informing the rescue services, leaving the Team chasing ghosts on the hill.

I also asked whether they were carrying a camera. The flash can travel for a tremendous distance and can be used to attract the attention of a helicopter crew or, fired off into the dark, bring a search party in more accurately than the most expertly taken bearing.

With phone and car numbers the police would run an identity check which would, first of all, confirm the caller's identity and, secondly, give us access to the family and, through them, such information as the climber's health and experience.

These procedures complete I set the Team in motion, tasking them to go to Point 1141 on the Fiacaill Ridge. At the same time, I asked the casualty if he preferred to wait for rescue or if we should try to talk him down. If so, he would have to accept responsibility for his own safety, keep his eyes open and react to what opened before him in ways that I could not. A competent hillwalker who was subject to a simple accident he elected to help himself.

I already had the OS map opened on the table in front of me and using headphones had both hands free. Locating his coordinates on the map I put myself in his boots and got to work with the compass, choosing what I judged would be the best route to Point 1141. On the Incident Report I have the bearings and distances I gave him by phone: 95 degrees for 250m then – 80 degrees for 500m then – 25 degrees for 1,000m. He adjusted his compass to the bearings I gave and counted paces to his next change of direction. It was impossible to be absolutely precise so the Rescue Party waiting at the cairn spread itself out across the hill. The alert had come to me at 17.55 and he walked into their good company at 20.50, safe and sound.

Not everyone takes the option of being navigated down. One couple called from the hill, thoroughly misplaced but also concerned about the diabetes one of them suffered. Given their state of fatigue and hunger they felt it best not to make the physical effort. No doubt they were correct in this. It was winter with white-out conditions prevailing and, since they had no GPS device and could not offer a location, or even had much idea, finding them was liable to contain some element of luck. However, when the couple described some of the close landscape details, I felt I had a good idea of where they might be.

Led by Chris Barley the Team set out with me remaining at base, using a mobile phone to talk to the pair and a radio to speak to the rescuers. The Team had to work on dead reckoning, counting paces while keeping an eye on the compass needle. Initially they drew a blank, while all the time the condition of the diabetic grew worse. We needed a more radical method. Thanks to this double communication, with Rescue Party and casualties, I was able to co-ordinate the firing of flares. I would warn the couple just before Chris and his party set off a flare. They would, first, listen for bangs and, second, look out for bright lights falling by parachute. Falling snow tends to diffuse the light, but gradually we were able to close the Team onto them and when they caught sight of each other I heard whoops of joy in both ears.

An incident more telling than either of these and, again, where use of a mobile phone was crucial, had occurred in 1999, the year before the new Rescue Centre was opened. On this occasion modern technology played a part more in creating the incident than resolving it. The file contains 16 A4 pages of notes made from calls through 19 hours of searching.

It began on 5th November at 19.45 when I received a call from the police. Two men in their twenties, both from Merseyside, were lost on the plateau and required assistance. The more experienced was a fitness instructor who had done 'a lot of walking in North Wales' and was described as carrying a 'pick axe'. His companion was said to be a 'computer buff' and apparently had no hill experience. They were on the Cairngorm Plateau in white-out conditions and not exactly sure where they were located.

I called them at 19.50 to learn they had decided to call for assistance around 16.00, as light was fading, to report themselves lost. At that time they were in a location with very little signal and had dumped their rucksacks, food and other equipment before setting out to find a better one. After a few minutes they tried to return but their footprints were filled with blown snow, it was dark and they could not find their rucksacks.

By this time they were thoroughly disoriented, uninjured but cold and hungry. Gloves and other protective gear were in the rucksacks along with their food, and they had little or no protection. Almost four hours later they at last located a signal. When I spoke to them it was apparent that they would be unprotected from the horrendous wind and snow for as long as these conditions persisted. Since the weather forecast did not predict a change it was clear they needed help.

Leaving their car at Coire Cas car park they had intended to walk along the rim of the Northern Corries to Cairn Lochain and from there to Ben MacDhui. This would be only the first day of an intended walk of five days that would have taken in several of the highest summits in Britain, a route they had read about in a popular outdoor magazine. To conserve the battery in their phone I told them I would call every hour on the hour and that they should turn it on at those times.

Asking Chris Barley to take charge on the hill I made a full Team call-out including Dave Riley and his dog, Rosie, and requested a helicopter. By 21.30 the rescue was fully underway, but it very quickly became apparent that the helicopter could not function in the conditions. It was also now apparent that these two young men were in serious trouble. With the loss of the helicopter we had a still greater need for numbers on the ground so I requested assistance from the RAF Team at Kinloss.

At 01.00 I contacted the two again to assure them that everything possible was being done. They were now anxious and their condition and morale were in no way helped by extreme hunger. Very obviously they would be vulnerable to hypothermia. It was while we spoke on the phone I came to realise they were very inexperienced indeed.

It became clear they did not really understand their predicament or that mountain rescue is not something that can be called up immediately on being phoned for, as the emergency services mostly can in the cities. They had not realised that conditions like these existed in these islands. Snow had begun falling at 15.00. It had not stopped since and the wind was blowing strongly. So hungry did they become they asked if a helicopter could drop food, but of course it could not so much as venture over the plateau.

The rescuers were now setting off flares and I asked the two men to be alert for explosions and bright lights which, even diffused, would give some indication of the direction in which to walk. I felt it was worth spending battery power by calling while the flares went off, in addition to my hourly calls. Chris Barley radioed that visibility was down to 30m, very low indeed. At 01.45 all contact was lost and I became extremely concerned.

Forty-two people were now involved in the search but the challenge of wide spaces, sub-zero temperatures and low visibility was a huge one. At the same time the likely consequences of failure were terrible. At 04.30 I requested that the Braemar and Aberdeen Teams prepare to assist us at first light, approaching the plateau from the south, and in the course of the night called up another tranche of Cairngorm members, asking them also to be ready at first light.

At 07.00 the two southern Teams joined us and we had five dogs involved and – at last it was possible – a search and rescue helicopter. We stood down the exhausted Cairngorm Team Members who had by now done a full shift and more, sending them to Glenmore Lodge for what turned out to be very few hours of sleep. With the fresh rescuers in place we now had a total of 43 people on the hill.

At 09.45 the first casualty was discovered near Stag Rocks above Glen Avon. He was hypothermic and described as 'heading towards death'. We wakened the personnel at Glenmore Lodge and sent them to assist in evacuating the casualty while the fresh rescuers continued the search for the second. For a time we had no fewer than 75 people on the hill. The first casualty was carried down below cloud level to a location where the helicopter could land and was in Raigmore Hospital by 13.30.

At 14.30 the second casualty was found and an hour or so later was following his companion to hospital. A huge, highly co-ordinated effort had been made and a great result achieved. Both casualties survived and made full recoveries, but the story does not end there. A few days later a passing hillwalker came across their abandoned equipment and reported it to Glenmore Lodge. The instructors there retrieved it and invited me across to see.

All of their kit was brand new and must have cost quite a bit of money to put together. They had ground mats, obviously never used, sleeping bags, new rucksacks, stoves and fuel and plenty of food, water bottles and spare clothes. In short, they had carried all they needed to survive. Some of it, such as gaiters and gloves, should have been put on before they left their car. A lack of knowledge of basic procedures, and a lack of appreciation of winter conditions, meant their lives had been at extreme hazard and almost lost.

All they needed to survive they had walked away from. Most poignantly of all, their compass was still in its case beside their map. I almost wept with frustration. It was clear these were fine young men who had been badly guided, perhaps even misled, in their assessment of the challenge. A willingness to learn was apparent, as was the commitment to resource. Speaking to them through the early parts of their prolonged rescue I formed a very positive impression of them and privately hoped the experience would not sicken them of the hills or prematurely end what could be a source of recreation and pleasure over the years.

This was a case where reliance on mobile phones played as large a part in the creation of the problem as it did in the solution, probably more. They had put a mistaken faith in the value of a call and the likely speed of response. A Mountain Rescue Service cannot be assembled and reach the scene as quickly as, for example, an ambulance to a road traffic accident. It has to be considered and planned. Distances to be travelled on foot are liable to be great and search demands are unique to every occasion.

How responsible the magazine which published the route was, for the way it was interpreted by at least some readers, is a moot point. A route in summer conditions is very different from the same route in winter. Any idea of following the informal paths, eroded by the boots of generations of hillwalkers, can be forgotten. In November there will be a coating of two or even three metres of snow and no paths to be seen. In either season a high-pressure day will present an enormous and beautiful vista from any of the high peaks. On a low-pressure day visibility can reduce to just a few metres. If accompanied by wind-driven rain or snow the conditions can be not only terrifying but lethal.

The outdoor magazines take a responsible attitude to safety but are obliged to assume a basic level of ability when they guide their readers towards locations of possible hazard. Our two casualties, it seemed obvious, had not reached that basic level, particularly in map and compass skills. They stashed their rucksacks, food and other equipment and set out to find a better phone signal, their footprints filling with blown snow as quickly as they made them. They were eventually successful but could not find their way back. They were uninjured but cold and hungry. Gloves and other protective gear were in their rucksacks along with their food and they had little or no protection.

I repeated this point several times in the correspondence that followed and was disappointed therefore, when *The Mail on Sunday* published a short article on the rescue that headlined, 'Saved, Thanks To Our Mobile Phones'.

I wrote to the editor in the following terms: 'In the Scottish Mountains mountaineers and hillwalkers should not rely on mobile phones, global positioning systems, or electronic watch type compasses. In bad weather in the Cairngorm Mountains their use is severely limited. Even with the technology available today there is no substitute for the basic navigational skills using a proper Silva compass and an OS Map.'

TWENTY-TWO

The problem of funding Mountain Rescue Teams is perennial. Scotland has 23 civilian Teams all made up entirely of volunteers, none of whom seek or expect any reward other than the satisfactions inherent in saving life, comradeship, and the mountain environment itself. There are also two RAF Teams, based at Kinloss and Leuchars, whose speciality is crashed aircraft but who are never slow to assist in other rescues. Grampian, Strathclyde and Tayside Police all run Teams. This amounts to 28 Mountain Rescue Teams in all. There is also a Scottish Cave Rescue Association and the Search and Rescue Dog Association.

All are members of the Mountain Rescue Committee of Scotland, which meets twice a year and is the representative and co-ordinating body. It is administered by an Executive Committee which contains eight officials as well as representatives of the Association of Chief Police Officers and ARCC and has the power to co-opt from many other mountaineering bodies. Its General Committee contains representatives of the Teams as well as the Search and Rescue Dog Association, the police, armed forces, and others.

In the United Kingdom the police authorities have responsibility for the preservation of life on all land above the level of high water. Enabling them to fulfil such duties means affording powers to suspend civil rights. This can be as straightforward as directing vehicles around traffic accidents or warranting temporary powers to enter and search a home or office. Between the levels of high and low water, and out to sea, the coastguard is responsible for implementing the government's maritime safety policy and co-ordinating search and rescue. Mountain Rescue Teams are very rarely called to assist the coastguard although it does happen, especially in the coastal areas of the North West Highlands.

The principal relationship is with the regional police force and it is traditionally they who have supplied funding to their local Teams. The logic is simple. The preservation of life in the mountain environment consumes many hundreds of person hours in the course of any year and is best served by dedicated and expert volunteers working in close conjunction with all the services but, particularly, the police.

A full-time professional service would cost a lot more money and all the questions that come with true professionalism would arrive with it. Would the service be free? Would walkers and climbers be required to insure, or achieve qualifications? 'Dedication' is a key word, meaning not only high commitment but a unique focus. To put it another way: the highest degree of professionalism possible within an amateur ethos. All of this was thoroughly established by the Scottish Office Committee which reported in June 1996. The question of funding though, had been left unresolved and would not be formally approached again until after the referendum of 1997 and the recalling of the Scottish Parliament.

Funding supplied by the police forces, again traditionally, came from within their normal policing budgets, a fixed amount within which Chief Constables have to work. In all but major incidents, when the government might be expected to step in, money has to be shifted around within the system. An unexpected expenditure here means a tightening of the belt there. Rising costs that must be met will mean a reduction in expenditure where it is possible to make one.

Throughout the twentieth century the use of hills for recreational purposes increased until there came a point, with increased wealth and leisure time, and under the influence of an increasingly large and vibrant literature, visitor numbers increased exponentially. Rescue funding, of course, did not. From my earliest association with the Cairngorm Mountain Rescue Team we had received £6,000 annually from the local police, now Northern Constabulary, along with other assistance such as free road tax and insurance for Team vehicles.

The Cairngorm Mountain Rescue Team is perhaps more fortunate than most in that we operate in a terrain suitable for our biennial sponsored walk, have the vigorous support of our community and the enthusiasm and skills to put in the work and reap the rewards for mountain rescue. Raising money by ourselves meant we were able to purchase more vehicles and other expensive equipment. In 2000 we achieved our long-term ambition of creating at Inverdruie a Mountain Rescue Centre that would not only accommodate us but possibly act as a model for future development elsewhere. Not only was this costly in itself, but it also considerably increased our regular running costs

By 2002 unrest among the Highland Teams was growing ever stronger. Rescue requirements had far outgrown resource, and showed no sign of tailing off. Because of our own fundraising the Cairngorm Team was not threatened, even with our increased costs, but as Leader I was aware that we were only one part of the Highland mountain rescue scene. There was no question of seeing ourselves as a case apart. Assynt with its remoteness, Dundonnell with its rugged expanses of wild land, Skye with the Cuillin, Glencoe, Torridon and the rest each had their own unique demands. Because of the nature of the terrain the Lowland Teams had especially different requirements and, possibly, outlooks.

I had already spoken with the Chief Constable in Inverness and agreed that the Cairngorm Team could use a further £25,000 on top of the original £6,000 per annum to function on an annual basis. This amount would cover annual running costs leaving our own fundraising income free for the purchase of new capital equipment and to maintain and improve the new Mountain Rescue Centre.

To give an example of capital cost: our 40 rescuers have to be completely re-equipped with clothing every two years at a cost of about £500 each. Stretcher carrying and arrested falls can be very demanding of outer clothes. To give another: flares cost £30 each, and later when we used 30 on a single rescue, all of which had to be immediately replaced, they would make a significant headline. A more recent example: a four-wheel drive ambulance we purchased recently cost £37,000 in itself. In addition, new health and safety legislation demanded a speedier turnover of certain equipment such as ropes.

The Highland Team Leaders met as a group and loosely agreed to this sum as a suitable amount to seek for each Team. We also agreed that it had to be ring-fenced, entirely and only dedicated to mountain rescue. The Chief Constable listened to this point and understood. However, he could not be entirely supportive. If anything, he was the opposite. Not only was the total sum beyond his reach but the loss of freedom to manipulate his own overall budget was not, and could not be, acceptable.

These points were taken but I began to wonder just when the police had last reviewed the mountain rescue budget. I wrote to the Chair of the Police Committee who replied that it had never been reviewed at all. It was apparent that our whole funding structure was an accident of evolution rather than a considered design. Learning this, we suggested that a review was not only overdue but that it should be repeated on a regular basis. The Chief Constable was unbending and perhaps, in considered retrospect, correct to take such an inflexible stance.

'We have a fixed budget from the Scottish Executive,' he said. 'Go to them and we will support you but, for now, there simply is not enough to go round.'

This gave food for thought because it was clear the problems of resource could not be ignored. It was also clear that the traditional route would not deliver the answer. The Mountain Rescue Committee of Scotland agreed collectively to lobby the Scottish Executive. On hearing this I groaned inwardly. Inconvenient lobbyists, however strong their case, are all too easily shifted from minister to minister, civil servant to civil servant.

The terms of the lobbying, and indeed of our case, needed

some consideration and I came up with the following argument. The Executive was actively promoting a healthier lifestyle among the population, and outdoor activities were a strong part of their strategy. They were actively encouraging people to 'get out there'. In addition, in my own area, they had created the Cairngorms National Park that contained four of the five highest mountains in the British Isles. For these reasons more and more people were visiting, some were getting lost, some injured, and a few even killed. Who would pick up the pieces? There was only one answer, and the Teams were being swamped. There may have been some element of exaggeration in the word 'swamped', but the principle was a true one.

The argument received practical support not long after when an American gentleman walked into the shop at Glenmore to buy a map before setting out on the long walk to Nethy Bridge. His guest house reported him missing next day and I instigated a search. The walk is entirely low level and so he was unlikely to be seriously injured. The Team had no great difficulty finding him, unharmed but slightly upset that he had got lost.

'I thought I was going for a walk in the park,' he said.

The press picked up on this and allowed me to develop my theme of increasing usage and the misconceptions that come with the word 'park'. The Cairngorms is by no means a rolling plain of flower beds and ordered lawns. In fact the funding issue began to generate stories across the press in a way that suggested things were coming to a head.

Other changes were in the wind and decisions had been made in the south that would put a new slant on funding. It is the United Kingdom, rather than the Scottish Parliament, which allocates radio frequencies. For many years all the Mountain Rescue Teams had shared Channel 53. Now we were to be given a new frequency with ten channels to share among us.

On the surface this was an improvement but it implied a capital cost in that we would require new radio equipment, replacement base sets, vehicle sets and individual sets. This would amount to an additional, unexpected expenditure of between £30,000 and £40,000 for the Cairngorm Team alone, with the total for all the Teams amounting to hundreds of thousands. Finding these sums, especially for the smaller Teams, was out of the question and we had to let the governments know that we could not make the change unless this money was forthcoming.

In March 2003 Scotland's First Minister, Jack McConnell MSP, visited the Ranger Base in Coire Cas to reinforce the safety message to walkers and climbers immediately before the Easter influx of visitors. At the same time he announced that the Scottish Executive would provide 'about £300,000' for new radio equipment. Willie Anderson was one of those present and took the opportunity to put a question that would alter the course of mountain rescue in Scotland. What it boiled down to was, 'What about the rest?'

In a short, public conversation that Willie describes as 'amiable' the First Minister was apprised of the wider situation. He seemed receptive and before being swept off by his diary-holders promised that a higher level of general funding would also be forthcoming. We felt he had been surprised by what Willie had to say and had perhaps spoken rather more off the cuff than most politicians would choose. The terms were vague but they gave our campaign an important toehold. Mr McConnell was to prove as good as his word but there was some way to travel before a complete solution was achieved.

Meantime press interest was gathering, and we took every opportunity to plead poverty. Willie was quoted in *The Glasgow Herald* as saying that we were 'fed up' of fundraising.

In May 2003 we were required to fire off no fewer than 30 flares on a single rescue. When we sent an invoice for the replacement 30, to the value of £991.40, the police at first refused to pay. The *Highland News* headlined this as 'Flares Fury of Cash-Strapped Mountain Heroes', and quoted me as saying, furiously, 'We do not want to be paid but we need the right equipment.'

In July the *Strathspey & Badenoch Herald* headlined, 'Mountain Rescue Teams Need More Cash' over a story that described not only much of our work but our own fundraising that enabled it. Inside, the editorial insisted, 'Politicians Must Come to the Rescue'.

A stingy, possibly exploitative, attitude towards the volunteers was becoming apparent. It was also becoming clear that the prize was a greater one than we had at first targeted. Where we had previously been seeking more money to allow us to simply keep going, we were now campaigning to put mountain rescue funding on a permanent, sustainable basis. It was worth persisting.

On 12th August, opening day of the grouse season, *The Guardian* headlined, 'Mountain Rescue in Plea for Funds' over a large picture of me with the Team's new, self-financed ambulance in the background. As a quote they boxed out, 'The government are getting us dirt cheap, they really are.'

'Dirt cheap' was only half true. The rescuers give their services for no financial reward. This point has to be understood. Equipment, transport, Rescue Centre all cost money, but if the point is 'value' then very few services can compete. The financial cost of any lost life, the heartache to survivors, the health benefits to the whole community of healthy outdoor recreation, might be priced by economists. I won't even try.

On 31st August the *Sunday Herald* ran a full-page story by Stephen Phelan under the headline 'Walk Of Life' with a large colour picture of a CMRT stretcher party on the moor. 'Today, the Team seem exasperated at the way the government and the police seem to take this work for granted,' he wrote. It was a telling sentence. There was no way the mountain rescuers would, or could, walk away from what they do. It followed therefore, that the Executive would have to respond in adequate fashion. Gratifyingly, Stephen Phelan also highlighted the 'national park' aspect. We had the feeling that now, at last, something was about to happen.

On 17th November the Scottish Executive announced a fourfold increase in mountain rescue funding. Speaking in Ballater, a beautiful village in the Southern Cairngorms, Jack McConnell outlined the scenario in the following terms, 'Scotland's mountains are one of our greatest natural assets and are enjoyed by many thousands of Scots and tourists alike.' Of the rescuers he said, 'They commit so much of their own time and money, often risking their own lives. It is only right that we support them.'

The First Minister and I exchanged some warm correspondence and I came to like him. The campaign, particularly the press aspect, had created some friction, but we were able to put that into a proper perspective.

This new funding is still accessed through the police but is, effectively, ring-fenced. Of course, the sum is limited, and since the Mountain Rescue Teams have differing demands that vary through time, the sharing of the money is a sensitive issue. Some Lowland Teams might have as few as one genuine mountain call-out in a year, although that rescue, and the life at risk, will be as important as any other. To achieve a fair cutting of the cake the Mountain Rescue Committee of Scotland now meets annually with the police, and the number of rescues undertaken in the preceding year, by each Rescue Team, is a factor. This takes the discussion into a sensitive area.

In recent years there has been a movement, instigated by the police but approved by the Mountain Rescue Committee of Scotland, to include mountain rescue under the more general heading of 'Search and Rescue'. This means that Mountain Rescue Teams have been obliged, more or less willingly, to participate in urban searches.

There has been no appreciable increase in call-outs for the Teams serving truly mountainous areas, but the mutual advantage to the police and the less busy Teams is obvious. The police have an additional resource of trained people to call on when engaged in urban searches for lost people. The Lowland Teams in this way increase their number of annual searches, and this is the figure that is fed into the following year's funding calculations.

This means there is a danger that the increase in non-mountain call-outs will reduce the funds available to Mountain Rescue Teams who involve themselves mainly, if not uniquely, in true mountain incidents. There has already been a year when funding for the

Cairngorm Mountain Rescue Team was reduced because of this formula.

Some of the Highland Teams take a dim view of these developments. There can hardly be any doubt that the Highland Teams carry out the greatest number of mountain rescues in the more difficult terrain. Nor can anyone doubt they were the principal activists in favour of change. Manipulation of mountain rescue resource, into general search and rescue, risks division between the Highland and Lowland Teams and could possibly provoke a breakaway by the Highland Teams at some future time. In this way the solution of one problem gives rise to another, and all must be wary.

The Cairngorm Mountain Rescue Team at the time of writing receives about £25,000 a year, close to the figure I agreed so long ago with the Chief Constable of Inverness. I would say we are satisfied with this. Other Teams have varying levels of satisfaction, or dissatisfaction, and act accordingly. Funding is an issue that will never be perfectly resolved. Even fair-minded rescuers who see well beyond their home patch will disagree about who should get what. The problem continues to be perennial, but now it has a framework for resolution and a realistic amount to be distributed. The Mountain Rescue Service provided should not be put at hazard by ambition and politicking within that new framework.

TWENTY-THREE

One morning in January 1997 three young men set out from Coire Cas car park with the intention of reaching Ben MacDhui after ascending to the Cairngorm Plateau from Coire an Lochain. Conditions were not particularly good, although not so bad as to be truly daunting to a competent and experienced party. During the approach one of the three decided he was too tired to continue and returned to the car park after agreeing to meet his friends there later in the day.

The remaining two continued into Coire an Lochain and began their ascent near Twin Burns, an area notorious for avalanches, and in the course of their climb were swept down onto the frozen loch.

Later theorising by avalanche experts suggested that, because the loch was not frozen solidly to the bottom, its icy surface flexed on impact and so absorbed some element of momentum. The snow will have changed its condition several times in its descent but eventually came to rest in lumps about the size of refrigerators.

The two casualties were trapped head to tail but this lumpy formation made it possible to breathe. One was buried completely. The other's head remained above the snow, as did one hand. It must have looked like the scene of some dreadful, but mysteriously bloodless, dismemberment except that the head could blink and the fingers move within their glove.

In former times avalanches in Scotland were not given the respect they were due. Seen as a phenomenon of much higher ranges it was perhaps felt they could not be compared in terms of size and destructive power and so were left not much considered. Indeed, it is true that avalanches in the higher ranges can be awesomely spectacular and destructive.

Only a few months before my time of writing an avalanche occurred in the French Alps that swept no fewer than 11 climbers into a glacier crevasse, burying them under many thousands of tons of snow. So complete was the trail of devastation there was no question of attempting a rescue. The disaster was on such a scale that no attempt was made to even recover the bodies which will now travel downwards with the glacier, eventually to emerge when it reaches its melt location somewhere far below.

This was the fate of the character known as Ötzi the Iceman who lost his life on a mountain traverse more than 5,000 years ago and whose body was finally given up by the ice in 1991. Since then his body and clothing have been studied as a sort of human archaeology and it seems likely he died of hypothermia. The process of travelling will no doubt be speeded by global warming, but I wonder what future generations will make of our present-day breathable clothing, ice axes and crampons, and what further advances will have been made by then.

As climbers came more often and ambitiously to the Scottish mountains it gradually became clear, at first only to a few but then to a gathering number, how frequently avalanches occur and with what lethal consequences. In 1985 two serious professional mountaineers, Bob Barton and Blyth Wright, published *A Chance in a Million*, the first close study of the phenomenon as experienced in Scotland. Both men continue to live here in Strathspey and are close friends of the Cairngorm Mountain Rescue Team. The book was no doubt a contributory factor in the founding of the Scottish Avalanche Project in 1988. In 1993, the Scottish Avalanche Information Service followed, not only continuing the study of avalanches but also providing an assessing and alerting service for those who go on the hills.

Led by Blyth Wright SAIS is a funded service located at Glenmore Lodge. It trains competent mountaineers in the means of testing snow and pays them to go, every day throughout the winter season, to selected locations across the mountain areas of Scotland to carry out their experiments. The results are sent to Glenmore Lodge where they are fed into a computer model, and Hazard Levels, together with more detailed assessments, are published on the Service's excellent website and through the broadcast media. Explanations of the Hazard Levels together with historical data and permanently relevant advice can easily be located on the website, one that all mountaineers and winter hillwalkers should have bookmarked.

Whether the two casualties we left trapped in Coire an Lochain checked the Hazard Level for the Northern Cairngorms is not known but they were not necessarily wrong in setting out. High avalanche risk should not be seen in the same way as a storm warning at sea, a wrong analogy that is frequently made. At sea the entire water surface is subject to the same winds, the same rain and the same patterns of pressure change. On the mountains areas of risk can be avoided by walking along ridges, keeping to rocky areas where possible and avoiding steep slopes. Caution must be exercised but competent mountaineers should not, necessarily, be put off their day's sport.

On recovering from the surprise of finding himself alive this will have been a fine point to the owner of the blinking eyes and wiggling fingers. With every other part of his body trapped he began to move his chin backwards and forwards in a sort of chewing movement, gradually winning more space from the snow in which to move his head.

The companion who had decided not to proceed called the police at 18.30 and they called me. I felt this was an early hour to turn out the Team but began gathering information which we would review at 20.00. Eric Pirie had been in the Coire an Lochain area and noted that the clouds were low. Wes Sterrit, who worked for SAIS, had been on the Cairngorm Plateau that morning taking and testing samples. An avalanche risk warning had been issued that day, and he also confirmed that visibility was down to 10m on the tops. This being so it seemed most likely that the casualties had misplaced themselves and would walk out safely in due course.

This was not a complacent attitude but one based on long years of experience. In the interests of information gathering, for a rescue that might or might not be required, Chris Barley agreed to go up to the car park and speak to the waiting man. He was about to set out when we received a call and he went to the police station instead.

The two men had, indeed, walked out with nothing worse to show for their experience than a few bruises and an amazing story. The chin had created space for the head which had given the shoulder some room to move. The moving shoulder had eventually freed the arm which had cleared the snow from around the chest and taken the hand to the compass. The compass, a small piece of stiff plastic looped around the climber's neck, had been used to chip and scrape away at the snow until the second arm was freed and then the body. The legs followed and the freed man set about liberating his companion. They had been buried at 11.30 and the second man was only freed at 18.00, probably the longest and most miserable seven and a half hours of their lives. The story has entered mountain rescue history as a legend of self-rescue.

Another avalanche legend grew around the incident in 2002 that came to be known as the Red Bull Massacre. In one of the biggest avalanche rescues to be carried out in Scotland thankfully no lives were lost.

The Cairngorm Mountain Rescue Team had been contacted by the company which markets the famous high-energy drink, Red Bull, who intended to sponsor and organise an extremely demanding endurance event named the 'Red Bull Northern Exposure'. Taking place through an April holiday weekend it would attract the sort of athlete who enters triathlons and Iron Man competitions. Ten teams of four would be challenged to walk, run, paddle and climb their way around the Cairngorms for three days non-stop (that is, without sleep) and all four would have to finish if a prize was to be claimed.

The race would close with a cycle ride into Glen Einich

followed by a climb onto the Great Moss where Team Member Jas Hepburn would remain, tented and self-reliant, for the duration of the event. A qualified physical education teacher fallen out of love with formal box-ticking systems, Jas makes his living as an outdoor sports consultant. He has an uncontested knowledge base and skill set (to use his own educational jargon) and on this occasion was employed directly by the event organisers to assess the snow conditions and decide when failing light should call a halt for the day.

The whole event was to take place over five days with Day One given over to arrival and preparation, and Day Five dedicated to an enormous hooley at Glenmore Lodge where Red Bull would create a beach from many tonnes of sand imported specially for the purpose. On the beach the competitors would relax to the sound of a Beach Boys tribute band and enjoy the barbecue that would also be laid on. Red Bull wanted us to advise on safety and provide first aid throughout the event.

Even if they had not offered money the barbecue would have been too surreal to refuse. We advised that climbing while exhausted was inadvisable but it is not the policy of the Cairngorm Mountain Rescue Team to police the hills or wag disapproving fingers. We agreed to stand by at various posts along the route.

On Tuesday the 16th I sat in a Land Rover at Whitewell, a group of crofts that look into the Lairig Ghru and just the perfect spot for radio communication with Glen Einich, Cairngorm, Braeriach and many other places. The weather had not been kind. On the first night temperatures had plummeted into freezing making river crossings even more strenuous. Later there had been a fall of snow. This, the final day, was understood to be the most strenuous of the three with the cycle ride into Glen Einich and climb onto the top.

Radio reports were coming to me from the various staging posts that competitors, especially the slower ones, were tired and clumsy and sometimes at the ends of their tethers. Some were stopping and a few giving up. Others would rest, eat and drink and recover enough to continue. One was so dehydrated he had to be assisted to the Rescue Base at Inverdruie and put on a drip.

We were uncomfortably aware of an overhanging cornice on the rim of the corrie and of the rising temperature that could only serve to destabilise it. With this in mind Gordon Stewart was tasked to go in closer to keep an eye on it. Gordon is probably the fittest of the rescuers and it was joked that if the cornice came down he was the one most likely to outrun the avalanche. Eventually we recommended a halt to this part of the event.

As so often the accident did not happen in the expected location. While the Rescue Team was substantially committed to the event a group of eight army airmen on a winter skills course was trekking in Coire an Lochain with a black spaniel named Breagh. Unknown to them, or unappreciated, the previous night's snowfall had landed on older, harder snow. A slip plane had formed and, as they trekked across the slope, the new snow began to travel downwards carrying the soldiers with it. In the course of its downward journey the slab broke up and the soldiers were thrown to the ground and swept against rocks many metres below. When they finally came to rest only the commanding officer was left standing and he used his mobile phone to summon aid.

The call I received at 13.55 from Aviemore Police Station spoke of seven casualties at grid reference OS: 985034 with the person reporting saying he could see Cairn Toul from that location. This seemed impossible so I sought confirmation while at the same time requesting the assistance of Rescue 137. Confirmation of the position arrived at 14.00 and I immediately redeployed eight rescuers to Glenmore Lodge, at the same time requesting support from that quarter.

Conditions were cold but fine with long-distance visibility, good weather that would contribute to a speedy and efficient rescue. The day evolved in this fashion:

At 14.45 Rescue 137 dropped five rescuers from RAF Kinloss MRT at the scene continuing to the Red Bull event where it picked up three Cairngorm Team Members and a stretcher.

At 15.20 it took in six more of our people and a supply of Entonox.

At 15.25 I learned the full extent of the damage. Seven casualties were, thankfully, on the surface although among rocks. Three of these had suffered back injuries, and of course the rescuers were alert to possible spine injuries. Two casualties had leg injuries and another had a stomach injury. The seventh, although shocked, was apparently uninjured. Four were stretcher cases, the rest walking wounded. The dog was well.

Rescue 137 continued to airlift rescuers into the area until we had 20 people working there. The rescuers packaged the casualties, secured them to the stretchers and began the 400m descent down the hill to where the aircraft waited.

At 15.31 I confirmed to Raigmore Hospital that the first casualties were on their way and was told that the Raigmore air ambulance, known as the heli-med, was available and could contribute to the speedy evacuation of the remaining casualties.

This was a constructive offer but I was reluctant to accept. The heli-med is a smaller machine than the Sea King, and its crew, while highly competent, are not trained for mountain emergencies. Their usual functions were at road traffic accidents, taxiing pregnant women to hospital from the islands (which of course means assisting with airborne births from time to time), and all other conventional ambulance duties that are required across a vast, more or less empty terrain. As events proved the heli-med crew's protocols proved to be different from those of the Mountain Rescue Teams and Air-Sea Rescue.

The heli-med protocols demanded that the crew shut down their engines as they would at a roadside accident. When I heard this I was immediately worried that the engine might not restart. No Sea King pilot would have taken this risk in the low temperatures that are typical at these heights during a winter rescue.

First aid had already been given and the casualties properly packaged for transport to hospital and a higher level of medical care. The Rescue 137 crew would not have hesitated to get them off to hospital. Nonetheless the heli-med crew was required, by the same procedures and training, to unwrap again and check that all was as well as it could be before taking the casualties aboard and flying them to hospital.

I felt that ten minutes had been wasted that might, in other circumstances, have been extremely valuable. Thankfully, all the soldiers survived without serious consequence and were later reunited with Breagh – which gave the press a superb photo opportunity.

The rescue went off in textbook fashion with the rescuers returning to the Red Bull event and, eventually, the surreal beach party at Glenmore Lodge. SAIS later confirmed that no avalanche of this severity had been recorded so late in the season for 50 years and I felt this put their excellent work into another context. An avalanche risk warning should be looked at as a guide and not a substitute for visual awareness and caution. Among the interesting features of the day was the difference in snow conditions in Glen Einich and Coire an Lochain, a relatively short distance apart, and in attitudes between the two groups.

Recognising their competitors would be pushing the envelope of endurance the Red Bull organisers put every possible safety measure in place and, when Jas Hepburn eventually suggested an avalanche in Glen Einich was possible, altered their plans without abandoning them.

In comparison, the Coire an Lochain avalanche was waiting to happen and evidence of avalanche activity was all around. Little balls of snow, known as sunballs, had formed and left thin tracks as they rolled down the slope. Immediately to the west of the avalanche site a crown wall, the mound of snow left after a soft-slab avalanche has come to rest, was there to be seen. With this visible evidence, and a straightforward awareness that new snow on old will create a slip plane, the party should have remained on safer ground.

Responsibility for their own safety rested with all three sets of climbers and walkers discussed in this chapter. In the first case a fair cognisance of the warning given would have kept the pair off the climb they attempted. It would not necessarily have thwarted their larger ambitions as another route to Ben MacDhui could have been chosen. The possibility of avalanche should be borne in mind when planning any outing into the Scottish winter hills. It is no infrequent occurrence.

TWENTY-FOUR

Mountaineering is many things to many people. For some it is a means with which to achieve change, to grow humbler or stronger, for others an inspiring and renewing process. Still others find spiritual experience, others art, science, wonders of all kinds. For me it is all of these things but, mostly, it is a sport.

W.H. Murray defined the expert mountaineer as one who is comfortable in all mountain locations in all conditions. Consciously or otherwise I was developing myself in this way from my first hillwalks with Martin. From walking ever more challenging hills the move into mountain rescue, then climbing and ultimately ice climbing in Scotland and the Alpine 4,000m summits was a natural progression.

By 1985 my competence had increased considerably. Here and there I was soloing ice climbs in Scotland although I had never put up a first ascent. I was also discovering my limits and, by now, keeping company with climbers who were better than I could ever hope to become. The positive side of this was that by climbing with them I could extend myself in relative safety, as well as enjoy the company of some of the best people I would ever meet.

In February of that year I felt that my standards had risen enough and that Smith's Gully on Creag Meagaidh was waiting for me. This route leads up out of Coire Ardair onto the rolling top of the mountain and of course I was mindful of my first call-out when Mollie Porter and Bill March had led the rescue of two young climbers from rocks near Easy Gully. It was first put up in 1959 by the legendary climber Jimmy Marshall and is given Grade 5. The SMC publication *Scottish Winter Climbs* describes it as 'a tremendous climb of great character, continuously steep and sustained' and goes on to say, 'The route takes a while to come into condition and the crux fourth pitch can be particularly difficult if unconsolidated.' I would find out the hard way how true this is.

Four of us travelled to Loch Laggan with my caravan one Monday night to camp beside the beach. This meant we could make the early start that is particularly important in winter, taking advantage of the ice before the sun softens and changes it, rendering it, sometimes, unreliable. We had already agreed our pairings. James Grosset would climb with Malcolm Sclater. I had the privilege of climbing with John Lyall who had by now become one of the strongest climbers I knew. He was perfect company to attempt such a difficult, classic route as Smith's Gully.

Next morning we were up early and into Coire Ardair where we broke into our two groups. For ice climbing two is the perfect number. Three brings complications when changing the lead climber at rope's end. John and I roped up, checked our equipment and made our way up Raeburn's Gully to the start of the more challenging climb. We had already decided to alternate the lead. This is the more speedy method since it means the second climber can simply climb past his companion without taking an awkward stance to adjust the ropes.

We each used crampons and two axes. In this kind of climbing one of those will be a normal ice axe with a pick at one side and a horizontal blade at the other, for cutting steps where necessary. The other axe also has a pick but the other side has a flattened head for hammering in ice screws, or at least for giving them a start so the climber can do the rest. The picks are used in the course of actual climbing with, depending on the condition of the ice, the picks entering perhaps as little as 2cm, perhaps as much as 10.

So we ascended, first one leading for the 50m-length of the rope and then the other, both of us putting in ice screws wherever we found a good, solid stance with a reasonable distance travelled. The climb's verticality was not completely unremitting. At times the leader would find a place where he could stop and lean forward on the points of his crampons. Here he would take one hand from his axe and screw in the protection. Alternatively, if the ice was hard, he would free both hands and hammer the screw in for a centimetre or two.

An ice screw is a hollow bolt with its thread on the outside. At the entry end it has four angled teeth that lead the cut. At the other it has a U-shaped eye standing out from the bolt's side for the climber, first, to grip as he makes his turn, second, to push the pick of his axe into should he require more leverage and, third, to pass the rope through. It is usual for the climber to put the screw in more or less level with his head, perhaps a little higher.

As I approached the crux fourth pitch I found such a location and put in a screw that I would later describe as 'bombproof'. That done I continued while John looked up from a sound belay position, a shelf that he had cut in the snow with his axe. The actual crux comes at a location known as Appolyon Ledge. To my eye there was very little sign of a ledge. Instead there was an overhang that absorbed my full attention.

Understanding I was approaching one of the climb's more precarious moves I put in another screw. Here though, I could find nowhere within reach where the ice was as solid as I would have wished. For that reason, and perhaps because recent solo climbs had increased my confidence, I made what I could of it and hastened on. Any other strategy would also have meant down-climbing, which is notoriously difficult on ice. Fortunately for us both, John had been watching my efforts from below and made an accurate judgement on how effective that final security was likely to be. He tightened the rope and braced himself.

Now taking hold of both axes I pressed down on my points prior to striking. On the higher levels of the climb and away from the shadow of the cliffs the sun had no doubt been working on this particular piece of ice: it came away from the wall in a sheet. When my body weight hit the first screw it gave up without a fight and followed me down. We were at least 200m above Raeburn's Gully and a further 300m above the floor of the corrie when I found myself plummeting downwards. The second ice screw held, as did John's grip on the rope although he was lifted from the shelf by the force of sudden arrest, and I found myself swinging in mid-air slightly above him, rattled that I had come off but not yet feeling any pain.

'That's good,' I said to him. 'The system works.'

John's reply referred to the screw that came out and was less than flattering. He had watched me fall in the knowledge that anything dislodged in such a gully by the lead climber was likely to descend on the follower, including the climber himself. As it was he had watched me bounce across the walls of the gully on my way down, protected by my rucksack from back injury.

'I'll just climb up again, then.'

The attempt didn't last long. On the way down my right foot had struck a bulge in the cliff and my body had pivoted around it, tearing the ligaments and cartilage of my knee and sending me on my way head first.

'I can't use my knee,' I said.

John pulled me in and we secured ourselves while considering what to do, but it was already apparent that we would not be completing the climb.

These were the days before mobile phones so, if I was to be rescued, John would have to make the descent alone, walk out and find a phone. It would take hours during which I was likely to become hypothermic. We both came out against this plan. It had personal costs built in, but there was another factor. As members of the Cairngorm Mountain Rescue Team, we were reluctant to admit to ourselves, and even more to others, that we had got ourselves into a position we could not get out of again.

To make it worse, Creag Meagaidh is on the borderline of the Lochaber Team's area and our own. There was a real possibility they might rescue me before our own people arrived, and the prospect of meeting them in bars and bothies afterwards was not to be countenanced. The nightmare thought of other Cairngorm members being obliged to enjoy their humour was appalling. We could never hold our heads up again. The decision to climb down ourselves was inevitable.

John lowered me to a location where I could secure myself and then abseiled down to join me. We repeated the exercise and, in time, reached Raeburn's Gully which I could slide down on my bottom, controlling my descent with an ice axe. Undignified as the strategy was it worked. Now safe in Coire Ardair I was able to look properly at my knee. It was swollen badly and very painful. John also noted a large dent in my helmet. With no sense of having a choice I taped the knee up, gritted my teeth and walked out.

James and Malcolm were already at the caravan when we returned at 21.00. They had noted we were later than anticipated but were too experienced to be concerned yet. Winter climbing often takes longer than anticipated, sometimes by many hours. Conditions can vary greatly; the weather can change. One climber might sustain a minor injury. None of these occurrences is unusual.

Through the mountain rescue years I would often have to speak with concerned relatives, reassuring them that a late return was not in itself evidence of an accident, far less a tragedy. Missing climbers often walk out the next day. Recognising the family as casualties too, if their anxiety was great I would often send a small group of rescuers to investigate. Under these circumstances it was the relatives whose needs were attended. If the climbers were in trouble news would come to us soon enough and a larger Rescue Party, with decisions on strategy, helicopter, first aid, would follow.

Tonight though, we were safe. Not only safe but our immediate needs were attended by cordon bleu chef, James Grosset. We ate like kings and on Wednesday the others returned to the hill.

At our local surgery I was attended by a locum who diagnosed damaged knee ligaments and prescribed only basic treatment. My leg was immobilised by being bandaged from ankle to thigh, I was given crutches and told to rest the injury. Time would do as much healing as was possible, or so the thinking ran.

Today the same injury would be iced to bring down the swelling and further investigation would at least be considered. If so, it might lead to surgery and a reduction of the consequential trauma.

In time the swelling went down and the pain reduced, finally to a level below normal awareness. Such fitness as had been lost in the rest period was quickly regained by cycling and walking and, in the summer of the same year I completed the Highland Cross within my target time of four and a half hours.

An event originally organised by the emergency services in Highland to raise funds for a new scanner for Raigmore the Highland Cross has gone on to legendary status. Performed competitively it is one of the most demanding endurance events available to the general public. From Morvich on the west coast we were required to run or walk the 20 miles to Loch Affric and from there cycle the remaining 30 or so to Beauly on the east coast. Every year there are entrants who fail to complete the course.

I did the event again in 1987, and in 1988 decided I would make a serious attempt to break my own record, to complete the route, in fact, as quickly as I possibly could. The knee gave me some pain and, never a good runner I lost time on the first section that I made up on the cycle. I loved the whole experience; at 46 years old I was as fit as I had ever been – or so it seemed.

Not long after, in July, a party of us went to the Alps as I continued my long-term ambition of working my way through the list of 4,000m mountains. On this occasion our twin targets were the Durrenhorn and the Hohberghorn, two peaks on the Nadelgrat Range. In terms of physical fitness getting up onto the ridge is the most demanding part of the challenge. Snow and ice have to be climbed, steps cut, strains are put on knee and ankle joints which the young and fit are barely aware of, but which are considerable. On the way up I had a sudden sensation in my right knee that was both painful and disconcerting. It would not respond to my mental commands and, when I put my hand to it, the patella wobbled.

'Something's wrong with my leg, boys!'

I remained calm but was aware that something was seriously

wrong. Willie Anderson and Gordon Stewart were closest. We conferred on my knee and at the same time noted deteriorating conditions. We had been encountering more loose objects on the surface and the snow had become distinctly sugary. In light of these observations the party retreated from the hill into Zermatt Valley. The weather continued to deteriorate over the next few days and so we returned home with the Durrenhorn and the Hohberghorn left unclimbed.

At home I consulted my GP who agreed that something had to be done. That being so I wanted it done speedily and decided to proceed privately. My consultant was based in Edinburgh and he had the joint X-rayed. This found a piece of bone that had been splintered by the accident on Smith's Gully and ever since been floating about in the fluid within the joint, sawing at the cruciate ligament as it went. The report said the cut was, by now, three-quarters through. In addition the medial ligament had been torn off, but had reattached during the rest period and calcified.

The operation removed the sliver of bone and cleaned the joint of excess material and fluid. This led to a great improvement that, in fact, kept me going through most of the 1990s when pain and discomfort returned. The joint was once again examined and further deterioration was confirmed. Nothing more could be done short of surgery that was described as 'serious'. My consultant suggested I attend his colleague David Finlayson, the NHS Consultant at Raigmore, one of the most respected knee specialists in the country.

This meant a longer wait for treatment but by this time I was beginning to accept that I was growing older, and it made a difference. I had lost some of the urgency felt at an earlier stage of life. He examined the joint and confirmed everything that had been said before. It seemed a partial knee replacement was required.

I was, frankly, daunted by the prospect. 'When?' I asked. 'I don't know if I'm ready for that.'

In retrospect I can see that Mr Finlayson was sensitive to the psychology of the ageing, injured, former athlete. 'You will decide when,' he said. 'Come back year on year and, when you are ready, let me know.'

I continued to live my active life as best I could but the knee, inevitably, deteriorated. Coming out in sympathy, as it were, the other knee also experienced pain. Soon both legs lost their straightness and I found myself walking with an uncomfortable rolling gait. Some hard truths had to be faced.

In the season of 1999 to 2000 I made the decision not to attend mountain rescues on the hill. Instead I would delegate that duty to my Depute, Chris Barley, and restrict myself to co-ordinating from the Rescue Centre where, it was agreed, my experience and talents continued to be of use. In 2007 I finally made the decision to have the joint replaced, and Mr Finlayson carried out the operation.

In hindsight I would say that the injury probably extended my mountain rescue career by putting me entirely into an organising role. Even my wish to see the new Rescue Centre fully operational could not have kept me shoulder to shoulder and up to speed with the younger men on the hill.

Also in hindsight, and with no element of blame, I would say that a sports injury required a sports specialist and not the attendance, as I think mine had, of a doctor with no great sympathy for sport and whose focus was purely on what might be called a 'normal working life'. For many of us sport is an essential element in the living of a full and satisfying life. Some will ask: why go to the hill – much as they ask, why kick a large ball around, or hit a smaller one with a stick? For those who need to ask there is no answer. For the rest of us there is no question.

Sport comes with risk and, eventually for most, some degree of physical damage. The door that had opened to me when I discovered the mountains, perhaps as early as that long view taken from Ben Loyal so many years ago, slowly closed with the deterioration of my knee. I came to understand that my time, even in Rescue

Control, would eventually end, but as one door closed another almost equally slowly opened. The aesthetic of sailing is close to that of mountaineering. The challenge of the journey, of navigation and reading the elements, the great wide vistas of hills and coastline, the way light plays on water, all echo between the two activities. In 2005 I purchased *Ticoyo*, a 20-year-old Danish Motor Sailor Type LM30, and took to the waves.

TWENTY-FIVE

'You're not going to believe this,' said Davy Burgon, Duty Officer, calling from Aviemore Police Station.

It was June 2004, high summer, and I had just completed writing a reply to the headmaster of Vale of Leven School. On learning that the Team had been turned out for his pupils Terry Lanaghan wrote a letter of appreciation that included a substantial donation. He promised a full analysis of the events that would include the staff involved. My report should have put his mind at rest. The teacher had acted in exactly the right way. He too had written in thanks, also enclosing a cheque.

Accidents will happen on the hill, and any school party is likely to contain a wide range of fitness levels. This being so he was alert and knowledgeable enough to recognise mild hypothermia. Since it was a fairly large party he called for assistance and everyone came through with no harm done. The Team was glad to attend and hoped very much that the pupils' appetites were whetted for further hill activities.

I checked my watch. It was 17.00.

'No?'

'Do you want the good news first or the bad?'

'The good.'

'Something's up on Meall a'Bhuachaille.'

'What?'

'A party of kids and a teacher.'

There is no hill in the Cairngorms without its challenges but

Meall a'Bhuachaille is one of the most benign. If something goes wrong on a summer's day on that particular hill it is relatively good news for the Mountain Rescue Team, certainly much better than the prospect of going into Glen Avon at night in a blizzard. It stands above Glenmore Lodge at a moderate height of 810m and is usually ascended by an erosion path that leads from Ryvoan Bothy directly to the summit. The bothy is an easy 3km walk along the track from Glenmore Lodge. The less fit may have to stop for a breather and it is possible to slip in wet conditions, otherwise it presents no problems. From the summit cairn a walker might return directly or continue for another half kilometre to the first low point of an undulating ridge and return to glen level on the path down through the Queens Forest to the hostel beside Loch Morlich. Either way there are no technical difficulties and no sharp edges to fall off.

'So, what's the bad news?'

'It's got a bit misty so the teacher called from one of the kids' phones and asked for a helicopter.'

'A what?'

'She's already tried to call the RAF. After that she called their bus driver to come and get them. Judging by the background noise they're pretty panicked. I think it's one for you, John.'

Davy passed the teacher's number to me. It was engaged so I tried again, and again every ten minutes or so. Eventually a female voice answered, one of the pupils. There was a good deal of shrieking going on so, yes, they did sound pretty panicked – or maybe just a bit excited, it was hard to tell. I introduced myself and asked to speak to the teacher. When she came on she reported that the all-girl party was frightened and needed help to get down.

'We need a helicopter!'

'It's just a short walk,' I told her.

'It's too misty to see.'

'Do you have a map?'

'Yes.'

'Take it out along with your compass.'

She procrastinated and I doubted if she had either.

'Are there any other teachers there?'

'No, it's just me and 39 pupils.'

'Thirty-nine pupils and only one teacher?'

'We started with four teachers and 60 pupils but the rest turned back when it started to rain.'

Since she neither would nor could help herself there was no choice. 'Keep calm,' I said. 'I want to make another call.'

The Principal at Glenmore Lodge at this time was Tim Walker, and I knew he could see the top of the hill from the window of his home in Boat of Garten. I also knew he kept his binoculars on the window ledge. He answered first ring.

'Yes, I see,' he said. 'The mist is isolated at the top,' he said, 'just a cloud that's parked itself there. 'Wait now, it's lifting. Yes, there they are. They're in the clear. No need for a call-out.'

I spoke to the teacher again. 'It's clear now. Look towards the main range and down. You should see Loch Morlich at the foot of the hill and a bit to your right. Just...'

It was no use. They were more frightened now they could see the wide open spaces than they had been before. 'We need a helicopter,' the teacher wailed.

'I think not. Hold on.' There was no getting away from it now. I called a group of ten rescuers away from their families, their evening meals and however they had intended to relax after a long day, to Glenmore Lodge and we made our way along the track to Ryvoan Bothy. Among them were Willie Anderson, Heather Morning and Nick Forwood, all teachers either at that time or at some other time in their lives, and I felt their experience would be useful. Heather, in particular, took her degree in Outdoor Education and understood very well how such a predicament should never have been allowed to develop.

When we looked up the hill from the bothy, lo and behold, a line of people was making its way down. It was the school party.

As they arrived in their ones and twos we silently noted their clothing. They wore soft gym shoes, skirts and blouses and those who were not wearing ankle socks had tights on. Five minutes of genuine wind-driven rain in a position of no shelter would have soaked them and chilled them through and through. Their idea of a windproof and waterproof shell was cuttings from black plastic bags, or pieces of blue plastic sheeting taken from a building site. Later I would speak to Richard Eccles, who ran the Nethy Bridge hostel where they were staying. A former soldier and good organiser, he had advised them against climbing the hill but, in his words, 'they insisted they knew better'.

As the girls filed into the bothy one of them ironically asked Willie, 'What kept you?'

An experienced teacher, and an acerbic wit in his own right, Willie is normally more than a match for a teenage pupil of either sex and the comment pushed him just a bit too far. He gave her a dressing-down she was not likely to forget, letting her know that the rescuers had turned out to help them when they had no obligation to do so, that they had left their families waiting at home, and that a modicum of gratitude, not to say respect, was the least they could expect.

The girls treated the whole experience, including Willie's rebuke, as a joke.

The teacher finally arrived with one or two girls who were limping. With those shoes on they almost certainly had blisters or twisted ankles or both. I tried to put her at her ease by offering to shake hands but she refused the gesture. I suggested we talk through what had happened and asked again if she had a map. When she said she had I asked if I could see it and she procrastinated again. A ripple went around the bothy as the girls each in turn said someone else had it.

'She's got it, her!'

'No, Emma's got it now.'

'Who?'

'Em-mm-ma!'

Asking about the compass brought the same reaction.

By this time the rescuers were coming to the boil, but especially the teachers who understood what it is to be in charge of pupils.

The idea of having the mickey taken under any circumstances, with no correction from the teacher, they felt was an insult from their own profession. They were also deeply unimpressed by the ratio of one teacher to 39 pupils in an environment such as this, and equally unimpressed that the original four teachers had allowed the party to be split in the way it had, three teachers returning with only 17 pupils.

The group was from a school in London, and Willie put much of what was wrong in perspective when he asked, 'Would they take a party round a London museum with this ratio?' The answer, of course, is that they would not.

No one involved had been hurt but Meall a'Bhuachaille, benign as it is, has wild moorland on its other side. If the party had descended the wrong way they might well have become lost, and a change in the weather would have put them at risk of exposure. The dreadful events of the Cairngorm Plateau Disaster were unlikely to have been repeated in these circumstances but it seemed the lessons so painfully worked through and learned at that time had, to some extent, been forgotten. Ironic, hurtful comments kept coming at us, to the amazement of our teachers. Five years of teaching at Plas-y-Brenin in Wales, and two more with Joint Services at Ballachulish, had not prepared Heather for this. She became visibly more annoyed.

We put the girls with sprained ankles and blisters into the Land Rover and Nick arranged the rest in pairs, marching them back along the track to Glenmore Lodge where their bus was waiting. Before they were allowed to leave though, Davy Burgon, now impressively attired in full dress uniform, interviewed the teacher while the others waited. This still did not bring home the seriousness of their actions and attitudes. It was a disappointing and frustrating position to find ourselves in but I was not without informal, effective recourse.

As Leader I had little left to do other than speak to the press.

'I'm not sure what attitude to take,' I said.

Normally the most moderate woman in the world, Heather was in no doubt. 'Go for the jugular!'

I felt we could not simply let matters rest. It was apparent that at least one school was sending pupils from south of the border into the beautiful and enriching, but dangerous environment of the Cairngorms with neither thought about the hazards nor preparation in environmental appreciation. What I did was simple. It may have had an element of cruelty but it was also salutary and it was important that parents and more senior teachers, people I was unlikely ever to meet, should hear and understand. The press ensured in no uncertain fashion that they did.

As a Rescue Team we are normally non-judgemental. The Leader prepares press releases and takes interviews as required. Well accustomed to the ways of the Cairngorm Team, the press would understand that if a different line was taken it was for a good reason.

Several press contacts had my mobile number, and our local commercial radio station, Moray Firth Radio, was first to call. To them I said that I had never seen 'such an ill-prepared, ill-equipped group in my life'.

When pressed I added, 'I think they broke every rule in the book. They were completely out of their depth and did not take on board the seriousness of the situation.'

When asked about the girls' attitude to their rescuers I said, 'Well, they were less than polite.'

This last comment became the most quoted I have ever made, which shows the value of understatement. Press calls came in thick and fast as word spread across the small world of British newspapers, radio and television. Time and again I was asked where the school party could be contacted but this I declined to say, feeling an unacceptable degree of harassment was possible.

However, reporters can check timetables as easily as anyone else. When the girls arrived at Aviemore Station a photographer was waiting. The pictures that were eventually published showed a group of healthy, happy teenage girls looking forward to getting home. In any other circumstances it would have been a delight. Under headlines such as 'Asking for Trouble' and 'Girls Wore Bin Liners Against Elements' it took on a darker hue.

A camera crew boarded their train at Peterborough and unsuccessfully attempted an interview. Another was waiting at King's Cross but had no more success.

My phone didn't stop. I received calls from papers in Glasgow, Aberdeen, Edinburgh and Dundee. The Aberdeen *Press and Journal* would next day quote a worker at the hostel as saying, 'They left early this morning, thank God. They left the place in a right mess.'

The London press was not slow either. *The Times* dedicated half a page, describing the events of the day as 'one of the worst examples of a group's failure to prepare for the dangerous and rugged terrain they had come across'. It also outlined the Department of Education and Skills 'Guidelines to Teachers'.

This intensity of coverage sent a shock wave through the education system in England that should, and probably did have a jarring but positive effect on attitudes. Of course there are many competent and dedicated practitioners who must have winced when they read these headlines. There will be many who spoke out in private. I certainly hope so. When a Mountain Rescue Team is obliged to turn out for a group of supposedly supervised teenage girls protected by plastic bin liners, and neither pupils nor teacher display an appropriate respect for either their rescuers or the Cairngorms themselves, it suggests a deeper malaise within the education system. I do not suggest it was necessarily widespread, but it most certainly existed at that time.

The school involved was what is known as a faith school. The Principal wrote in apology for the events of the day and the bad attitudes displayed. Many practitioners of the faith, who were not in any way involved, also wrote. I will say here that neither I nor any other rescuer places any responsibility at all on the faith involved. Nor would we normally have anything critical to say, but the girls *were* less than polite.

TWENTY-SIX

Beside the road that runs between Aviemore and Coylumbridge, close to the junction with the Feshiebridge road, the Ordnance Survey map shows the little plus sign that means a church is stationed here. In 1895 building work began for the Free Church of Scotland on land acquired from Rothiemurchus Estate, and in 1896 St Columba's was formally opened with a service conducted in both Gaelic and English. Its ownership eventually transferred to the Church of Scotland and, later still, it fell into disuse. Like many churches it was conceived along the lines of an upturned boat, a symbolism that will do as well for the Rescue Team as the fishers of men.

It has a belfry at one end and narrow, arched windows along its length. The stained glass of the windows could not be more plain, 10cm squares held together by a mesh of beaten lead so they resemble, if anything, a draughts board. Plain and unpretentious it sat at the crossroads as though secure in the knowledge its time would come again. Like many people I drove past it for years, hardly noticing it existed. Now it is the Cairngorm Rescue Centre, owned by the Team, and I come here often.

The building was acquired with a fair amount of land and sat beside a stand of Scots Pines, some of them ready to topple. Much of the area has now been cleared because the rapid arrival and departure of rescue vehicles demands room for movement. Clearance also allowed us to build a large garage close to the main building for our Land Rovers and an ambulance that was supplied by the Order of St John, a charitable organisation that traces its origins back 900 years to the hospital of St John in Jerusalem.

The original doors are still in place, affording entry from the car park into what was the vestibule, where a succession of ministers donned their vestments and contemplated God before entering the church proper to face their successive congregations. Now it is a kitchen. In addition to being the Association's present Chairman and also one of the Team's two Depute Leaders, Donnie Williamson brings his skills and initiative to the position of Base Manager. In the course of his daily work he rescued kitchen units which were destined for the skip although good as new. Sinks, refrigerator, kettles, cups and saucers, pots and pans, and cooker were all acquired. Gordon Ramsay could work here without complaint.

Another wooden door opens into what was the church proper, now divided into two rooms. The first is our small lecture theatre where the original communion table has been retained. The pulpit is gone but its wooden backing is still in place, rising vertically to curve over the speaker's head and throw the spoken word forward as it rises. This structure is now given over to shelves filled with books on mountains and mountaineering and at the top has a plaque that says, *The Christopher Barley Memorial Library*. Chris was the Cairngorm Mountain Rescue Team's Depute Leader from 1989 to his death in 2004. He bought every book on mountains he could lay his hands on. At each side of the room is a window. Because speakers are likely to show slides it was necessary to put blinds in place. The blinds we chose are also used as projection screens.

The next room is where the Team gathers before rescues. It has coat hangers, shelves, a drying area, and two smaller rooms that lead off. One is the store where we keep the standard kit the rescuers take with them. Plastic boxes contain survival bags, flares, much more. Elsewhere we have emergency survival shelters, harnesses and karabiners, stretchers. Boxes of flares come in three types. Maroons ascend to a great height where they explode loudly and give out a powerful light. Paraflares are for illumination and descend on a parachute. Among their virtues is the message they give to the injured climber. Help is on the way. Do what you can for yourself. Do not despair. The third type are smoke flares; hand-held they emit a highly visible orange smoke that pilots can guide themselves towards.

Opposite the store is the Control Room where the rescue co-ordinator works in partnership with the police. There are maps on the wall, a powerful radio, and a television to relieve what can be long hours of waiting as the rescue unfolds.

Donnie was also busy upstairs in the roof area where a wooden platform now gives more room than the ministers would have guessed at. Of course, they raised their eyes for other reasons. Here there are comfortable seats and another television. The coffee table is made from the seat the ministers used in the pulpit. Team Members might be either men or women, although most are men, so we have toilets and showers for both. The women's showers are individual and the men's collective, superb, suitable for Manchester United's first 11.

Off the mess are four small bedrooms, each named for one of the main Cairngorm peaks, MacDhui, Cairngorm, Braeriach and Cairn Toul. Each room has four bunks where members can snatch some rest if they are involved on a long rescue. Otherwise they can be used by the rescued when they are uninjured but exhausted. We have paintings on the wall, and inexhaustible supplies of tea and coffee.

I visited the other day, more than a little proud to show a friend around. We left by the side door that faces onto the garages and by chance met Donnie. I made my first trips to the Alps with Chris Barley and, in later years, Donnie, who already had Alpine experience, joined us. More people arrived while we were talking, Willie Anderson arrived with Willie Ross, his wife, Lea, and their son, Niall. Donnie's predecessor as Chairman, Peter Finlayson, drove the ambulance in. A high-sided box on wheels it looks like no other ambulance except it reminds me of those used in the First World War.

I think of these people and more such as Martin, Mollie, Pete

Cliff, many policemen and volunteers. None would describe him or herself as a hero but if dedicating yourself to training, equipping yourself mentally and physically, venturing into the worst of winter conditions to save others, finally dealing with their injuries and grief is not heroic then nothing is. Intelligent, outgoing, filled with fun, I am glad to have spent so much of my life with them.

The Cairngorm Rescue Centre was created by foresight and ambition aligned with goodwill, community action and an altogether different kind of faith. The story of how it transferred from one kind of salvation to another is worth the telling.

When Martin and I joined the Team in 1972 it met upstairs in Aviemore Police Station and the force awarded us approximately £6,000 a year, a substantial sum, but not enough to allow for development and growth. The police also provided one of their garage spaces for storage. Until 1974, when Grant's Whisky provided our first Land Rover, the Team had no vehicles. Delighted and grateful for their generosity we gladly displayed their logo on the door panels.

By the 1980s the level of professionalism in the Team had been significantly raised, we had acquired more equipment, and the requirement for increased storage space had become pressing. About this time the police were to relocate to new premises within Aviemore. It was agreed that we should be allocated space but there was debate about how much. Like us the police could foresee increasing rescue demands leading to greater requirements. In short, whatever space they might allocate was likely to prove inadequate in time. The police were our great allies but almost certainly not the providers of a permanent solution.

Changing times can provide solutions as well as problems. One of our members, Dave Morris, worked for the Nature Conservancy Council in a large, rambling building at Achintoul, just outside Aviemore. NCC management was thinking of leaving for other premises because reduced budgets and altered government priorities had led to a reduction in staff levels. Dave suggested to his employers that offering us space would at least ensure that part of the building was utilised to good effect. This argument prevailed and we were given a room for storage and use of the conference room. The Meteorological Service already used the top floor so, when the police agreed to pay our rent, the Cairngorm Mountain Rescue Team became the third party in the building. It also meant a sort of unity of ethos was established and that we had ready access to the latest weather forecast.

We moved between 1983 and 1984 and immediately benefited from such apparently minor improvements as a warm room to meet in and use of the kitchen. In addition, we were allowed to build a garage outside although not to purchase the land it stood on.

The thing about changing times is that they continue to change. This was a more than satisfactory arrangement until well into the 1990s when natural heritage became, once again, more valued, and the Nature Conservancy Council became Scottish Natural Heritage. Staffing levels were raised which, in turn, increased the number of vehicles in the car park. Repeatedly we had to ask for them to be moved for rescues until at last we decided that we needed our own premises.

We felt the Team should have a financial cushion. Fundraising, and especially sponsored walks, ensured we carried a surplus of around £50,000 which we placed in an interest raising account. Money arrived in other ways. After we had searched out a crashed mail plane the widow of the pilot donated a large sum for which we were very grateful.

With this surplus in hand I approached the Right Honourable John Grant, who owned the Rothiemurchus Estate, with questions that amounted to, 'Any old buildings?' or, 'Any land we could build on?' John contemplated for a while and answered, 'I might have just the place.'

It was the disused church at Inverdruie. When his far-seeing ancestors sold the land they insisted that, should the church ever be deconsecrated, they would have the right to buy. This had happened in 1988 and John had, ever since, been trying to find a use for it. We visited together.

The church was just as the final congregation had left it, the pews tidily arranged with hymn sheets laid out for their successors, the pulpit prepared and ready for the next minister. The floor would require levelling but otherwise I was convinced on sight. This would be our ideal home.

I put it to the Association and we organised a succession of visits. Everyone in the Team thought it ideal. It was environmentally sound and on the road that led to the ski area and so to the Cairngorm massif. It was an important part of our Strathspey heritage and, of course, it lay unused. The decision was made and we formed two committees of three, one to decide on design and construction matters, the other to organise funding. I was with the funding committee. We had a survey done and a price was agreed. We agreed not to compromise on standards or quality, always a mistake in the long run. The roof repairs alone would cost £40,000 and we would require at least another £200,000. It was a daunting sum although the developed building would represent tremendous value for money.

We put our heads together and came up with three funding sources. Firstly, direct donation from others; secondly, sponsorship of the Team, which would mean the use of logos on vehicles, outer clothing and the likes; thirdly, we would seek sponsorship to reduce the expenses of our coming biennial walk. This walk, which we would label the Millennium Sponsored Walk, would be bigger and better than ever and we hoped to raise £60,000.

The *Badenoch & Strathspey Herald* came on board with free publicity and very soon the local community was pitching in. Out of the blue we received a legacy of £89,000. The Scottish Sports Council donated £10,000 and the Mountain Trust the same amount. The Lottery Fund took so long to decide that we began to contemplate a loan, but they finally came through with the final £86,000.

The building committee had similar good fortune when Laing's the Builder tendered an extremely competitive price, a generous offer it seemed. Suddenly everything was in place and, yes, it did feel like a miracle. We formally entered the premises when they were opened in April 2001 by the great mountaineer and rescuer Hamish McInnes.

Wonders had not yet ceased. By some strange coincidence the Order of St John, who hold property in Aberdeen and donate their income to worthy causes, decided they would make a major contribution to mountain rescue, building Mountain Rescue Centres for at least some of the Scottish Teams. Whether or not this was inspired by our success is impossible to say, but we had just raised not only the bar but levels of expectation. Our position presented them with a problem, although we had no intention so to do. How would they deal with us when we had already led the way?

Their answer was to offer to buy the premises and allow us to remain rent-free. We gave this long consideration. A large sum of money was involved that could be reinvested in equipment and training. Against that, the Rescue Centre had become something more. It was an example across Scotland, and locally a symbol of accomplishment and source of pride. Among all the lessons we had learned over the years one of the most valued was the need to be self-contained in our decision-making and standards. We declined the money with thanks, although we continued to accept such valued donations as a Land Rover. Our independence was important to us.

A great concentration and focus fell on the Millennium Sponsored Walk in 2000 since it would be the single greatest effort the Team would make in commanding its own destiny, and the most ambitious.

We had organised walks every second year since 1973 and they had become fixtures in the calendars of enthusiasts all over Britain. Not only that, many aspirant hillwalkers found the confidence to venture into the hills for the first time under the protective umbrella of our checkpoints and expertise. From there they had advanced into training and, sometimes, become accomplished themselves.

The Millennium Walk would fall in 2000, breaking the pattern of

1. Pygmy Ridge in winter.

3. Arrival at the top of Fingers Ridge.   4. Setting up the belay.

2. A high line, frequently used with the aircraft service.

5. Controlling the lower.

6. A complex belay of the type used on the Fingers Ridge rescue.

LEFT:

7. Boots on the ground,
a stretcher carry in winter.

BELOW:

8. Boots on the ground,
a stretcher carry in summer.

TOP LEFT:

9. Avalanche debris in the Chalamain Gap.

BOTTOM LEFT:

10. Probing avalanche debris in the Chalamain Gap.

BOTTOM RIGHT:

11. CMRT and ski patrol attending a casualty.

12. Good relations between mountain rescue agencies.

13. The team's new branding.

14. The Can-am Commander at the Cairngorm weather station.

15. Sunrise over Cairngorm Plateau from near point 1141
(often pronounced 'Eleven 41').

16. Drone activity with Iain Cornfoot.

17. Land Rover versatility.

18. Propeller Belay from the crash wreckage on Beinn Eighe.

TOP LEFT:

19. The cairn at Point 1141.

BOTTOM LEFT:

20. The scale of a winter search can be enormous.

BOTTOM RIGHT:

21. Overhanging cornices are to be avoided.

22. The potential danger of a collapsed cornice.

23. Remote Knoydart from Loch Nevis with Sgurr na Ciche in the background.

odd-numbered years. Most of the walks had gone through the Lairig Ghru but, in the 1990s, we had varied this with what we termed The Derry Way and The Feshie Way. In 1999 the Corrieyairack Pass, from Fort Augustus to Newtonmore, was added.

By this time most of the environmental objectors to such walks had either been persuaded onto our side or decided to retreat and keep their powder dry. The walks in 1993 and 1995, for the first time using Glen Feshie and Glen Derry, had attracted much critical attention. 1993 attracted letters of objection from the Save The Cairngorms Campaign, the Mountaineering Council of Scotland who had been writing since the mid-1980s and were particularly tenacious, the Scottish Mountaineering Club, and the Badenoch and Strathspey Conservation Group.

Any one of these groups would have represented a considerable weight of expert opinion. Together they were quite formidable. Their main concern was erosion of footpaths and, indeed, erosion is a problem throughout Scotland's mountain areas. With the rising numbers of people who go out to enjoy the hills this becomes increasingly visually intrusive and obvious.

In 1995 The Cairngorm Club added its voice, as did the Scottish Wild Land Group. All were answered respectfully, even when one suggested that the Rotary Club had 'taken note of remonstrances and not organised a Spey/Dee massed event'. I replied with perhaps a touch of irony that, 'I do not know where you were in June last year but around 400 persons walked through the Lairig Ghru wearing Rotary hats and tee-shirts.'

Time and again I pointed out that many of the objectors were, themselves, drawing people onto Scotland's wild land. Sometimes this was directly, in the course of their work as mountain guides or through Outdoor Centres. Sometimes indirectly, by publishing in magazines and bringing out books, by establishing and naming new climbs and publicising them in route guides.

No publication can have done more to attract walkers onto the hills, and direct them onto single routes, than the beautifully produced book *The Munros*, published by the Scottish

Mountaineering Trust, with its enticing photographs and descriptions. Directing walkers to a single route virtually invited erosion and many hills suffered as a consequence.

My feeling at the time was that our sponsored walk was a soft target for people who might better look to their own activities. Our walks began and ended on hard tracks and much of the central sections were on established paths. I felt we did not do as much damage as was being suggested. I also felt that a two-year gap between walks gave good time for recovery where professionally guided walks occurred every day and gave none.

Commitment was very great on all sides, as is usual in environmental matters, and we were appreciative when the Mountain Rescue Committee of Scotland informed the Mountaineering Council of Scotland that 'offering advice in this sort of fundraising is somewhat inappropriate'. It also suggested, 'if the MCofS would care to act positively on this matter, it may consider donating a percentage of its members' affiliation fees to Mountain Rescue'.

As with the debate over the Curran Shelter the emotional vibrations are impossible to miss. I took comfort from our parent body's stand and also from a dissertation on the subject of footpath erosion that was prepared by a student named Sarah Jane Hart in 1993 for her honours degree in Environmental Science. Sarah Jane used our 1991 walk through the Lairig Ghru as a case study.

In it she writes, 'Some highly conclusive results were obtained from this project. Following the sponsored walk in 1991, erosion levels were not found to be statistically significant, although a small amount of path widening was evident.'

Cairngorm Mountain Rescue Team is as aware as anyone of the destructive effect of increasing numbers of walkers on paths and other surfaces. So much so, we volunteered to spread a product known as 'daggings' across eroded, soft areas around the Lairig Ghru after the RAF had flown in several huge bales of the stuff. This experiment was less successful than the sleepers we placed on the Creag Meagaidh path, but in these ways and more our Team has many times demonstrated its commitment to the mountain environment. Never more so, it must be said, than when hand-spreading daggings, the faeces clogged clippings from a sheep's rear end.

Personally, I have only two regrets about the walks. The first is that when we introduced the Feshie Way we took people into one of my favourite areas, one that I would selfishly choose to keep to myself. The second is in my feelings for people walking the other way on the day of the Walk. There is a natural courtesy among people on the hill, but 500 to 600 people travelling in the other direction is a lot to say hello to and can use up a lot of time.

The level of hostility we experienced in the 1990s was, to me, inexplicable and even now I harbour a certain degree of resentment. Mountain rescue eats money. To heighten standards of training, equipment, communication, to establish and develop a Rescue Centre such as Inverdruie, while at the same time maintaining operations, takes more than most casual observers could even guess. It also requires a steady flow and, to ensure this flow, a capital reserve is required.

In 2002 we introduced the Gaick Way to our list. Organising the walks in sequence now gives eight years of recovery time to the ground. Objection and correspondence has, for now at least, died down. When it returns we can do no more than point to those recovery periods, refer to Sarah Jane's dissertation and any other research that may be available, emphasise need, and otherwise politely ignore.

Soon I will have to mention the TAF Club. Not yet though, first a word about the organisation of the walks. We laid on buses to take the walkers around the mountains to the start, most often at Linn of Dee near Braemar, where to ensure they were properly counted out they would have their tallies punched by a group known as Chris's Clippers. The Chris involved was Chris Barley.

The tallies having been clipped the Clippers would usually walk through, accompanying some of the less well prepared, keeping them going and, on the rare occasions when they could not continue, helping them out. Checkpoints were ranged throughout the walk and for the Lairig Ghru one of these was at the Pools of Dee where I was generally stationed. It was a longer day for Chris than me, since he had to get up at 04.00 for the three-hour drive to the walk's beginning.

For the Millennium Walk we quickly got the permissions in place and set about organising sponsorships. Experience told us we had to make our requests a year in advance as advertising budgets tend to be determined in that period of time. Anne and I decided to put the name of our pharmacy business, P. Grant, Chemist, on the sponsorship list. We had been informally supplying office and secretarial services from the beginning.

I have long said that, with charities as much as anything else, you have to spend money to make money. We made up our list of expenditure and found it came to a whopping £15,500. The largest single unit was the hire of buses. The second was the colour booklet that had become a collector's item for many, and of course we wanted it to be particularly special for this event.

In fact, our walks had enjoyed increasing success through the years with ever higher sums being raised. Tennent's, the brewer, sponsored the organisation of the 1987 Lairig Ghru Walk, and we enjoyed a quantum leap in earnings. Our reputation had been rising over the years, as had popularity, but it was then that we reached the level where such a large sponsor deemed it worthwhile to join us. The TAF Club also made a major contribution, not only with sheer effort but also in amplifying the already warm spirit. At halfway points they provide some form of food and this has become one of the walk's great traditions. Although the service has never been guaranteed it has never been lacking.

So, what is the meaning of this word TAF? A closely guarded secret, members say they have to kill any outsider who finds out. Membership is by invitation only but certain criteria have to be met. Aspirant members have to cook and consume porridge at a level of over 2,000ft or perform a musical turn on the summit of a Munro before two club members. Again, they have to swim in a

Highland loch or burn in winter or read that day's *Glasgow Herald* on the summit of a Munro. Do you have it now? Meaning is beside the point. Sociability and fine malt whiskies are at its heart.

TAF was originally asked to support the walks by providing extra personnel. This was not enough for them as a stylish flourish is required in everything they do. At the Pools of Dee in 1985 they provided ice cream. One member, whose name may have been Bill Allen, worked as a chemical engineer in the food industry. On a scorching hot day the ice cream was carried in on a stretcher, kept cool by chilled carbon dioxide. In 1993 a Scottish theme was maintained with haggis and tatties cooked at the same location; in 1995 it was pasta. Chilli and tortillas were conjured up in 1997.

Their greatest logistical challenge was the Corrieyairack Pass in 1999. Celebrating the Auld Alliance they decided on a Gallic theme with *vin rouge* and pommes frites. The pommes frites were not particularly distinguishable from chips, 129kg of which were carried in, as were 45l of cooking oil, 400 packets of soup, 40 baguettes, 400 cartons of orange juice, and *beaucoup de vin*. To cook the chips they hauled in three 200kg generators providing 12kw of power to a large oven and a deep fat fryer as well as four double burner cookers. Arthur Duffus, a local gamekeeper, helped with his Land Rover and so became an honorary TAF member.

This was the first year that pipers played at the high point, which is where this magnificent repast was served. Walkers would later reminisce happily, not only of the pipes calling them onward as they trudged uphill but of the kilted warriors who leaped out of the heather and chased them the last few metres.

Two years after the Millennium Walk was the Queen's Jubilee Year where, somewhere in the Gaick Pass, surrounded by the flags of England, Scotland, Germany and the United States, we ate roast beef and Jersey Royal potatoes. The Stars and Stripes was provided by an American aircraft carrier, but since I am not sure the skipper was aware I will not mention the donor. Not only were pipers present but also our friends the kilted warriors who attacked each other ferociously with claymores on top of the Mountain Rescue Land Rover.

The Millennium Walk itself was described as 'the highest whisky trail in the world'. We doled out miniatures to all the adults at suitable stages and at the end, where they also received certificates and rather high-quality medals. Disappointing weather conditions were alleviated at the Pools of Dee where we served smoked salmon and black pepper on Philadelphia cheese and brown bread. Otherwise, it went like a dream and we raised just over £57,000, all of which went to the new Rescue Centre.

Between our Lairig Ghru quantum leap in 1987 and Feshie in 2007, nine walks in 18 years, we raised over £500,000. In addition, we provided a lot of fun for a lot of people as well as a guarded entry into the outdoors for a good number of beginners. Hundreds of people participated as organisers, checkers, chefs, dogsbodies and directors. To the best of my knowledge they all enjoyed themselves.

It has not all gone perfectly, of course. Over the years a number of walkers have turned ankles or been insufficiently prepared. In 1999 an 80-year-old man named Douglas Simpson passed away not far from the Chalamain Gap. His daughter wrote to us saying he had ended his life doing what he wanted to do. All of us in the Team understood. Walking in the hills, alone or with good companions is what we all want to do. It is all the better knowing there is an umbrella of safety, or at least recovery, with a well-funded, adequately trained and provisioned Mountain Rescue Service in place. When my time comes I would be glad to go in such a fashion.

It is a long way from Glen Derry to the Alps but, in the end, the world is just one place. After discovering these magnificent mountains I visited on a yearly basis with a number of friends, but none more often than Chris Barley. No one gets more than a few real soul mates of the hills and Chris was one of mine. Over the years we walked and climbed together, bothied and camped. We shared tents and snow holes and the occasional dram. In terms of temperament we complemented one another because where my energetic and volatile nature drove us onward and upward his cautious and thoughtful side would be constantly checking and ensuring. He was also a brilliant navigator.

One year we did *Le Tour Noir*, this time accompanied by John Lyall on his first Alpine peak. We were coming off the peak in bad weather, unsure which way to go when we met a professional guide from Lyon and his client. There should have been a glacier close by and that would have been our route indicator, but we couldn't see it for the mist. It was natural to confer together to decide which way we should turn.

Almost at our feet was an inviting gully, a couloir, which both the guide and I believed offered a speedy and safe route down into the Vallé. The discussion went round as we gradually convinced ourselves, and soon all of us but Chris were keen to go down. He kept the map in his hands and defiantly told us this was not the way. We had to climb to the Javelle Ledges, out of France and into Switzerland, swinging back into France and, not before then, go down.

He was obstinate but correct and had pieced the puzzle together beautifully. Where the rest of us had allowed fatigue and wishful thinking to influence our judgement he remained true to procedures and objective thinking. Later I revisited the location in good conditions. If we had descended the couloir we would have had a terrible time among crevasses and broken ground and would eventually have been obliged to climb back up, even more fatigued.

Over the years I have steadily worked away at climbing all 61 of the Alpine 4,000m peaks. With seven to go and my leg as it is I do not now expect to complete the list but, no matter, completion was never really the point. The Weisshorn, near Zermatt, took five attempts, and Chris accompanied me on them all. The first attempt we took my son, Michael, then in his teens, but got lost on the way up. The second time I became unwell and we rightly turned back. The third time Chris became unwell and, again, we retreated. Chis and I approached the hill with great determination for my fourth attempt, this time accompanied by Donnie.

Snow conditions in the Alps tend to deteriorate in the course of the day under the warming effect of the sun. This tends to limit the climbing day, but for the more experienced and better prepared there are alternatives. One of the great experiences on these high mountains is to ascend while climbing conditions are good and remain high overnight. There is nothing like watching through the jagged peaks as the sun rises, its heat on your face after a night in which temperatures have fallen far below zero.

That night we bivouacked at 4,000m, intending a shorter ascent than usual in the morning, but we reckoned without blizzards and the temperature dropping to minus 15 degrees. In the morning we were so chilled we only managed another 200m or so of ascent before turning back. Donnie's feet took four hours to unfreeze.

On the fifth attempt we stayed at the Weisshorn Hut and next day got everything right. I will never forget the narrow inverted V of snow-covered rock we, at last, ascended to the summit. Exhilarated, I was barely aware of Chris fishing around in his rucksack and producing a bottle of champagne. It looked slightly travel weary, this bottle, the label faded and dog-eared. 'This is for you, John,' he said, 'on your favourite mountain – it must be; you've tackled it so often.'

He had carried it up the mountain five times, each time intent on opening and celebrating with me right there, with the sun shining brightly and the world at our feet.

On return journeys he would insist on our visiting his parents near Peterborough. Invariably, we would arrive late and bivouac on the lawn in our sleeping bags. Chris's mum would say that when she saw these man-sized sausages on her lawn, she knew to get the frying pan out and a full English breakfast sizzling.

Chris was an Englishman who loved Scotland. They are not small in number, those guys. He visited often, touring and walking the hills with friends, then with his wife, Denise, before an opening appeared in dentistry in Strathspey. They arrived in 1974 and joined the Team together in 1977. He once told me that his life's one regret was that he had not been born in Scotland. From time to time I would tease him about this but, defiant as ever, he wore his 'Scotland's For Me' tee shirt with pride wherever he went.

'Character is destiny,' someone said, and I think there is a lot in that. Unfortunately, genetic inheritance and chance also play their part.

The fortnight leading up to the Derry Way walk in 2004 was an intense one for the Team. We were called out for the Vale of Leven School group and also for the group of London schoolgirls on Meall a'Bhuachaille. A walker broke her ankle near the Pools of Dee and Chris, as Depute Leader, led the Team that located and attended her, stretchering her below cloud level where the Sea King could pick her up.

Two days before the Walk Chris collapsed at his surgery after complaining of chest pains. He was rushed to Raigmore in an ambulance where his condition was stabilised. Denise visited us at Inverdruie at 22.00, where we were discussing the coming walk under, obviously, a new and unexpected cloud. She told us she had left Chris sitting up and feeling much better. His mind was on the coming walk and he was intent on playing his usual part. This was not to be. At about 02.30 on the Saturday his blood pressure fell dramatically, the attending staff could do nothing to halt it and he died.

Denise was present and called me soon after. It took some time to absorb the shock but then I called Willie Anderson. Willie by this time was a thoroughly established senior member of the Team and a close friend. In time he would become the obvious candidate to succeed me as Leader. We discussed the coming Walk and decided not only that we had no choice but to continue, but also that Chris would have wanted it.

People die, and there is no point dwelling on either the thieving nature of death or its seeming treachery. Anger is pointless but grief is not. In all the history of the Cairngorm Mountain Rescue Team we have not lost a member during a rescue, but the normal rhythms of life apply to us as much as to others. Our predecessors in St Columba's had much to say on the matter and, in times of large families, disease, wars, living close to the land, more frequent cause. I stand before Chris's books where the pulpit used to be and feel glad we memorialised him in this way. We continue to go out without him, continue to climb, continue to rescue. It is a feature of our species that we can, if we choose, maintain the memory of loved ones without being crippled by them. Our business is not ends, or for that matter beginnings, but continuance.

TWENTY-SEVEN

In recent years the police have come to regard fatal accident locations in the mountains as potential crime scenes and ask of the Rescue Teams that they be treated as such. The logic is obvious: in a risk-filled environment, opportunities are plentiful to nudge someone over an edge, fail to secure a belay, or commit some other act of commission or omission that might take a life. The culprit's motivation might be insurance, inheritance, sexual jealousy, career advantage or any of the others you might find in a well-crafted detective novel.

This burden of automatic suspicion must increase the distress of survivors but there were two cases in recent times, neither involving the Cairngorm Team, where the police seemed to truly believe that murder had been committed. Short of confession the onus of proof is almost impossible to satisfy, and I have to say that all my experience is with police procedures and protocol, rather than nefarious criminals.

In the early evening of New Year's Day, 1980, the police received a call from two men who were having difficulty finding their car in Coire Cas car park. Shortly after 17.00 the officers turned out and took down details of the vehicle, its registration number, colour and model. During what amounted to no more than a quick look around the car park they discovered the vehicle exactly where the men had said it should be, and not at all difficult to locate.

On further questioning it became apparent that they were somewhat confused, as they might be if suffering from hypothermia.

Only then did they mention there had been a third man in the party and that they had left him 'up the hill'. Gradually the story was pieced together.

The three had crossed the plateau from the north on 30th December, intent on descending into Glen Avon to spend Hogmanay and New Year's Night at the Shelter Stone. Instead they were caught in a storm and spent their first night beside Loch Avon. By morning they had taken quite a beating and so altered their New Year plans. They decided to recross the plateau and descend into Coire an Lochain where Jean's Hut would offer more substantial protection from the weather.

Although still in his twenties one of the men had a pacemaker fitted to his heart. The weather worsened and they were obliged to force their way through a very severe Cairngorm blizzard. The man with the pacemaker felt unwell throughout the trip and, as if this was not enough, on their journey across the plateau the snow gave way beneath him and he dropped into the March Burn. The others helped him out, but between his soaking, the low temperature and the wind he was literally perishing. They made the decision to climb down into the Lairig Ghru where they anticipated the wind would be less and that some shelter might be found.

Working hard in deep snow the two fitter men stumbled and dragged their unwell companion along the course of the Burn, to eventually drop into the pass. Morale must by now have been very low indeed, but the weather was not yet finished with them. As they erected their tent it was snatched from their grasp and blown away by the high wind. By now they were deeply fatigued and almost certainly hypothermic. With no possibility of continuing as a threesome they bivouacked as best they could and, in the course of the night, the third man died.

The survivors put his body in an orange bivvy bag and in the morning made the decision to leave. Wisely leaving their companion's remains they made their way slowly northwards in a miserable day-long trip to the Chalamain Gap and the path into Coire Cas where, it seemed to them in their confused state, their car had been stolen. The ski areas were shut at this hour so they were on their own. They called the police and it was only when they were about to leave that word of the deceased man was given.

The police called Mollie and she discussed the matter over the phone. She had a reasonable idea where the body lay, but the area around the Pools of Dee is quite extensive and at night we might not come across it right away. She had also to think of the safety of the rescuers in a case where urgency was not a feature.

Starting at 06.00 we walked through falling snow to the pass accompanied by two CID officers. The Pools of Dee are not particularly difficult to access so, in daylight, we quickly located the bivvy bag and the body, by this time frozen to the ground. The police took pictures and examined the scene thoroughly and only then were we allowed to free the casualty's body. It has to be said that the rescuers felt bad about this investigation. It seemed obvious to us all that what had happened was an unfortunate mountaineering mishap and that anything which might increase the distress of the survivors should be avoided.

Sometime later we were required to attend a short course of forensic lectures where we were taught to look for anything 'out of the ordinary' and to protect the scene until the police could arrive. Immediately, a number of issues arose. It is by no means easy, or even possible, to arrive at the scene and not 'interfere'. For one thing the casualty may be alive when the Team arrives but die later or in the course of the rescue. For another he or she may be dangling at the end of a rope or trembling on a ledge. For yet another, the safety of the rescuers has to be considered and they cannot be asked to wait in severe weather until CID arrive.

Inevitably a compromise was reached and the Team Members now carry disposable cameras. Where we can we take pictures of the bodies and the scene around them and only wait for the police where there is good reason to do so – and when it is practical.

In 2000 a young German couple holidaying in Newtonmore set off together to traverse Creag Dhubh. Virtually a roadside hill it is relatively low at just over 700m, but it has some hard climbing routes on its eastern side, the side facing the A86. Otherwise it is a fine walking ridge with wonderful views to the Monadhliath mountains in the west and the Cairngorms in the east. For the most part, and in good weather such as they enjoyed that day, it is reasonably safe unless the walker should stray too far towards the crags.

Feral goats roam its slopes and, as climbers themselves, albeit in search of food rather than challenge, occasionally come to grief. On its south side it has a natural feature which is also historical. Cluny's Cave has Jacobite associations and is a minor tourist draw.

The German couple had been over the hill the day before so it was a repeat walk for them and, on this second ascent, the woman was happy to potter along while the man walked more quickly. They agreed to meet at the top and, in due course, she reached the summit cairn but found no sign of him. Expecting to find him at the other side, possibly investigating the cave, she continued.

Still not finding him she returned to Newtonmore and their hostel and at 22.00 the hostel owner reported the man missing. The Team located his body at 01.00. It seemed he had wandered too close to the edge and fallen to his death, landing in more or less the same location as the goats.

This was one of those rare cases where a mountain accident is also a roadside incident. The officer in charge was the local sergeant from Aviemore whom I knew well and I remember standing at the roadside discussing procedures with him. At that time his Chief Inspector was based many miles away in Nairn. When the Chief Inspector was informed he insisted that the location be treated as a crime scene and demanded a full investigation. This would mean the Team standing by until CID had finished taking pictures and searching the area before we could complete our duty of removing the body.

I made a quick mental calculation. It was now just after 01.00 so it would be 05.00, perhaps as late as 06.00, before CID would arrive from Inverness. They would require statements from the woman and the hostel owner as well as the Team Members and all this would take time. Through the sergeant I let the Chief Inspector know we would take pictures with our new disposable cameras and we had a police constable in the Team who could make all the necessary verifications. After that, the hour being what it was, along with the demands of family and work, I would have no choice but to stand the Team down.

There was a brief face-off but, in the end, common sense prevailed and we removed the body from the hill.

It had become apparent the police could not attend scenes in the mountains when weather conditions were too extreme or the simple practicalities of access made it too hazardous. This was only sensible, but we lived on a two-way street and if the Team could be trusted to create such records as were required in those conditions I felt we could be trusted by the roadside. Asking us to stay out all night for the sake of protocol was unreasonable. As ever when changes are made, it took some time for a practical, common-sense settlement to be reached but, gradually, we relaxed into the new requirements.

We could not be entirely relaxed though, when behind the figure of the Chief Constable hung the wig and gown of the procurator fiscal. The loss of a life is a serious matter, especially when a criminal action might be involved. In addition, the requirements of health and safety and 'duty of care' brought new levels of responsibility. The shadow of a possible prosecution falling across us was all too real.

In November 2006 a university group from an East of Scotland University organised a trip to the Cairngorms. Its purpose was two-fold: to undertake winter routes in the Northern Corries and to attend a seminar in Glenmore Lodge. No doubt the students had a third objective: to have a great and raucous time. Four former club members came along, two in their own vehicle and two hitching a ride in the club minibus.

They climbed all day Saturday, and on Sunday looked forward to meeting together and talking about the hills. The weather had turned very much for the worse and most felt that, under the circumstances, they were better off inside. The four guests though, decided to attempt routes in Coire an t-Sneachda. On the same day some members of the Cairngorm Mountain Rescue Team went into the same corrie. Strong as they were, when they saw the conditions they decided that discretion was the better part of valour and came out again.

One party consisting of a 24-year-old man and his 19-year-old companion set their sights on Western Rib, a Grade 4 climb. The other pair decided on an adjacent route. The younger of the first pair was reported to be particularly fit. Bound for a career in the marines he was known to go running with boulders in his rucksack.

Each pair was in sight of the other as they climbed, until around 16.00 the second pair topped out into high winds. The first pair had a distance to go and would be some time, so the second pair shouted to tell them it was bad on top and that they should abseil down, either from their present belay or when they completed the climb. With no motivation to remain they returned to the car park and drove home.

Back at Glenmore Lodge the other two had still not returned by the time the club members were ready to depart. This meant the minibus could not leave, and most of the others went to the bar to wait. When they became concerned they called the police, and at 22.00 the police called me.

The story as I received it was that two experienced climbers had entered Coire an t-Sneachda to attempt Western Rib. They had the necessary equipment of ropes and ice axes and had not given the adjacent climbers any concern at last sighting. I called our Depute Leader, Willie Anderson, and we agreed that anyone going out in the prevailing conditions who was not completely green must be extremely experienced. Given that the others had been unconcerned at last sighting I saw no reason to turn the Team out at that time and instead arranged for a first light search to be undertaken if they had not turned up by morning.

I went to bed but couldn't sleep and at 23.30 got up and called Nigel Williams, then Depute Principal at Glenmore Lodge. Nigel confirmed that the two had not appeared and that the other club members were still waiting at the Lodge. He had driven up to the car park for a look but seen no one. Not only had the weather not improved but his Land Rover shuddered when it was buffeted by the wind. On return he had engaged the club members in conversation and discovered that the pair was not as experienced as had been assumed.

The younger, very fit, man had worn crampons for the first time only the previous day. A Grade 4 route would require a fair level of expertise in their use. Still more disturbing, the same young man had tried to borrow overtrousers from the others before starting. He had not been successful but continued anyway. Without them he would certainly be severely compromised. On the walk in he would generate a good deal of body heat which would be dispersed while they prepared at the foot of the climb. On the route he would be obliged to wait for long periods while low temperatures and wind chill sucked the heat from his body. To make matters still worse they had very little food with them.

Alarm bells were now ringing. Such a climb *must not* be tackled in such a way. Expertise, full shell covering and plenty of food are *necessities*.

I called Willie again and we arranged for John Lyall to lead a party of four particularly strong and able rescuers into the corrie immediately. The others were Al Gilmour, Hamish Irvine and Gary Ford.

John's transformation from a young forestry worker to a respected and very competent mountaineer had been completed in 2000 when he qualified at the top European level with the *Union Internationale des Associations de Guides Montagnes* (UIAGM). Now a professional guide he spent at least half the year out of the country, climbing and guiding in the Alps, Andes and Atlas mountains, in Norway and the Himalaya. In the winter months he did the same job in the Cairngorms and we were fortunate to have him available to participate.

As it happened, he already had a personal connection with the casualties having been involved in arranging the course and, by coincidence, suffering a slight vehicle knock with their bus that morning. 'Enjoy the first part of the day,' he had said. 'It's going to be bad in the afternoon.'

The weather improved slightly but conditions were still very poor so even a group of this standard would go in with their hoods tied up and heads bowed to the conditions. There would be no pausing to look around over a wide and lovely vista, no hanging about to enjoy the night. The snow would certainly be deep and wet, and swirling mist would reduce visibility to a small circle around them. John would later liken the conditions to a time on the plateau when he was first blown over then lifted from the ground by the wind. Such conditions would demand considerable hardihood and determination.

Willie went in to co-ordinate from Rescue Control which allowed me to take my 64-year-old self back to bed. He could report developments to me through the night as required, and there would be plenty to do in the morning anyway.

On the hill John brought his tremendous depth of experience to bear on the situation. He considered the route it was most likely the two would have come out on – if they had come out – and advanced along that bearing. The four spread into a line and entered the corrie as observantly as conditions allowed, shouting, whistling, firing flares and making as much noise as possible. Reaching the foot of the climb they discovered ropes hanging down, descending out of the mist and entering a fall of broken snow, apparently avalanche debris. They gained the impression of a climb either completed or abandoned and the climbers either swept down the mountain or engulfed at the bottom. This last they felt to be least likely since it is usual to find a hat or glove or similar evidence on the surface, and there was nothing to be seen. Nonetheless, since speedy retrieval from the snow would be imperative if the students should have been avalanched, they reported back to Willie at Control and began to probe. At 04.00 Willie called me at home to report.

The avalanche theory seemed more than likely but there was still the possibility the two had come out of the corrie and got lost on the return journey. If only lost they would most likely survive. By keeping moving they would maintain body heat, and there was the possibility that they may find shelter behind a boulder. I now called for a first light search, asking the rescuers to report directly to Glenmore Lodge.

At the same time Willie requested that the RAF Kinloss Team turn out to assist. The conditions seemed to preclude the use of a helicopter so he was surprised by the suggestion that one could fly into the corrie in the dark, but new technologies are in constant development. With an infrared heat-seeking device on its pod it would have a wider sweep and different sensitivity than our human resources on the ground. Of course, we agreed. Shortly after this a Sea King swept in and made several runs without finding even a glimmer of heat.

Our four strong rescuers kept digging among the avalanche debris until the others arrived shortly after daybreak, many of them flown into position by the helicopter. At 09.30 the aircraft crew changed in the normal course of their shift pattern and at about 10.00 Willie called me again. We had taken huge resources onto the site but uncovered nothing, no sign, no clue, and he had come to believe the two were not where circumstances indicated. That being so they could be anywhere.

If they had abseiled down without being avalanched, and succeeded in coming out of the corrie, they would surely have headed for the car park.

If hypothermic, they may have been in a state of confusion and wandered downhill to Rothiemurchus Forest.

If they had topped out they may have set off in the wrong direction across the plateau.

If their wanderings took them into Glen Avon they may have reached Faindouran Bothy, or even found their way to Tomintoul.

These uncertainties meant extending the search area considerably and we decided to concentrate first on the area between the corrie and the forest.

By now conditions were improving and the helicopter's first

flight across the area located the first body beside the Sneachda burn. It was close to the path that runs from Lurcher's Crag into Coire Cas, about a kilometre from the car park. A dog handler found the second body close by a short time after.

The reasoning our advance party strong searchers had applied the previous night had been impeccable, as was their strategy of entering the corrie in a line. What defeated them, and ensured a long and difficult search, the expenditure of enormous resource and, no doubt, an extended period of anxiety for those waiting, was the weather. They may well have passed close to the bodies without noticing.

The press made much of the short distance from the car park, headlining as 'Twenty Minutes from Safety', and in fact there was quite a fuss. For some reason it seems difficult to understand that, when the whereabouts of a casualty is unknown, the area of search amounts to the whole of the Cairngorms and the method cannot be to completely cover every inch of ground in a slowly expanding circle.

As a Team we discussed the events of the night and all that led up to them. Low temperatures, wind chill, lack of preparation and food, inadequate clothing; these were the reasons for the two deaths.

Soon though, I received word from the Chief Inspector at Aviemore that the father of one of the deceased had approached the procurator fiscal asking for an investigation into the Team's decision-making and actions. A report was required to show that everything that could be done had been, or in what ways we had been deficient.

I could understand the distressed father's position. It must be difficult to accept that your beloved son has lost his life, particularly to accept that no other party was responsible. For the family's sake as much as his own he would have sought that elusive quality known as 'closure'.

We were aware of different police attitudes, now requiring that all incidents be investigated as potential crime scenes. No legal action had ever been attempted against a Mountain Rescue Team and, in fact, would almost certainly be filed against the police authority if it was ever to happen. We dealt with the situation as professionally as we did all mountain rescue challenges.

Willie and I carefully composed a report of four A4 pages that was entirely truthful, extremely full, and completely non-judgemental. We made it clear not only that our initial decision under the circumstances was to do nothing, but also that this was the correct decision. We could not be expected to second-guess such a lack of equipment and experience. We also noted the companion climbers who had seen nothing unusual or distressing on the route, so much so they felt able to leave the two to their own devices. We listed the human and material resource expended, all the 'extra miles' that had been walked, and made especial, creditable reference to the four rescuers who had first ventured out in search of the two.

Willie and I signed the report together and let it be known we would be happy if it found its way to the grieving relatives. We passed it through the Chief Constable's office to the procurator fiscal and heard no more. Later though, I noted a further report from an inquiry in England that quoted ours almost verbatim. For all of us, rescuers, police and procurators fiscal, the incident was thankfully over. Not so for those who remained alive with aching hearts.

TWENTY-EIGHT

We often have call-outs around the New Year period. Mountain rescuers have to be prepared to give up at least some of their most precious time, time which the family will feel a prior claim to.

I had been contemplating retirement for some time; my period as Team Leader was already longer than any before and, to some extent, I was seeking new challenges such as those that sailing would present. The yacht *Ticoyo* was still in the future but, for these reasons, the turning of the year held certain 'end of an era' feelings.

Against all this the early death of Chris Barley had badly affected us all and there was perhaps a need for 'least disruption', at least for a while. I was and always will be enamoured of the Cairngorms and the Mountain Rescue Team and still felt fully competent in my position as Team Leader, albeit from a sedentary position at the Rescue Centre. Its conception, planning, funding and construction at Inverdruie had taken so much effort I wanted not only to enjoy it but also to see it thoroughly established and operating efficiently.

At all times sensitive to the Team's thoughts and feelings I could detect no movement to suggest I should leave immediately and so decided to continue. It was on Hogmanay of 2004, the last day of the year, that we faced one of our more technical rescues. As so often the use of a helicopter was crucial.

I was driving through Aviemore on the way to Inverness when I received a call from the police on my mobile phone. A male climber had reported an accident on Finger's Ridge in Coire an t-Sneachda. He was part of a father-and-son climbing pair who, when leading a pitch, had dislodged a large stone and sent it tumbling off into space. Below him his father was secure on a belay stance about halfway up the route. The rock had struck him on the back, taking him to his knees. The son had climbed back down to find his father in considerable pain and unable to move. He was unable to climb either up or down and continuing was out of the question.

Using my mobile phone I called them on their belay stance and ascertained what conditions were like. As I thought, they were gusty and overcast, although relatively mild. This kind of accident has become more common now our winters are more generally mild. Winter climbers of an earlier era could expect the snow and ice that covered such a route as Finger's Ridge to be frozen hard and therefore reliable. Now, in these warmer conditions, they could put their hand to a rock that might come away. The result might be a fall for the lead climber, or again an injury to a following climber who might as easily come off the route.

Instead of continuous, reliable winter climbs in the Northern Corries we are faced with variable conditions that are much more dangerous, routes that at times can be slippery and loose.

More alarming was the leader's description of his companion's condition. As he went through point after point suspicion altered to conviction and I realised we were going to have to effect a difficult rescue in the shadow of what might be a serious spinal injury. I set the full Team on course for Inverdruie and called RAF Kinloss to ask their Team for assistance and for the use of a Sea King. Both were provided without question and without reference to the date.

The Sea King flew in to the corrie at 14.45, but the weather had worsened so much it could not make a close approach to the casualties. Few climbs are on precisely vertical rock. Most are on sloping ground however steep, and sometimes an expert pilot can take his aircraft in so close that the rotors can be kept clear of the rocks while the winchman is lowered onto the ledge. It takes an iron nerve and a high degree of skill and neither of these were ever in short supply. However, on this day the wind in the corrie was growing increasingly turbulent.

The pilot made his decision and returned to the landing area at Inverdruie. By this time our Team Members were ready and they piled aboard. They had strops to be lowered by, ropes, dead men, radios and stretcher. I was increasingly concerned at the possible spinal injury which, even if not confirmed, would make the rescue more complex.

When a stretcher can be lowered vertically the descent, generally, presents no great problems, especially if belays can be attached to reliable rock. A single rope will be suspended from three rock belays so for each rope that is in use on the face there will be three connecting it to the rock belays at the top. All three must be tight to be effective and on the strength of this arrangement the safety of both rescuers and casualty depend.

The stretcher comes with a metal cage that drops over the casualty's head to protect him or her from any more falling rocks. With the head protected and the casualty strapped securely in place it can be lowered down easily. There will be some bumping over bulges and ridges but the stretcher descending in the vertical plane will generally slide over them until the rescuers on the ground can take hold.

In the case of a spinal injury even the casualty's self-weight can have a crushing effect that might do irrevocable damage. In such cases the stretcher has to be lowered in the horizontal plane, creating increased difficulties and even risks for the rescuers.

Unable to reach the casualty, the pilot performed a minor miracle of the flying arts by riding the wind on the lip of the corrie to lower both Team and equipment onto the plateau above the casualties. As they began laying out the belays he returned to Inverdruie to take the Kinloss Team into the corrie and as close to the foot of the climb as possible. By 15.45 all the parties were in place and he returned to Inverdruie. For now the Sea King's task was done and all our attention was on the two Mountain Rescue Teams deployed on the hill.

On this occasion the Rescue Party at the site was led by Jas Hepburn. A fearless climber he would not, on this occasion, go over the side. Instead he would organise directly from the corrie's rim. With the helicopter gone he established contact with me by radio and supervised the Team as they laid out their equipment. Because of the suspected spinal injury they would need twice as much as usual. It was already growing dark and the wind was gusting wildly. By 16.00 he had established communication with the climbers.

The stretcher having to go down horizontally would require two ropes, in turn requiring six rock belays, the belay ropes attached to each end of the stretcher. To be most secure the belays have to be located as far from the drop and as widely apart as possible. The first party worked quickly to secure the ropes while, at the same time, Duncan MacDonald abseiled to the ledge to make a better assessment of the casualty's condition. At 16.45 our worst fears were confirmed; a spinal injury was indeed likely. It was going to be a long and difficult rescue.

Al Gilmour, another strong climber, now abseiled down to assist Duncan in securing the casualty to the ledge and preparing further belays to receive the stretcher which was now made ready and lowered down. John Lyall went down beside it, tasked with preventing it snagging on the cliff face and preventing any further rock displacement. Jas kept me informed by radio.

At last there were five men, three rescuers and two casualties, standing together on a narrow ledge, over an almighty drop, with the stretcher gusting about in the wind beside them. They had to secure themselves before they could be of further use and so set about cutting a wider ledge with their axes. The essence of this cutting action is to let the weight of the axe do the work, to take a relaxed stance and to swing it like a pendulum against the ice and snow so that it breaks away in chips and shards and eventually a safe foothold is formed. In these circumstances it is by no means easy and precious time was wasting away. Expert as they were it took an additional 15 minutes, while the casualty's condition got no better, and for those of us waiting anxiously it was all time, time, time.

After what seemed an age they were ready. Our three rescuers grabbed the lines that were trailing from the stretcher, drew it close and got the casualty aboard and secure. He was now lying horizontally and so keeping as much pressure as possible off his spinal column. Even at this stage the risk to his future well-being was reduced, but there was a tricky ride ahead.

John opened the karabiners on his harnesses and secured himself to the centre of the stretcher between it and the cliff, all in conformity with training and procedures. With the six rock belays high above transferring the combined weight of John, casualty, stretcher and ropes, into the ground they swung out into space and the lowering operation was begun.

Inevitably it was a slow process as the rescuers above let the ropes out as evenly and steadily as possible. The cliff face, although not precisely vertical was not far removed from it, so John in the middle kept the stretcher clear by lifting his legs and walking down with his feet, pushing off here and there and shouting instructions to Jas. Slowly as John went, the bumps and nodules that decorated the rock face came up at him all too quickly, and of course it was impossible for the men above to lower both sides at exactly the same rate. This was the crux of the rescue and I was not the only one listening carefully to the shouted conversation. The RAF rescuers were laying out ground flares on the floor of the corrie and as the descent came close to its completion they lit up the whole area.

At about 20.30 they were down, the stretcher grabbed and taken to ground by the Kinloss Team with the casualty kept as comfortable as possible. His son was lowered after him. On the plateau and ledge the Cairngorm Mountain Rescue Team cleared up their belays and ropes and abseiled down into the corrie.

At Inverdruie I heard this news with relief and made a call to Aviemore Police Station to let the police know that Rescue 137 was about to fly into the corrie to uplift the casualty.

Our aircrew took off again, heading into the corrie to meet the Teams as they carried the casualty out. Sadly, the weather had worsened horribly and the pilot radioed to me that they could not go in. I transferred this news to the carriers who met it with loud moans and ironic season's greetings. There was no choice but to carry the casualty all the way out. At 23.30, almost New Year, we put both father and son into the Cairngorm Mountain Rescue Team ambulance and got them away.

By that time the curries I had ordered earlier in the evening from the Royal Tandoori in Aviemore had arrived. Well used to our more eccentric orders they like four or five hours' warning before delivering 40 curries to the Rescue Centre, and this was how we brought in the New Year, stuffed with Lamb Madras or Chicken Vindaloo and rice, with single malt whisky for those who did not have cars to drive or, for that matter, helicopters, with glasses raised high to toast our friends in the air and our families at home, and hoping that many more years would come for all of us, not least the casualty now safe in hospital.

TWENTY-NINE

Everyone who sees the cartoon remembers it, the tree on a snowy hill-side with ski tracks running towards it, the tracks breaking impossibly to either side, reforming downhill of the trunk, back in parallel and running together to who knows what destination. Funny, uncanny, a mistake miraculously unpunished, it encapsulates some of the 'other' aspects of mountain rescue which visit us from time to time.

October can be one of the most delightful months for walking in Scotland. The low-angled light of autumn picks out the hills' features. Plants, animals and birds are still plentiful and the air is rich with scents. One evening a lone hillwalker, weary after a long and satisfying day, beginning his descent from Cairngorm into Coire na Ciste, noticed that the chairlift was still in operation. No one was on any of the chairs though, no one to witness him giving in to temptation.

When he reached the middle station, which is not open to the public, he jumped the fence and climbed aboard a passing chair. Unknown to our friend a maintenance engineer in the lower station, having just completed his work, was about to throw the off-switch, lock up and leave for home. On the hill the chairs juddered in the air, one more than most since it carried the weight of a tired and hungry hillwalker.

It must have been a rare experience to hover there above the mountain, the great Strath opened below him, the mighty River Spey carving its route across the floodplain, scribbling its destiny across the tremendous land. No one could be less than awestruck at such a sight and I imagine he entered a wonderstruck trance as the sky blackened. Soon he was hovering in darkness with the lights of Aviemore seemingly reflecting the stars, lost in space.

For all of October's attractions to the hillwalker, warmth at night is not one of them. As it grew colder our friend decided that something really had to be done or he would freeze. He was a tantalising few metres short of one of the safety nets that are placed at strategic locations to protect innocent passers-by from falling ski poles and the likes. With no chance of leaping across from the wobbling chair perhaps he could clamber out of it, dangling to the full length of one arm and drop the remaining distance to safety? Maybe, but how long was the fall? It was too dark to be sure.

To test it he dropped his rucksack over the side and waited for a – *thump!* – that took far too long to arrive. Oh dear. What monstrous height above the ground was he, and what should he do now? As the temperature dropped he decided to put on the spare clothing he had, as a sensible, well-prepared hillwalker, that morning packed in his...

He had climbed aboard the chair at about 16.30. At 21.00 his wife alerted the police who called me. Soon there were 18 Cairngorm Mountain Rescue Team Members searching the hill, Willie Anderson and John Lyall among them. Since they had a good idea of the missing man's itinerary, they divided into several parties and followed the routes generally taken by returning mountaineers. After scouring the hill for several hours someone heard whistling and shouting.

'What's that?' he asked.

'Uphill!' called a rescuer.

More whistles and shouts.

'Downhill!' called another.

They searched to no avail, and yet the shouting and whistling continued. This went on for some time. Search here, discover nothing; more whistling. Search there; more shouts. Groups of three and four got together to scratch under their woolly bonnets and ponder. Where was all the noise coming from?

At 01.25 Willie decided to invest a paraflare and, at last, they found our forlorn friend floating in the firmament. Alas, his ordeal was not yet over. It would take at least two hours for the Chairlift Company to return and restart the machinery. The Team was faced with a new and unusual, and to this day unique, rescue situation.

Ladders are by no means an unusual climbing aid on the larger mountains of the world. Occasionally in the Himalaya ladders are laid across crevasses for mountaineers to clamber over. To the best of my knowledge they have never been used in the Cairngorms before, but the ever-resourceful John Lyall located a set and reappeared with a gleam in his eye.

Extended to its full length the rescuers raised the ladder a towering 10m into the vertical to find it was still just short of sufficient height. They had a hurried but intense conversation with the casualty and, undaunted, clambered onto the safety net to send it, wobbling and barely under control, toppling towards the chair. Decapitation of the casualty was thankfully avoided, but the crisis was by no means over. It remained for him to transfer his all too vulnerable body from chair to ladder.

'Are you sure you want to go through with this?' Willie called up. 'There may be health and safety issues.'

While not exactly keen the casualty seemed determined.

'The Chairlift people can be here in a couple of hours!'

'I'll fuh-fuh-reeeeze in that time!' our friend replied, and with the ladder leaning on the chair swung himself onto the rungs with everything moving, net, ladder, chair and self, as if with minds of their own.

At last he was across and gripping tight (probably his fingerprints are still pressed into the aluminium runners), but swaying precariously and still 10m above the hard, cold ground. Accompanied by shouted encouragement from below he began his descent only to come off a few steps down, but far enough across to locate him above the safety net.

In fairness to our friend, when he stopped bouncing he was capable of laughing at himself, and I hope he won't mind me poking some easy-going fun in his direction now. Paul Hunter quoted him in our local paper thus: 'I watched the chairs come up and got onto one of them. It wasn't too long before I realised something wasn't right. I'll be more careful in future – that is, if my wife lets me out on the hills again.' I am sure his wife was very pleased to have him safely back.

The press has a sense of humour too, although they tend to keep their faces straight in public. In July of the following year I received a call from the police who had, in turn, received a call from a Mr Adams, at that time a journalist and resident in Ballater. Mr Adams was acquainted with a man named Tom Robertson, then 68 years old and described as a ghost hunter/author. It seemed Mr Robertson had gone on to Ben MacDhui with a younger man named Derek Blake. Mr Adams had tried to dissuade them from this adventure, possibly in mortal fear of the Great Grey Man of whom I had read but never seen a trace.

Around 06.00 Mr Adams narrowly failed to get to his phone while it was still ringing but found a message left on his answering machine. It was Derek, who was on his way down having been obliged to leave Tom who, it seemed, was 'having problems with his heart'. Derek sounded as if he knew what he was doing, and quite confident. Mr Adams attempted to call their mobile phones but they simply rang out.

At 06.20 the police called me and I agreed to turn out right away. Shortly after, Derek Blake spoke to the police to say he had arrived at the skiing area and was at the Coire Cas car park. He had no grid reference for his friend whom he had left 'three miles up'. In the police report 'three miles up' is followed, not surprisingly, by a question mark. More worryingly, he reported 68-year-old Tom as experiencing dizzy spells and maybe having heart problems.

At 06.45 Mr Adams called again to correct some information. The police report notes as follows: 'Transpires he (Derek) also phoned a colleague of Adams in Glasgow – David Leslie who works with the *News of the World*.'

More cynical minds than mine might have taken a dim view of

this turn of events, but that was not a luxury we could indulge with a possible heart attack to deal with. I questioned Derek and learned that their tent had been destroyed by the wind around 04.00. They had evacuated the site and begun their walk out leaving the ruins behind. Some distance along the way Tom became unable to continue and was now in a sleeping bag located beside 'a track'. Such were the limits of our information.

Seasonal holidays had depleted our numbers. I therefore requested numerical support from the RAF Kinloss Team and got on with co-ordinating the rescue. Soon ten Cairngorm Mountain Rescue Team Members were on the hill and at 09.15 another 15 more from RAF Kinloss joined them. With visibility at around 200m requesting a helicopter was not an option.

Duncan MacDonald, whose physique has evolved with the sole purpose of running across hills, arrived very quickly, as did the equally speedy Graham Leggat. Fit as a fiddle and feeling frisky they were keen to set off on their own. With Donnie and his group following I decided to let them go and at 11.50 they came across the slumbering Tom in his blue and red sleeping bag, apparently comfortable on the ground some distance from the Coire an Lochain track. Visibility at this location was down to about 50m so there was still no question of utilising a helicopter. Fortunately, after a speedy examination, it transpired that Tom was feeling much better. Duncan radioed back and the three met Donnie's group on their way down, with Tom managing the walk out unassisted.

The very next day the *Daily Mail* gave the incident a column headlined 'A hunter of ghosts…lost in a shroud…' in which they accurately reported that the two climbers had their tent blown away. *The Press and Journal* more soberly reported 'Ghost hunter in climbing alert'. They added 'A ghost hunter risked becoming a ghost himself when he searched for the Highland version of the Abominable Snowman…'

We laughed all this off and hoped the two men weren't embarrassed about it all – although Tom might like the publicity for his books. When visibility cleared a few Team Members gave themselves a pleasant hillwalk across the plateau and retrieved the wreckage of the tent. We dropped it on the floor of the Rescue Centre and there it lay for several weeks until I received a call from one of the tabloids. Could we send them down the remains?

It seemed a pointless request but I agreed provided they would provide the postage costs. 'Why do you want it?'

'To see where the claws went through,' I was told, 'and to get a DNA test done on the saliva.'

Approximately two months later, on 4th September an unsuspecting reading public, at least those discerning enough to take the *Daily Mail*, opened a two-page spread that can be accurately described as 'fabulous', even 'fantastic'. Headlining 'TERROR OF THE SCOTS YETI' half a page was given over to a visual representation of a hairy, fanged sub-human monster, above a smaller photograph of the two men, looking pensive and wary.

Tom was quoted as saying, 'I saw a very broad, hairy chest, a massive arm and the outline of a huge head. It was covered with white and grey hair. It looked like a giant grey gorilla. It is a sight I'll never forget and it still upsets me.'

Derek had previously been sceptical of the monster's existence. Not anymore! The *Daily Mail* quoted: 'When I began hearing this thing moving around, the hairs on the back of my neck and arms went up. It was terrifying. There we were in the middle of nowhere, and this thing was feet away from us. We had no way of defending ourselves and, as we were thrown around, I was waiting for the thing to come into the tent. All the time it was making this loud mumbling sound. It was massive and seemed to have huge strength.'

Neither man had made any mention of being attacked by the monster during or after the rescue.

I myself was quoted thus: 'I couldn't say what caused it, but the Cairngorms are hit regularly by 100mph winds.' So they are, and they remain my sole theory for the destruction of the ghost hunter's tent.

Only two days after that call-out we attended a rescue of

altogether different character. A man aged 47 had taken his 13-year-old son into the Lairig Ghru the previous afternoon. There they pitched their tent and enjoyed a pleasant evening together before turning in. In the morning a mist was down and visibility much reduced. The two packed up and continued their walk into the pass with their map to hand but without a compass, and soon became misplaced.

At 14.13 the father used his mobile phone to call the police. They called me with his number and I called him back, 'somewhere in the Cairngorms'. There was no indication of panic but it was evident, from both his tone and the information he provided, that he was anxious about his son. The temperature was low, they had no waterproof overtrousers and both were cold, wet and miserable. The only clue the father could give about location was that they stood beside a 'big pile of stones' with mist swirling around.

I went through my set list of questions, among them asking the location of their car. In fact they had no car. They had travelled by bus to Aviemore from a city some distance to the south. A second bus had taken them to the foot of the mountain, the ski bus had carried them up to the car parks and from there they had walked.

From his description of their surroundings I deduced they had somehow left the Lairig Ghru, and since they seemed not to have made any particularly steep ascent I suspected they had inadvertently turned into the Chalamain Gap. If so they were most likely now in Coire an Lochain, a theory that fitted the father's description of their surroundings although, in fairness, they could have been in any one of many places.

I asked him to turn off his mobile phone to conserve battery power but to call at regular intervals. That done I called out the Team and requested assistance from the RAF Leuchars Team who were in Newtonmore at the time. By 16.30 eight rescuers were in Coire an Lochain, reporting that the mist was lifting and visibility improving. By the time they reached the headwall we were pretty sure the casualties were not at this location. This was rather disturbing since it implied a search area that was very wide indeed.

At 17.00 the rescuers were joined by five more Team Members, moving together into Coire an t-Sneachda as the next logical location. By 18.00 21 rescuers were involved, but drawing another blank. In both corries they had fired off paraflares that descended casting an eerie green light, and maroons whose explosions echoed back from the cliffs. I was in regular touch with the father who had neither heard nor seen them but was now describing his 'big pile of stones' as a cairn, a man-made object that implied a significant location.

What seemed most likely, from the father's description, was that they had somehow ascended to the plateau and were now at the cairn above Coire an Lochain that marks the rim's highest point. Several of the rescuers now made their way upwards and around the corrie's rim where they did, indeed, find the pair at the cairn. The wind at this exposed location would have made it impossible to hear the maroons and the mist would have obscured the flares.

Both father and son were cold and miserable but the rescuers were carrying hot drinks and soup and these made an immediate and positive difference. The two were escorted to Coire Cas car park and from there taken to Inverdruie in the Team Land Rover. Arriving after 21.00 they were too late for the last bus home, but even if a bus had been available there was no question of sending them off shivering and exhausted.

In these circumstances the new Rescue Centre came into its own. After getting them into the hot showers we managed, between us, to round up a complete change of clothing and cooked a more substantial meal than the soup that had fuelled their descent. The son went to bed in one of our bunk rooms while the dad stayed up to share a beer with me. When I assured him I would be happy to drive them to Aviemore for the bus next morning he asked an unexpected question.

'Will there be any publicity about this? I wouldn't like that.'

I told him it was likely but he shouldn't worry too much. He had acted responsibly and done all the right things after becoming lost.

'It's not that,' he said. 'You see, I'm divorced and my ex-wife has custody of our son. If she hears about this she'll go off her head and my access to him might get cut off.' It was clear he was genuinely frightened.

I had already warmed to the pair. In fact, I felt that anyone who saw them together would have felt the same way. Writing now, remembering the father's anxious face as we talked, I feel the same positive emotions. Their weekend had gone awry but they had not come to grief and their bond of love and trust was not in any way weakened. As a father who has taken his son not only into the Cairngorms but also the Alps I can do nothing but applaud his motivations. The journey anticipated and planned together, the introduction to one of life's finer experiences and to a great sport, the deep togetherness, not to mention the memories he would retain would all be to the boy's great benefit through his future life – or should be. The thought of their relationship being threatened because of such good intentions was a chilling one.

'I'll do my best to minimise publicity,' I told him, knowing I could ensure they would not be named. 'Now best turn in.'

Accompanying him to the room he was sharing with his son we found the boy at the point of sleep, but not quite across the border to the Land of Nod. 'Thank you for saving Dad,' he said.

From what? I wondered, but the question is perhaps best left open. In the morning I left them at the bus station, their future before them, catastrophe avoided, travelling together side by side at least for a while longer.

THIRTY

Three brief notes that flutter from the files speak unconsciously of human values and priorities, and how helicopters have their limitations too. They come with a sheaf of press cuttings from *The Glasgow Herald*, Aberdeen's *Press and Journal* and *The Sun*.

The first is handwritten on a card showing a dramatic sea rescue as painted by the artist Michael Powell. A hovering Sea King has lowered a rope to two men struggling in icy waters and on the point of being dashed against cliffs. Waiting in the background is the trawler from which, presumably, they have fallen. The message is addressed to 'John, and all at Cairngorm MRT', and it runs, 'I am writing to thank you all for your magnificent response to events over the past few days and, particularly, for looking after my people and aircraft stuck on the hill. A great job, much appreciated – by all at 202 Squadron.'

It is signed by Bunny James, Wing Commander, Officer Commanding No 202 Squadron.

202 Squadron's D Flight, based at Lossiemouth, normally consists of two helicopters. It is quite usual for only one to be serviceable at any one time such is the requirement for maintenance. The RAF, like their sister armed forces, use call signs, and it gives away no secrets to say that the helicopters are Rescue 137 and Rescue 138. The call sign is not assigned to either machine but to whichever is on mission at the time. So, the machine in the air will be Rescue 137 and the machine at base will be Rescue 138. This second call sign only comes into play on the rare occasions when both helicopters

are in action together – as on one occasion towards the end of February 2006.

I had purchased a cottage near Boat of Garten with the intention not only of turning it into a sort of retreat, but also of making it as ecologically sound as possible. With Donnie Williamson's professional help I had a well dug and lined with concrete rings, using a pump to supply the house with fresh water. We installed solar panels to provide some environmentally friendly electricity, supported by two diesel generators in a shed at the rear. The noise from the generators at times was too great so we later constructed a bund, a mound of grassed earth, between shed and house. Internally we placed two handsome wood burning stoves, and with a plentiful supply of birch always to hand there was no reason ever to feel cold.

The cottage is located approximately 2km from Boat of Garten on the Speyside Way and in summer the steady stream of walkers and cyclists is usually happy to linger and talk. On the other side of the Way is a clearing in the birch wood and beyond that the rail tracks used by Speyside Railway for its steam locomotive, now quite a tourist attraction. What all this amounts to is a wonderful, uninterrupted view of Braeriach, the mouth of the Lairig Ghru, Cairngorm and the Northern Corries.

It is the sort of project that can never be truly completed, but since the cottage became watertight and heated it has been temporarily inhabited by more than one rescuer. The months of planning and building were good months, with my mind ranging between present work on the cottage, plans for retiring from the business, and the yacht *Ticoyo* which I had now bought and was falling increasingly in love with. While work continued on the cottage I remained in touch, with the Team and the rest of the world, by having not only a mobile phone close to hand but also one of the Team's radios.

On the particularly fine winter day that was 27th February Donnie and I were busy with the generators when my mobile phone rang. It was the police in Aviemore, passing on a plea for help they had received from Coire an t-Sneachda. A party of three had been climbing The Seam and the leader, a young man named Martin W, had fallen onto a ledge. It seemed he had broken either his ankle or his leg, but they were not sure which. In either case he would not be walking out unassisted. It was 13.37.

The Seam is a technically demanding route that begins some way above the point where the cliffs grow suddenly steeper and climbers normally stop to put on helmets, extra gloves and other warm clothing. The route was first put up by John Lyall and James Grossett, who also gave it its name.

One of the three, Peter P, had left his two comrades at the low point of the route and walked out for assistance. He had met another climber and borrowed his mobile phone to call the police. I called Peter back.

Now he had made contact he was, naturally, reluctant to retreat any further. He wanted to return and assist his two friends. Since he sounded calm and confident I viewed this positively, feeling sure he could be of most use back in the corrie. My concern was that having returned the phone to its owner he would afterwards be out of contact. I wanted to be sure that as much preparation was complete as possible before that time. From Peter I learned that another group of three had joined them and were waiting with Martin W, the casualty. Again this was good, the more hands available the better.

I knew rangers Ewan MacLeod and Iain Cornfoot, who were both also members of the Mountain Rescue Team, were on the hill and so radioed and asked them to trek into the rescue box in Coire an t-Sneachda to pick up a stretcher.

A word about the rescue box is appropriate here. The Team had kept an unlocked box in the corrie since before I joined, but in recent years we had made important improvements. When we noticed the old box was growing dilapidated Donnie not only designed a new one but persuaded his friends at AI Welders in Inverness to donate the materials and fabricate it for us. About the size of two large baths butted together it is constructed of mild steel. After it was delivered to Glenmore Lodge it was attached to a net and flown by a Sea King into Coire an t-Sneachda as far as conditions would allow. After that it took 20 mountain rescuers to carry it to its final location. Not only heavy, it was awkward. The method Donnie devised was to push ladders underneath so that several carriers could take a grip at each corner. Even so they were glad to put it down for the last time.

The box is kept unlocked and the many people who enter the corrie regularly, rangers, weather watchers and mountain guides are all aware of its presence. It contains stretchers, casualty bags, shovels, avalanche probes, and other hardware that will not be affected by low temperatures. Having it so close to the most likely scenes of accident means the rescuers have less gear to carry in. It also encourages self-rescue and assistance in the corrie that suffers the largest number of accidents in all of the Cairngorms. In a short, two-month period of the winter following Martin's rescue five people lost their lives in the area and many more suffered injuries of varying seriousness.

Because of the location I had concern about getting a helicopter in close enough to effect a lift. Although at the foot of the cliffs the casualty was nonetheless at the top of a steep slope. I asked Peter to return and, if possible with his companions, carry Martin to the foot of the slope. Great care would have to be taken since there was no way of assessing the extent of his injuries. Since he was conscious, it was more than likely he would tell them when the pain was too great. I told Peter I intended not only to request a helicopter but also to get a Rescue Party moving on foot. This gave him important work to get on with back in the corrie and also allowed him to pass on realistic reassurance to Martin. It was also as much forward planning as was possible. With the helicopter the ordeal would be over quickly. Without it they should be ready for a long walk, and stretcher carry out.

Donnie and I looked up at the plateau from the cottage garden. Earlier in the day we had taken flurries of snow but now the sky was blue. The mountains were so clear they might have been cut from a postcard and pasted onto the sky. We put our heads together and agreed the whole thing would be over in half an hour.

I called the police and asked them to contact ARCC to request a helicopter. ARCC called me back to report the weather at Lossiemouth. Heavy snow was falling, driven by strong winds. This seemed strange to me. Conditions on the plateau had not altered much in the course of the day and, from our side, there was no prospect of a change for the worse.

'Up there,' I told them confidently, 'there are bright skies for a hundred miles all round.'

ARCC agreed to send Rescue 137, reckoning the journey would take about 20 minutes.

I now called Willie Anderson at Kingussie High School, where he taught, and described the position. We agreed we should send in support, more because some element of technical rescue might be required, and in case the lie of the land prevented the pilot getting close to the casualty, than with any sense the weather might change.

Willie agreed to break off what he was doing, round up some other Team Members and have them trek into the rescue box to join Ewan and Iain. It took them very little time to get to the car park and make a start. I also called Heather Morning who at that time was working at Glenmore Lodge. With three other instructors she started the one-and-a-half-hour walk in at 17.32 intending to meet the others at the rescue box.

So, Rescue 137 was in the air and we had three parties walking into the corrie. That is, belt and two pairs of braces. The skies remained blue and everything was under control, or so it seemed. Donnie and I had resumed our renovation work when a voice came through on the radio.

'Cairngorm John from Rescue 137: we are to the east of the range and fighting our way through a blizzard. What are conditions like on your side? Will we continue?'

From the garden we again looked up at the mountains.

'The hill is clear as far as the eye can see,' I said. 'Come on in.'

The helicopter flew over the top of the hill and over Heather's party as they walked in. Yes, the pilot agreed, the weather was clear on this side. He dropped into the corrie and hovered as close to the

casualty as he could while the winchman lowered himself down.
As ever, the downdraft and noise were too severe for the aircraft to
remain above the scene for long. The pilot backed off and waited
for an assessment.

How badly injured was the casualty?

Could he be lifted from where he lay or would he first have to be
moved further downhill?

At that point the storm he had already flown through blew in
with frightful suddenness, racing across the plateau and filling the
corrie with billowing snow. Visibility was reduced to such a short
distance there was no question of the pilot manoeuvring between
the cliffs. With the wind gusting strongly there was also no question
of him remaining in position. This left him no choice but to set
down and wait for the storm to pass. This he did with expertise, but
the storm did not pass. Instead it intensified and the light dimmed
as pilot and co-pilot sat turning and burning. None of us realised it
at the time but the storm had set in for days.

At Boat of Garten we were amazed by this sudden change and
immediately scaled up the ground operation. Donnie and I now
removed ourselves to the Rescue Base where we mobilised still
more people and encouraged the ranger and ski patroller, who
were closest to the corrie, to continue with the stretcher to the
foot of The Seam. However, communication proved difficult and
we moved on to Glenmore Lodge to co-ordinate from there. At
18.30 the Cairngorm Mountain Rescue Team reached the scene
of the accident, assisting the winchman, comforting the casualty
and encouraging his companions who had endured a long, anxious
wait. Martin was still in a high and precarious position although the
winchman had by now carried out all first aid that was possible and
given Entonox to minimise the pain he was inevitably suffering.
That done the Cairngorm Team secured Martin in the stretcher
and carried him to a position from which he could be evacuated in
safety by a stretcher lower.

Temperatures, already low, plummeted and the helicopter rotors
began to ice up. At 18.50 the pilot realised he had no more to offer

the rescue operation and would not be able to fly the helicopter out until the weather had properly cleared. He did not want either himself or his crew added to the casualty list and so reluctantly made the decision to shut down and abandon his machine.

I heard this over the radio and remember thinking, 'We've lost a helicopter. They're not going to like this. Good grief, there'll be hell to pay!'

I called for assistance from the RAF Kinloss Team now that a long carry out, even more complex than could have been antici-pated, was assured, and knowing the RAF would want a ground presence close to the machine. I also redeployed Heather and Team Member Tom Mullins to the stricken aircraft.

Unlike the winchman the rest of the helicopter crew, pilot, co-pilot and navigator were not dressed for the hill. They were not entirely unprepared though, since their normal gear included immersion suits against the possibility of being forced down at sea. The Team Members carry spare kit as a matter of course. This was shared and Heather navigated the party sympathetically out of the corrie. The others continued to the foot of The Seam.

It was 20.00 before Martin could be lowered from the cliff and the carry out begun. Heather and the aircrew reached the car park at 20.35. The carrying party reached the rescue box at 21.30 and were off the hill at 23.33. All through these procedures Donnie and I hung onto and considered every nuance of the rescue as it unfolded, constantly considering next moves and available resources, and were only now beginning to relax – so much for our easy half-hour rescue.

The downed helicopter became an object of much attention over the next week. I had been concerned about the attitude the crew's superior officers might take, but this proved to be without foundation. Even a cursory consideration showed that the pilot and co-pilot had not only made all the correct decisions but carried out their tasks with expertise and courage.

What I had not appreciated was the emotional power of a downed helicopter. The press fastened on it and the public gaze never wavered until it was out of the corrie. Conditions remained poor but people made the trek in to look at the machine. Conscious of security the RAF kept their guard team in position while, over the course of a week, the helicopter became increasingly iced up, more like a living creature in trouble than an assembly of aluminium and wires.

Sandy McCook, a professional photographer who was also son of our former Team Leader, Alistair, took possibly the most heart-rending of all the photographs. Rescue 137's rotors, by this time, were hung with icicles and its windows blinded by frozen snow. More than once the RAF tried to get in with other aircraft but were repeatedly beaten back.

More and more people walked in and more and more pictures were taken. When some humourist put a picture on eBay saying the 'buyer must collect' I felt a strong sympathy with the flyers forced to abandon their craft in the course of one of our rescues and whose charge had become not only a sort of tourist attraction but also a butt of low comedy. When the storm finally abated the RAF sent in a specialist cold country maintenance team who were immediately busy at the scene, thawing out the engines and gearbox, checking the moving parts and electrical equipment.

Knowing when the attempt was to be made I watched from Boat of Garten while listening in on the radio. The second Lossiemouth helicopter, Rescue 138, carried the crew in and lowered them into the corrie. No doubt to their delight the engines started first time. Then the two aircraft came out of the corrie together and it was only then I realised they had never stopped referring to the first machine by its original call sign. For all it had been down for a week it was still the lead aircraft on an uncompleted mission, a mission that would not be considered 'complete' until the helicopter was safely recovered.

Rescue 137 came out of the corrie low over the trees with Rescue 138 at all times close by. Keeping as clear as possible of roads and housing it made its way to Glenmore Lodge where it put down for more exacting repairs. I admit to feeling a lump in my throat as I watched them through binoculars from the cottage. I thought of the Wellington bombers of World War II accompanied by Spitfires on the last legs of their return journeys. That was away back in time to the earliest years of my life and I had received the knowledge almost as legend. Today I felt and understood the strength of connection. Like the rest of the public my attention was on this homecoming and it took some little time to see and return to what was really important.

The air-sea rescuers, like the Cairngorm Mountain Rescue Team, exist for a purpose and that purpose had been fulfilled in difficult circumstances. The return of Rescue 137 was really only the final tidying-up of the main mission. This brings me back to the other two notes that fell from the file. The first was from Martin W, whose lower leg had been broken in six places. He said, 'Dear All, Just a note…amazing to see so many people working together so well in the "challenging" weather. I have just returned home from having another op down here in Glasgow. Lots of metal work in my leg but it should turn out well.'

The second is from his mother who says, 'I am writing to thank you from the bottom of my heart for rescuing my son.'

THIRTY-ONE

Wander of an evening into any one of a number of Community Halls about the Highlands and you are liable to find yourself interrupting a lecture on sports development delivered by a squarely built enthusiast wearing a Groucho Marx moustache, but without the cigar. Jas Hepburn qualified as a physical education teacher at Jordanhill College of Education where he continued the journey into the outdoors he had begun in childhood.

The school system could not contain him though. Achievement targets and form filling conflicted with his own more traditional values and the teacher's mission of providing learners with the intellectual tools of discovery and understanding. To speak with him, at any length at all, is to be reminded that an hour of physical activity in any day will improve all other performance in addition to servicing the emotional and spiritual welfare of any human being. He now works freelance.

Qualified as a Mountain Instructor and kayaking coach he ranges all across the Highlands, lecturing wherever a client can find a hall, instructing and encouraging. Among his clients is the Highland Institute of Sport. Tasked with locating and developing young talent in its area it employs Jas as strength and conditioning coach, working in the weights gym with gifted young athletes in many disciplines from rugby to curling.

Unfailingly positive he is also a fearless, highly skilled climber. Roughly contemporary with John Lyall and Simon Steer they form the backbone of the generation of Cairngorm rescuers following

Willie Anderson and Donnie Williamson. Given all this he is an ideal man to have on one of the Team's regular training days, ranging across the plateaux, practising navigation, cross-country skiing in season, and climbing.

On 8th January 2006 we had just such a group out, practising the full range of winter skills. Among them, on this occasion, were two of our most experienced and accomplished mountaineers, Jas Hepburn and Simon Steer.

As Leader my role was straightforward. I met them at Inverdruie in the early morning to discuss their coming day and how they might best use it to advantage, and later made myself available for communication. At 64 years of age and with my knee condition steadily worsening there was no question of joining them. In fact, I knew I could not put off my knee replacement operation for too much longer. I was becoming increasingly aware of new generations of climbers coming through and that the steady and beneficial processes of change were continuing.

Later in the day the police at Aviemore received a call from Hell's Lum in the Loch Avon basin. Three climbers were cragfast with one injured and in a precarious position. They in turn called me at the cottage.

Hell's Lum is a beautiful area littered with many good climbs for both summer and winter. Overlooking the Shelter Stone, it faces eastward to Beinn Mheadhoin and along the great length of the loch to The Saddle. South-facing, it takes most of the light and heat that is going. Being that bit more difficult to reach than the Northern Corries, it tends to attract more serious climbers, and enthusiasts for unspoiled, wild land. With the upper reaches of Glen Feshie it is probably my favourite area in the Cairngorms.

The police gave me the men's number and I called them back on their ledge. One experienced climber had been leading two novices on the route known as Kiwi Gully when he fell. The two had been properly roped and belayed and this is what saved his life. Their climbing strategy had been standard and, in itself, competent. Properly equipped with an ice axe in each hand and crampons on his boots the experienced leader had led each pitch, cutting and supporting his way up the snow and ice-covered route to some suitable, relatively safe ledge. His less experienced companions followed, belaying at that point and remaining while he led the next pitch.

About 17m above where the two now stood he had reached a point where the ground steepened, the crux of the climb, and come off. The snow and ice he pushed his crampons into were not firmly locked to the rock face and, when it shattered, he fell with it, plummeting past his companions. His fall was arrested by the rope the same 17m distance below, swinging him against the cliff. He put out his foot to act as a shock absorber as the shards of ice smashed on the rocks far below.

It had been a long drop and his companions thought he had 'hurt his leg'. Now he swung beneath them, probably injured, certainly unable to reconnect with the cliff face and climb back up. His companions had not panicked but were very frightened and unsure. From my call it was apparent they could climb neither up nor down, nor could they lower him to the ground. It was now 16.45 and Jas, Simon and the others had returned to base, tired but fulfilled by their efforts.

It was getting dark, the temperature was falling and a severe worsening of conditions was forecast when I asked the rescuers to return to the hill. The prospect of an injured climber hanging overnight in temperatures that would fall well below zero was not to be contemplated. The additional factors of wind chill and an anticipated change for the worse in the weather, would almost certainly take his life. None of them hesitated.

The situation was uncomfortably reminiscent of the predicament faced by Simon Yates and Joe Simpson on Siula Grande in the Andes when Simpson fell to a position where he was swinging free and therefore helpless. Yates was pinned by his companion's weight and faced with the prospect of them both freezing to death. With no prospect of assistance the situation was irretrievable. Not knowing what kind of drop Simpson would face, Yates cut the rope assuming he was sending his companion to his death. In fact both survived and Joe Simpson wrote one of the greatest of all mountaineering books about the experience, *Touching the Void*.

Like most mountaineers I have contemplated and discussed what I would have done in Simon Yates's position. I have no doubt he made the right decision and this would be true even if Joe Simpson had died, because two deaths are worse than one. Whether or not I could have used the knife I do not know. The bond between climbers that the rope signifies is greater than the fabric itself. It goes to the heart. That said there is no point in giving your life for nothing. The principle is recognised in the first rule of first aid – do not be the next casualty.

The *Touching the Void* predicament was much worse than our climbers' because Yates and Simpson were in a more isolated position, much higher, and they had extended themselves far more, but the tenuous linkage was enough to take the story into the national press.

There was never any prospect of me advising the cragfast climbers to cut the rope on their leader, but I was acutely aware of how important time was. A few years earlier, on a neighbouring climb named Escalator, a casualty had lost his life in this area, freezing to death while we attempted to reach him. Use of an aircraft was imperative, not so much for the technical rescue as for flying the Team in and out. To get one to us as quickly as possible I called ARCC and requested the assistance of a helicopter.

Calling them ensured that the most convenient aircraft from across the services would be brought into play. Usually this is Rescue 137 from Lossiemouth but not always. Jas was making a list of kit we would require for the rescue; ropes, dead men, stretcher, figures of eight, when I learned that the RAF could not supply a helicopter quickly from Lossiemouth, but that HMS *Gannet* could send Sea King Rescue 177 from Prestwick. We arranged for it to fly up and meet the Team at Glenmore and that I would oversee the operation from there. As on the Finger Ridge rescue the Team would be led on the ground by Jas Hepburn but this time, as it proved, he would go over the edge.

They went up in two trips, Jas on the first. It was still a beauti-fully clear night, cloudless and starlit, with visibility of many miles. For those who are experienced and prepared the plateau is a joy to visit in such conditions. The helicopter flew in noisily and the sound of its rotors whipping the air must have echoed back to the stranded climbers from the crags of the mountains opposite raising their downcast spirits. The pilot though, was inexperienced in these conditions and found it difficult to assess height above the featureless whiteness. The solution was to lower Roger Gaff down, to provide perspective simply by his physical presence.

For those on board the aircraft the white snow of the plateau glowed under its lights as they landed close to Hell's Lum. With the rotors slowed to 'turn and burn' Jas led the Team out of the side hatch, hauling the equipment after them. It was 20.00. The weather remained fine, a clear night lit by a full moon, but a major storm was forecast and we knew it would not be long in arriving.

Descending from the most suitable position was obviously vital but locating the cragfast climbers with sufficient accuracy proved difficult. Consequently Jas tasked Chris Stuart to descend by Coire Domhain where he would have an uninterrupted view upwards and could report back by radio. With their location established the Team set about preparing for a descent.

The helicopter flew our second group in to assist and then returned to Glenmore Lodge where the crew shut down the engines and joined me while the rescue unfolded.

In winter conditions, if there was no possibility of establishing rock belays, the equipment termed 'dead men' could be used in their place. Dead men are large metal plates that the Team Members bury in the snow to take the strain of the single rope that will be used on the descent. They are placed as widely apart and buried as deeply as possible and it is important to arrange them in such a way that they take the strain together. It was now 23.00 and the fallen climber had been suspended above Glen Avon for seven hours. Reports indicated that the weather was closing in and so we decided not to spend time in setting up a winching system.

With the ropes and dead men in place Jas harnessed up and was manually lowered by his colleagues to assess the situation. Simon Steer now took charge topside.

Jas found the cragfast climbers to be still physically well but frightened and desperately cold. On the end of the rope the fallen climber was bruised and shaken but was conscious and reported nothing to suggest more serious injury. Jas returned topside to confer with his colleagues and with me by radio at Inverdruie. Since none of the three climbers was in a seriously bad condition the decision was made to bring them up without delay. If they had been badly injured it would almost certainly have been necessary to lower them to the floor of the glen and possibly carry them out.

Jas then tied a loop into the rope about two metres above where his head would be. Onto this he clipped both himself and a spare karabiner. That done the others lowered him past the cragfast pair to the fallen man. When they met Jas first clipped the man to the spare karabiner and then unclipped him from his own, original system. Now he undid the loop and lowered himself to the extent of the remaining two metres of rope, to a point where the man's flailing boot could not strike Jas's head. He called up to Simon Steer who co-ordinated the pull and the two of them, casualty and rescuer, bounced and walked their way up the vertical face to safety. Afterwards Jas climbed down to the other two and the process was repeated with them one at a time.

The aircrew and I had been in touch by radio all along and when we learned that the last man was on his way up they ran to the helicopter, landing in a swirl of loose snow as Jas appeared over the rim. At the same time Simon Steer looked up and saw a horizon-wide bank of black clouds covering the moon and rushing towards them. The fallen man had injured his ankle, but with the weather deteriorating rapidly we decided not even to put him into the stretcher. Instead Simon demonstrated the aptness of his call name 'Sumo' by opting for what he would later describe as the TLC treatment, Total Lack of Compassion. He took hold of the man's collar and dragged him backwards across the snow to the helicopter – needs must when the devil drives.

The helicopter made two speedy journeys to Glenmore Lodge, the first with the casualties and some Team Members, the second carrying the rest of the Team. At Inverdruie an ambulance was waiting and ten hours after we received the call the rescue was complete. Other than the lead climber's hurt ankle no great damage had been done, but all three climbers were cold and shocked and it could have been very much worse.

So often time is of the essence and rescuers often refer to the first hour after an incident as the 'Golden Hour', the decisive hour when lives are lost or won. The ten hours for the casualties were hours of deep suffering, physical pain combined with freezing temperatures, fear for themselves and anxiety for their companions. No doubt there was also some level of self-recrimination. They survived though, and although the modern combination of mobile phone and helicopter was crucial, more so was the resilience of our Team Members after a day on the hill that would have bankrupted most people's energy reserves and will.

Otherwise their survival would have been dependent on luck. In the first instance some other climber would have had to happen past or seen their plight from another crag. That climber would then have had to walk out and raise the alarm. This would have taken hours. With the alarm raised the Team would have to assemble and walk back in to effect the rescue, taking at least the same amount of time again. Carrying in the amount of kit we actually used would have been difficult. Since the two cragfast climbers would by then be hypothermic, if they were still alive, they would most likely be unable to assist in their own rescue. They would have to be hauled up and carried out on stretchers.

Getting to the fallen man from either above or below would be a job for at least two experienced, accomplished mountaineers. Operating without the dead man belays and a physically strong team they would have been lowered to the glen floor and a location which another group would have to reach with a stretcher. The carry would be long, hard and cold and it is likely that any injuries already suffered would be worsened.

I took great satisfaction in how the Cairngorm Mountain Rescue Team had shrugged off fatigue and performed. Such a combination of skills, equipment, physical fitness, energy and comradeship would never give in and almost always succeed. When the time came for me to retire, not long now, I knew not only that I would place the Team in good hands, but that in time more good hands would follow theirs.

The press made much of the *Touching the Void* similarity and took the opportunity to publish diagrams, maps and, in one case, a still from the film. In a way the casualties were lucky because, unlike on Siula Grande, no one had been seriously injured. Had the lead climber suffered, for example, a broken leg or, worse, a spinal injury it would all have been much more complex. Carrying him out from the head of Glen Avon, over The Saddle and down the snow-covered, narrow path in Strath Nethy, would have taken many hours.

The Times quoted me thus, 'To say they were grateful when we reached them is an understatement. I think they were maybe wondering whether they were going to die.'

It is hard to see how any of the casualties on either Siula Grande or Hell's Lum could have survived but what can look like miracles sometimes do happen. The comparison the papers made was always tenuous but the consequences would have been the same if the worst had happened. As always when someone dies on the mountains, the void they create is touched not by them but the loved ones left behind.

THIRTY-TWO

Among the more photogenic of our rescue colleagues are the search and rescue dogs, for which the public maintains a great affection. Another cutting sits in my files. This time from our local paper, the *Badenoch & Strathspey Herald*, it is dated 27th March 1986. Brief enough, it opens, 'Police Constable Jimmy Simpson and his German Shepherd dog, Northcon Rocky, have won the Scottish Region police dog trials' – and there is the uniformed Jimmy standing proudly to attention beside a table loaded with trophies, and there is Rocky lying in front of his haul. Ears up and alert, he is enjoying the attention.

Rocky was one of those big, hairy German shepherds, darker of muzzle and coat than the smoother-haired dogs, and sharp of eye. In the Team we knew he was as ready to deal with criminals as search through snow, and we watched our ankles. The time I best remember him in action was just a few months before the picture was taken.

It was another of the many rescues we have been called to during the New Year period. On the day before Hogmanay of 1985 a party of three spent the day in Coire Cas. Up on the rim, immediately below Point 1141, the slopes hold their layers of snow longer than probably any other location in the Cairngorms. Because of this sureness with the snow, the nature of the slopes and proximity to Aviemore it is an excellent area for practising winter skills, fastening on crampons and walking surefooted across ice, cutting steps with the axe, and arresting falls. Since daylight time was short, and training if your attitude is right is also play, this is how the group spent their day.

Perhaps thinking of the revelries ahead one of them left his ice axe by mistake and, no doubt, cursed himself overnight. He went back on his own the next day, Hogmanay, to retrieve it. When night fell and he had still not returned his companions raised the alarm. Pete Cliff, who was Team Leader at the time, questioned the others and received good information. They were able to describe very clearly where they had been and therefore where the missing man would most likely go to retrieve his axe.

At midnight we went directly there but could locate no sign. There was some loose snow that looked like the debris from a cornice collapse but I did not believe such a slight fall could possibly have taken a life, far less hidden the body from sight. It simply did not look like much of an avalanche.

Pete was less sure and had us perform a line search. Taking our snow probes we stood each within an arm's reach of the next rescuer and advanced across the snow, probing as we went. Neither on this occasion, nor on any other, have I personally found a body using this method. The element of chance is very great but the great thing is to take all possible resource to the search and to cover all possibilities. Line searching is one resource. So are dogs, and on this occasion it was Jimmy and Rocky who made the find. They were slightly away from the main group, as is usual, so that noise and conflicting scents would not confuse the animals. I was at the end of the line closest to them, working steadily, when Rocky became very animated, whining and scrabbling at the snow with his forepaws.

It did not take him long to reach the body and the human rescuers did the rest. The climber was dead, fallen victim to the collapsed cornice which must have swept down and round him, eventually burying and suffocating him.

I was impressed by two things, the first being how small the avalanche had to be to take a life. Although I have suffered accidents in the hills, not least to my knee, I have never been avalanched. Others have described how helpless they found themselves. The snow that appears to be, and is, soft, hardens immediately it stops, taking a set as cement does, and anyone trapped beneath the surface finds him or herself unable to move and soon unable to breathe.

The second is the usefulness of dogs: how they can sense what no human can sense when chance takes them to the right spot. I know I would have walked past the casualty if left to my own devices.

The body responsible for training and regulating these dogs is called the Search and Rescue Dog Association. SARDA Scotland is a charity dependent on donation and it states with pride, on its website and in its literature, that 'our dogs work anywhere 24 hours a day 7 days a week'. It is affiliated to NSARDA (where N stands for National) as are equivalent associations in England, Ireland and Wales.

SARDA Scotland's standards are rigorous. Anyone wishing to become a registered handler is required to already be a member of a Mountain Rescue Team. They must have the written approval of their life partner and their employer. They must also be competent mountaineers with high levels of skill in all areas of mountain activity. Physically fit, they are required to commit themselves to driving anywhere in Scotland at short notice.

There is no requirement that dogs be any particular breed. German shepherds and border collies are frequently used. Bearded collies are less frequently found on the hill but can be excellent, as I know from experience.

Although required to be members of a Mountain Rescue Team the handlers and their dogs become, as it were, liberated from that Team. SARDA has a controller who receives requests for the use of dogs, assigning whoever is best placed and available on any given occasion. Cairngorm Mountain Rescue Team is sometimes joined by a dog and handler who drive down to help from Tongue, on the north coast. Long drives at short notice, such as his, demonstrate the level of commitment required. Between those demands and the requirement for regular training updates and assessments it is unlikely that any person and dog team could maintain these standards for long periods – and yet some do.

Denise Barley was one of our handlers for several years. She and Chris kept bearded collies and, in fact, Denise has for a long time been a breeder and show judge. I dropped by her house the other day to talk about this book, reminisce about dogs and, to some extent inevitably, about Chris. The dogs were always mostly Denise's interest, to the point of fascination, and they continue to be. As a trainer, shower and breeder she takes great care in deciding who may or may not buy her puppies.

In 1984 Denise achieved some level of fame when an article on her and her dogs appeared in *YOU* magazine. A human interest story it described her rescue commitment of that time and outlined a few other details of her life. It was accompanied by photographs of Denise at home with her dogs, Bessie, Charlie and Bobby, others showing her walking on the hills with Bessie, Charlie braving the elements, Denise thawing poor Bobby out in the sink.

Bessie had been her first dog but, by the time she reached eight years of age, developed arthritis to such a degree she could no longer manage the work. Charlie's temperament was suspect and he was early retired. The third dog, Bobby, has the best story. Denise bought him as a show dog rejoicing in the name of Quinbury Stormdrifter – which turned out to be appropriate. He took to the hill as though bred for it rather than the show ring but, in fact, was equally at home in either. Shampooed but neither beribboned nor flounced – beardies are shown in their full natural coat – he won many prizes. Even on the hill he was a bit of a poser, but he was also a great search and rescue dog who claimed a place in my heart that is sadly empty now. His energy was without bounds and he seemed impervious to the most demanding weather.

Denise used to organise training sessions to keep him up to his hill mark, burying some willing volunteer in the snow and tasking Bobby to seek him out. She thinks deeply about them as creatures close to the wild, about their domestication and work, and their relationships with humans. She was quoted in the article as seeing search and rescue as a return to work for many breeds whose purpose had gone, or at least diminished. We sat around her hearth and spoke at length while she reminisced on Bobby's first call-out, the first time he showed his worth in practical terms.

In the summer of 1982 a little girl went missing at Dulnain Bridge, a small community not far from Grantown on Spey. The River Dulnain sources in the Monadhliath mountains, flowing below the A9 at Carrbridge, winding on through one of the most scenic areas in the Highlands to reach Dulnain Bridge and its woodlands before joining the Spey. The bridge was built in the eighteenth century and there must have been a community of one sort or another there ever since.

News of the missing child brought all the neighbours out and the area was thoroughly scoured. Family members kept themselves as busy and positive as they could by making tea and sandwiches for the searchers. The police were called in at an early stage and, somewhat later, the Cairngorm Mountain Rescue Team was invited to help in what was, for us, an unfamiliar environment. With others I entered the forest and swept through it as tightly as we could manage although we were continually forced apart by thorns, bushes and other vegetation.

Denise and Bobby took themselves away from the hubbub of sound and scent to walk along the riverbank, Bobby delving in and out of the wood. The river was high at the time, running quickly and gathering loose branches and other debris. At one point Bobby dived without warning into the water. The river was in full spate and Denise was concerned he would drown, so she called him back and looked around for some sign of the missing child but saw none. Shortly afterwards he dived in again, once more without warning. Again Denise called him out. This was not normal behaviour when the dog was wind scenting but there was no explanation and still no sign of the little girl. They continued along the bank as far as was practical and then returned.

Later a Sea King helicopter performed the manoeuvre known as 'hover-taxi', which is to say it flew slowly and at low level along the length of the river with the navigator and winchman staring down into the water. It was they who saw the child's body submerged in the middle of the river. By some mishap she had entered the water and been swept away, and it is virtually certain that her life was forfeit from that moment. With no adult to help she would have been helpless in the powerful current. Bobby had somehow taken her scent off the water surface but it was an unusual experience, especially for an inexperienced dog. Denise had done all that could have been done and the pair had played their full part in a rescue that ended, ultimately, tragically. It was clear though, that neither the dog's nose nor his courage were in any way wanting.

In an earlier part of her search and rescue career the then Secretary of SARDA, Kenny MacKenzie, asked Denise to design a harness for dogs to be winched in and out of helicopters. She did her homework thoroughly and eventually created an elaborate device of fabric and straps that was based on a First World War design for unloading horses from ships. The design was so successful it was soon used all across the country.

Bobby loved helicopters and used to sit with the winchman and look out of the open door. He also had a healthy appetite. One winter we were flown into Coire Garbhlach, at Glen Feshie, to carry out a snow search. The pilot couldn't put down on the severe slope but went as low as possible to allow us to jump onto a drift. The rucksacks were dropped first, then Bobby, then we all jumped. We probed the snow for hours while Denise and the dog searched through deep, stamina-sapping mounds until he was almost exhausted. By the time we stopped for lunch he looked pretty well done but knew me well enough to ask politely for a piece of my pork pie and I am pleased to say it revived him completely.

By 1985 the other side of Denise's life with dogs was growing stronger. Sitting by her fire she reminded me that as a result of giving more time to the show ring she was losing at least some of the physical fitness that is required of dog handlers. She said they have to be 'at the top of their game as mountaineers' and felt she had dropped below that rarefied level on the occasion we were called out, in 1985, to Creag Dubh.

Again it was a low-level event, this time occurring at the Creag

Dubh cliffs near Newtonmore. A family was holidaying nearby and their ten-year-old son, whose name was Lee, was highly taken with the cliffs, although reaching them meant a road crossing that had his parents' hearts in their mouths. Naturally he was expressly forbidden to cross the road and equally forbidden to climb the cliffs. Equally naturally, he circumvented his parents' orders at every opportunity. His interest had already cost him a few scoldings.

When his father reported him missing to the police they called the Team. We talked matters over with the Chief Inspector at Aviemore and while we were talking a report came through of two newly arrived casualties in Raigmore who reported seeing just such a boy.

Peter Cotton and Kenneth Clark had travelled north from Dundee to tackle one of the more difficult Creag Dubh routes. When they were about halfway up they heard a high-pitched calling for help. Against all reason it sounded like a child's voice, but as they climbed the cries grew louder and eventually they saw Lee close to the top of the route.

Being at a low level the Creag Dubh cliffs have a lot of vegetation about them, clumps of grass, stunted trees growing from cracks. Somehow Lee had managed to haul his way up to this level by a roundabout route before losing his nerve and becoming stranded. Peter and Kenneth were immediately alert to the dangers of sudden movements, and equally aware he could not be left while they went for help. They made their way to the boy, consoled him and got him to the top. They unroped and had made a start at walking Lee back down by the path when Peter slipped and fell down the cliff face. He plummeted 100m, apparently to his death.

Kenneth was now faced with another emergency while still in charge of young Lee. His most direct route was to climb down and, since Peter was at least injured and possibly killed, this he felt obliged to do. The path was a relatively safe one though, and he felt that by instructing Lee to return directly to his parents he had discharged his duty. He would report what had happened and check on the boy after doing whatever circumstances dictated when he reached his friend.

Peter Cotton had miraculously survived his fall but sustained a compound fracture of the tibia, now known as an open fracture. This is to say the broken shin bone had pushed out through the skin. Kenneth gave him a shoulder to lean on and they hitched to the surgery at Kingussie where a more expert diagnosis was made before they were taken to Raigmore by ambulance.

As far as the police and the Team were concerned this was all to the good, but Lee was still missing. We put ourselves in the lad's shoes. His parents had warned him against crossing the road and climbing the cliffs but this is exactly what he had done. It seemed likely that he would be afraid of the consequences. To compound his fears he had been involved in what appeared to be a fatal accident that would not have happened had he been a 'good boy'. Possibly he had been too frightened to go home and headed in the other direction, onto the moor and out towards the hills. We organised the search under those assumptions.

Two hours had by now passed since Lee's final disappearance. Probably he would turn up safe but tearful and chastened. We were reluctant to request a helicopter for what was probably a minor incident and so organised a line search of the moor. Denise and Bobby were passing the foot of the cliffs on their way to higher ground when Bobby picked up Lee's scent. He 'fetched' Denise and climbed onto a ledge about three metres above the ground and barked down at her. Unknown to any of us Lee was keeping quiet because he didn't want to be found. In fact, he had fallen into a gully at just this point and was lying in a wee heap with a broken ankle. Denise assumed that Bobby had seen Chris, who was also at the foot of the cliffs, not far away. She called him away and continued the search further and further away from the, no doubt, relieved Lee.

With darkness approaching we requested the assistance of a helicopter. From the bubble window of the aircraft Lee was easily spotted as we hover-taxied above the cliff. We winched a rescuer down and first aid was applied before winching the two of them up again. Lee had learned a hard lesson that might have been much harder, and Bobby had shown again that his instincts were usually reliable.

Denise described missing Lee as the final straw in her decision to leave mountain rescue. Time and travelling were also factors. She had journeyed all over Scotland to participate in rescues and had been doing so for a long time. This was the year Bobby won Best of Breed at Crufts. Widening and deepening her off-mountain interests she was about to begin her career as a breeder. She decided she had 'moved on' and it was time to go.

We spoke at length about these incidents and more, and it was good to reminisce. She played a hugely positive part in many rescues as did Quinbury Stormdrifter, better known as Bobby, and Bessie before him. The search and rescue dogs are a wonderful resource for mountain rescuers to call on and it is frequently they who make first contact with a casualty. Their nose and instincts add an extra dimension to our own reason and experience, and of course our bonds with them go back through the centuries.

I had not seen Denise for over a year. It was good to talk, and good to know the same warmth is there as always, but memories of Chris do not fade for either of us and I left with a certain melancholy, a feeling that a time in our lives had passed.

EPILOGUE:

THE SEA

Under a bright, blue sky in late May the yacht *Ticoyo* nosed out of Plockton Harbour into the wide outer reaches of Loch Carron.

I had her under power to ease her between the many other yachts and cruisers moored in the bay but, as soon as we were out and into open water, cut the engine, handed the wheel over to my crew of one, a burly hillwalker named Bob, and raised the mainsail. These things done I pushed the wooden tiller into its slot at the stern and steered from there. From my seated position I could see into the cockpit, over Bob's shoulder to the computer navigation, the sounder, and the compass fixed above them. The dinghy as it dragged behind, left a widening trail of wake that flickered and glittered in the sun.

We turned west of north, leaving the lighthouse of Eilean a'Chait to port, freshly whitewashed and bright, then west and south of west, round a scattering of rocky islands, until the Skye Bridge came into sight. Guillemots bulleted across the waves and seals dived from the rocks. Cormorants ducked under the surface. We left the hills of Applecross and the flat plain of Strathcarron behind and the day held more beauty than it seemed possible to absorb, the blues of sky and sea, mountains sharp-edged against the sky, the sun on our faces, the breeze in our hair. At this stage in my development as a sailor I made a point of not venturing out when the wind was more than Force 5, at most 6. On this beautiful day there was no such danger.

Anne and I had sold our last two shops to Boots and I felt that handing them over to my first employer made a nice closing of the circle. There was still quite a lot of tidying to be done, which has travelled roughly parallel to the writing of this book, mostly in my old office with ready access to all the Team's files and records and scrapbooks. At the same time I finally made the decision to have a partial knee replacement. The procedure was carried out at Raigmore Hospital after which Anne and I took a break in Cyprus where I began the rehabilitation process by cycling as far and wide across the island as possible.

After retiring from the pharmacy, and still more importantly the Rescue Team, *Ticoyo* became my second home. I had been fascinated by the coastal waters of Scotland since childhood. In addition to the occasional trips with my father and his employer, the Sloan Line, the family took some of its holidays in steamers down the Clyde, a tradition that was strong in those days, but that increased prosperity and affordable flights to the Continent has ended. When Anne and I moved north with the children we had very little money. Nonetheless, when a 13ft motorised dory, then owned by our friend Raymond, became available at a more or less affordable price we took the opportunity with both hands. The *Hilda May* became a feature of our west coast holidays and our own children's introduction to the sea.

I fell in love with sailing almost at first encounter and very quickly knew I had to have a boat. *Ticoyo* was also owned by Raymond and when he eventually decided to replace her I felt in my heart that the sea, or at least our coastal waters, could go some way to replacing the mountains for me, the mountains whose tops I could no longer reach thanks to my deteriorating knees. No licence is required to sail; there is no test. I boarded her and pushed off.

In fact, I sailed her more in the first season after acquiring her than Raymond had in five years. Soon she became my space, an extension of my fingertips and mind, and I came to think of sailing as mountaineering on water. The comparison might seem tenuous at first, but similar skills are required for both. Awareness of safety and weather were already thoroughly instilled. I was an accomplished navigator on land and comfort-able with radios. Now viewing the mountains from the sea became a new pleasure.

On this occasion it was the mountains that were on my mind. I was still in close contact with the Team. Friendships with the new Team Leader, Willie Anderson, Donnie, now Chairing the committee, and many others continued, and I was gratified by the surge of enthusiasm and energy they brought. Change is usually for the best.

On this weekend some members were staying at the hostel at Torrin on Skye, beside Loch Slapin, for two days of climbing and exploring. The visit would be part social and part exercise, designed to further cement the bonds and personal understandings that are so vital when the going is extreme and lives are at risk. My ambition for the trip, a small one but precious, was to sail into the anchorage and join them for the night.

In the present though, the bridge's graceful arch lay ahead. I picked a line directly under the centre and sailed *Ticoyo* through while Bob scanned the shore with binoculars. The water had more of a chop on it here, with the current picking up through the narrows, but it was nothing that could be described as a problem, far less a hazard, and only served to carry us through.

As we left the narrows behind the breeze picked up and filled the main sail, the only canvas we had up at the time. While Bob kept his binoculars trained on the hills of Skye I found my attention turning to the village of Kyle of Lochalsh on our port side.

As my mother grew older our business was thriving and I found myself able to take a couple of weeks off each year to drive her and my aunt around the Highlands. Thanks to this business success we could stay at good hotels, including one here in Kyle. My sister, Helen, carried the burden of our mother's declining years on a more or less day-to-day basis. I was lucky, sharing mostly good experiences with her, and count them among my life's great privileges. We would drive around the Highlands and across the islands, stopping where we wished to get out of the car and drink deep of the scenery.

By that time Helen was Secretary to Sir Alexander Gibson, conductor of the Scottish National Orchestra. She was indispensable to him and worked from an office in his Glasgow West End home. When we celebrated our mother's 80th birthday among a large gathering of the extended family the last thing she expected was for the great man to lead a group of classical musicians from the, now, Royal Scottish National Orchestra, into the room to play for her.Leaving Bob at the tiller I donned my life jacket to go forward and release the jib and adjust the sheets. The wind carried us along at never more than five knots. It was not speedy, but we were in no hurry, and I wanted to make the southward turn from Lochalsh into the narrows at Kylerhea when the tide was at its most full. At this meeting of waters, when the tides are wrong and the weather doesn't co-operate, there can be considerable turbulence and a skipper can come to grief. Not as dangerous or unpredictable as the notorious Corrievreckan tiderace near Jura, it is nonetheless a passage which requires care. When it was safely accomplished Bob asked me about the letters after my name.

In November 2000 I tossed a letter from the Prime Minister's office across the breakfast table to Anne.

'It's an MBE,' I said, but of course she knew. The Prime Minister's office had enquired of Northern Constabulary if they had a suitable nomination and Sgt Morris MacLeod had asked Chris and Anne for my CV.

That it was offered to the Leader of the Cairngorm Mountain Rescue Team, rather than John Allen, pharmacist, was obvious. On the Team's behalf there could be no question of a refusal, but other thoughts were in my mind. It was one of those occasions when, with a full acceptance that passing time removes the older generations as it ushers in the new, I could not help but say, 'I wish my parents were here.'

I was implicitly sworn to secrecy but felt that Helen should know. She was cruising in the Indian Ocean on the *Queen Elizabeth II* at the time. I faxed her in a not-so-subtle code. 'I have to tell you that the Prime Minister has informed me that the namesake of your ship has requested my presence at the big house.' I meant, of course, Buckingham Palace. She got it first time.

When the news came out the media made a huge and embarrassing fuss and, to my relief, all said the honour was deserved. The BBC, Grampian Television, the press in general, all focused on the Team. 'Mountain Man Flies High', the *Daily Mail* proclaimed at the head of a two-page spread that went on to profile eight other Team Members. As a result I received an astonishing number of cards and letters, some from people going back to my days as a student.

In fact we were invited not to Buckingham Palace but to Holyrood House, the Queen's official residence in Scotland, in July. The location delighted both Anne and me, and we decided we would make the day as much of a family event as we could. By chance we spotted a white stretch limousine in a magazine and decided, then and there, to hire one for the event. We stayed for a couple of days in Edinburgh and, with loads of time to spare, had a champagne-fuelled, chauffeur-driven tour of the city on our way to Holyrood. At Calton Hill we stopped so the chauffeur could take our picture against what we felt was a suitable backdrop, only to be joined by a busload of friendly Japanese tourists.

An official put a little hook into my lapel on our arrival and it was here that Her Majesty hung my medal. Later, along with Joanne and Michael and their partners, Anne's mother and Dougie, our best man, and about 20 others, we adjourned to Mama Roma's for a lunch that went on until after 18.00.

Before reaching Isle Ornsay we arrived at Loch na Dal, a remote inlet edged with a scattering of houses and a hotel, and decided against the more popular moorings. Leaving the lighthouse to port, we entered and dropped anchor. Bob prepared dinner while I put up the stern awning and opened a bottle of wine.

In no hurry the next morning we slept until a reasonable hour. The day was again bright and promising and a breeze blew across the island. Between us we raised the anchor and motored round the loch to put her bow almost directly into the wind while I raised the mainsail. Cutting the engine I took over at the wheel and took her out into the Sound of Sleat.

Leaving Isle Ornsay behind, we made our way rather west of south passing, on the starboard side, the small, coastal villages of Teangue and Armadale, communities that in recent decades have seen a rapid change of population as better-off incomers arrived, mostly from England but also from Lowland Scotland and abroad, while others have left in search of work. Although they come with a certain social cost, these changes have brought not only new blood but new energy and money.

As the morning wore on the strengthening sun demanded a coating of sun block, which we applied with more than one eye on the unique landscape to port. The mainland here is the most fragmented section of the West of Scotland's 2,000-mile coastline. Most especially Loch Hourn, on the north side, and Loch Nevis, to the south, create the peninsula known as Knoydart. Roadless but not trackless, the only ways in are on foot or by boat.

In Knoydart the John Muir Trust has performed what looks like a miracle on Ladhar Bheinn by fencing off Coire Dhorcaill and Coire Li from deer and sheep and attended to drainage. Native trees such as birch and rowan that the Trust regards as pioneer species have sprung up spontaneously, altering the nature of the ground and preparing it for the arrival of oak and pine. A helping hand was given here and there with plantings that had been nurtured from seeds harvested in nearby Barrisdale. Fifteen years after planting the same trees are producing cones and seeds of their own and the future seems assured.

The Trust looks on the venture as one of its most successful but needs to maintain fences against what are still high deer numbers. Following the trees, birds and other wildlife have returned and the quality of the soil continues to improve. Time, it seems, is the wisest investment.

I checked my watch to find we were progressing too slowly.

Putting Bob in charge of the tiller I once again unfurled the jib and *Ticoyo* picked up her pace. Going at it this way, not exactly 'goose-winged', but with more ambition, we were quickly on schedule once again. My ambition was to sail, rather than power, through Loch Slapin's narrows and into its upper reaches below the Black Cuillin outlier, Blaven.

Turning north to round the Point of Sleat we were thankfully still blessed by fine weather, but were becalmed near Ringill, across the water from the abandoned village of Suisnish. The scattering of ruins was plainly visible along the coast, among the remains of the field system. We looked at them for half an hour, speculating on the lives the population of the time must have led, living on a hard landscape and taking from a still more demanding sea.

The breeze picked up again and we sailed to Torrin, also owned by the John Muir Trust. The contrast with the Suisnish landscape was remarkable. Here on the slopes below the Red Cuillin, with Blaven towering across the loch, a living crofting community was situated among lavish stands of hazel and hawthorn. With spring moving into summer the hawthorn was in flower, with loads of buttery white petals basking in the afternoon sun.

Here the Trust has done little to promote regeneration. Nature was adequate to the task herself. The changing rural economy in these parts has reduced sheep numbers, and therefore grazing pressure on a naturally rich limestone soil. Hazel, and to a lesser extent hawthorn, have never been completely removed. In earlier times hazel was to some extent cultivated to provide firewood and materials for creel and basket making and later it hid away behind stone dykes and rockfalls. Only recently when arable use of the land came to an end, and sheep and cattle numbers reduced, did the woodland break cover and extend itself. Now the quality of the soil gradually recovers.

Near the beginning of this book I noted the effects of global warming on the Cairngorms. Close to the end I can point to at least the beginnings of regeneration and renewal.

*

I dropped anchor close to the hostel, glassed the shoreline and lifted the radio handset.

'Cairngorm Willie, Cairngorm Willie, this is Yacht *Ticoyo*. Do you read? Over.'

There was a click and crackle. 'Yacht *Ticoyo*, Yacht *Ticoyo*, this is Cairngorm Willie hearing you loud and clear. Over.'

'We will be coming ashore if you are ready to receive. We have supplies and could use a hand.'

'We have all we need here, Yacht *Ticoyo*. Curries from Aviemore Tandoori, beer, coffee. You are welcome as ever.'

Another crackle and click interrupted us. 'Cairngorm Willie, Cairngorm Willie, this is Cairngorm Heather – can we have two lattes and a double chocolate muffin delivered to the Clach Glas Ridge, please? We're sitting here looking down on you, *Ticoyo*!'

At that we moved to a more social radio channel and chatted for a few minutes more. By the time Bob and I waded ashore the Team was ensconced in the hostel, the curries were heating in the oven and one or two beers were being opened.

Two years previously Heather had acquired Millie, a smooth-haired collie of working stock from a local farm. Both had worked hard at training and Millie had qualified a couple of months previously. Now in her SARDA waistcoat she gave us a well-mannered, cold-nosed greeting and went off to lie in a corner, exhausted from her day on the hills

It is a qualification Heather can put beside the Mountain Instructor Certificate she gained from Plas-y-Brenin, the highest possible British qualification. Our Rescue Team has eight such members at the time of writing. With the even higher international qualification, *Union Internationale des Associations de Guides Montagnes*, held by John Lyall, Eric Pirie, Jonathan Preston and Alastair Cain, all professional mountain guides, this makes us one of the highest qualified Mountain Rescue Teams in Britain, a fact in which we take great pride.

Willie and Donnie were locked in banter as usual, this time with Willie speculating over Donnie's recovery from a shoulder operation. Years of working with a hammer, of pushing himself past normal limits in many ways, had taken their toll on his shoulder. 'Could be *finito*,' Willie said wryly.

'I think you will find this is a *comeback*,' replied the offended Donnie.

Since his day had included 900m of ascent, 2km of narrow ridge walking, and the upper body strain inherent in a dangling-in-space free abseil, it did indeed look like a comeback. Willie knew this of course, the corners of his mouth gave him away.

Mountain rescuers, probably everywhere but certainly in the Cairngorm Team, develop a sense of humour that can be too easily seen as flippant and even cruel. Instead it is a necessary defensive reflex, a sort of psychic armour that is occasionally pierced by tragedies involving children or a high degree of suffering. Writing this I recall the night of talking Roger Wild and I spent after Helen Mallinson's death. In units of two or three, this is how a good Team self-heals. We have never had need of counsellors or psychiatrists, but beer might be involved or a fine malt whisky.

We sat down to eat and more bottles were opened. Aside from Bob and me, and of course Millie, there were ten rescuers present. Tired by the day's climbing they were not too tired to contemplate more of the same tomorrow. I thought about them as people and of their qualities. Willie has an acerbic wit he uses to keep people on their toes. Donnie is a skilled joiner with his own business. Heather, in addition to being a SARDA handler, is a ranger with Cairngorm Mountain. Fran Pothecary is an Outdoor Access Officer for the Cairngorms National Park Authority. New member Leo Crofts is that modern phenomenon, the house-husband. Alastair Cain is a professional mountain guide, a superb climber. Gordon Stewart is a teacher but also a very serious runner. Before retiring Roger Gaff was an instructor at Lagganlia. Hamish Wylie works with medical equipment for the Health Service. Peter Finlayson is a Quality Improvement Officer in Education.

All of them are superbly fit, with Alastair the climber and Gordon the runner lean as greyhounds. All are experienced and highly trained with some, like Heather the dog handler, having special talents. For some time Bob had been speaking to them in ones and twos and, at one point, I heard him ask Hamish how he felt when he had to miss 'a recent rescue' through immovable work commitments.

To say the least, Hamish was disappointed. He, like the others, is a highly motivated individual who has brought his love of the mountains into our specialised discipline and added to it physical and mental training, almost all his recreational time and every kind of preparedness possible. When a casualty has faced possibly the worst experience in life, perhaps even the end of it, almost invariably with great courage, rescuers will often refer to their sense of privilege at being involved and given the opportunity to do their best. There is also an adrenaline surge associated with rescue, and that is a necessary part of their make-up because an element of danger is inherent within every set of rescue circumstances. All of this amounts to a sense of belonging to the Mountain Rescue Team that has, as its underside, a feeling of exclusion when a call-out cannot be answered.

They are a varied bunch, as all rescuers are – everywhere – but their principal characteristic is reliability. When asked to turn out all will do so if they can, and it takes a lot to stop them. They turn out knowing the possibility of injury is real, giving rescue priority over the normal course of their jobs, placing strains on marriages and family, again and again working against time in terrible conditions only to cope with the disappointment of a casualty who is already lost. Sound Team finances mean they are as well equipped and trained as possible. Otherwise their rewards amount to weekends like this, sometimes in other parts of Britain, sometimes as far away as Spain, the occasional rewarmed curry and a bottle of beer after a rescue, and Willie Anderson's sharp tongue to keep them alert. For all these reasons and more they are the best of, and best possible, friends.

Time wore on and I became aware of the turning tide. Bob and I made our way back to the dinghy and *Ticoyo*. On board I poured him a Glenmorangie, and from nowhere remembered how, every year on the anniversary of Chris Barley's death, those of us who loved him gather in a bothy to share stories about our good friend and drink to his memory.

'What did you ask when you got them on their own?' I said.

'I asked how mountain rescue had changed them.'

'And?'

'Developing expertise in turn increased confidence, which I would not have said was ever lacking in any of them. They most valued comradeship, but also said they had learned not to be critical. Accident is largely a matter of circumstance, of being in the wrong place at the wrong time. They said it made them more forgiving, more accepting – if you like, more "allowing". They were uniform in this.'

I was tired and decided to turn in, but Bob was still engrossed in the night and remained by the tiller. I went below, leaving him with the Glenmorangie, the silhouette of Blaven against the turning stars, a cool breeze on his face, the splash of a fish on the loch, perhaps with an otter in pursuit, the rich smell of hawthorn and whatever memories of his own all this might evoke. At one point I looked out and saw him tip his glass towards Old Lady Moon.

'Thank you, Ma'am,' he said.

Beyond our skills and strength, expertise and experience, we must accept the world as it is, including change however tragic. All we can do is mind how we go on the earth and look after each other and, if we cannot turn sadness into joy, or death back into life, friendship and remembering will have to do.

TEN YEARS AFTER

1. Rescue from the Air

A lot will change in ten years, mostly, but not always, for the better. As I write these additional chapters I am looking at a small piece of history. On my desk is an ornamental cut-glass plaque in the shape of a rock. It is inscribed:

Presented to
JOHN ALLEN
Happy Retirement
From All Your Friends In The
NORTHERN CONSTABULARY
2007

For me it represents the excellent and mutually supportive relationship which existed between the Cairngorm Mountain Rescue Team and the local police both at Aviemore and Inverness.

In April 2013 all police forces in Scotland were amalgamated into one organisation called Police Scotland with one Chief Constable. From my point of view, the loss of Northern Constabulary, and with it the loss of mountain rescue's local connection, was bound to be diminishing. For example, recently, in response to a 999 call, an ambulance arrived at the Cairngorm Ski Ground car park looking for a climber with a suspected broken leg. After some discussion with ski patrol staff it became apparent that the call had come from an injured climber in the relatively inaccessible Coire an Lochain and was therefore a task for the Cairngorm Mountain Rescue Team. The rescue was begun some two hours after the original call. My belief is that had the local police station been involved, this inconvenient delay would not have occurred. Rapid and accurate communication is essential, and something practical has been lost along with the relationship on the ground. Local knowledge is irreplaceable.

In the decade following the first edition of *Cairngorm John* I kept in touch with the Rescue Team on a regular, if intermittent, basis. In a Team with such a depth of skills and experience my advice was rarely needed, but old habits die hard and I maintained a continuing interest in rescues and developments. I also embarked on a programme of public talks given to a variety of interested organisations, always at their request. These helped to raise the profile of the Team and so it was in my interest to keep up with current activities.

Friendships with Team Members continued. Every summer I would sail around the Western Isles with friends such as Team Leader Willie Anderson, and Donnie Williamson, now a Depute Team Leader. Listening to them and to others, while keeping an ear open for the news, it seemed to me that two dark clouds currently hovered over mountain rescue. One was the continuing frequent requirement to assist mountaineers who had ventured into the winter hills poorly prepared and with inadequate equipment. The other was the change in the helicopter service since its privatisation in 2015. It was to discuss this last point that I drove to the Rescue Centre at Coylumbridge near Aviemore, to meet Willie and Al Gilmour. Willie is now retired from his post as a technical teacher. Al is a professional mountain guide who also serves as the Chair of the Rescue Team committee.

The Rescue Centre itself is in continuous development, and when I arrived preparations were being made to clear ground for a paving contractor to make necessary improvements to the car park. Inevitably, I thought, Donnie Williamson was hard at work clearing overgrown vegetation. Donnie is a powerhouse of a man whose contribution to the Team over a period of nearly 40 years is probably unsurpassed. On top of his steadfast commitment as a Team Member, he has applied his services as a skilled joiner to the Rescue Centre, his wisdom and experience to committee discussions both strategic and tactical, and his support to the bereaved. He has also acted as a mentor to trainee rescuers. About 20 years prior to this visit, he developed and gave leadership to a group who became known as the 'Wee Team', four aspirant Team Members in their mid-teens. Donnie's hard work paid off as illustrated by 'Wee Team' Member Iain Cornfoot who became an accomplished mountaineer and is now, like Donnie, a Depute Leader.

Not only is the Rescue Centre in continuous development but also, as new technology becomes available, innovative equipment is acquired. Three things, however, will remain the same no matter what: the basic unit of mountain rescue will always be the individual boots-on-the-ground Team Member; the second is that support from the air is as valuable to the mountain rescue Leader as it is to a general in battle; the third is Team training which, as a means of sharing information and transferring experience from one mind to another remains unsurpassed. I met Willie and Al around a table beside the shelves of the Christopher Barley Memorial Library, within the Rescue Centre.

June 2017 had been a demanding month, in which one week stood out, and they began by discussing incidents in the Northern Corries, an area first accessed by climbers in the early twentieth century. At that time, they were faced with a long walk in as the road between Aviemore and Cairn Gorm ended at Glenmore. The Northern Corries were therefore much less visited than they are now.

The 1928 edition of the Scottish Mountaineering Club Guide reports that the only definite climb worked out in the Northern Corries of Cairn Gorm was the Fiacaill Ridge, the arête between the two corries, describing it as an 'enjoyable scramble'. This ridge is visible from Aviemore. Various ascents were completed in 1904 but they were not identified or documented. The relevant point to note is that even at this early stage, the rock they found was described as 'broken and vegetated'.

One of the most popular rock routes, first documented in 1954, is Fingers Ridge in Coire an t-Sneachda, which has one or two different technical finishes leading to the plateau at the top. As the route became more popular both in summer and winter the condition of the climb deteriorated. In the 1960s the road from Glenmore was extended into Coire Cas to facilitate the booming skiing industry, and improved access dramatically increased the numbers of climbers. The increased amount of 'traffic' on Fingers Ridge in both summer and winter inevitably resulted in lots of loose rock, making the route even more hazardous.

Ron Walker, a former member of the Cairngorm Mountain Rescue Team, is based locally and provides qualified guiding in mountain sports. In early 2017 he became concerned about the dangerous condition of the route, and in June of that year posted notes on various websites warning of the extreme danger associated with loose rock on Fingers Ridge.

On Saturday 13th June Ron and a climbing partner, Andrew, decided to try to improve the safety of the route and went to Fingers Ridge to attempt to remove areas of loose slabs of rock. They cleared rubble from the first two pitches, but, at the top of pitch three, a large slab slid off with Ron still attached. He describes it as the size of a small fridge. Fortunately, one of his protecting runners held and he remained attached to the rock face, although suspended upside down, 5m below his safety belay. He was struck by one block which injured his right arm, but Andrew managed to attach him to a sling and lowered him to a small ledge.

Andrew phoned the police to report the incident and the Rescue Team along with coastguard rescue helicopter 951 were called out. In misty conditions Team Members were airlifted to just below cloud level from where they walked to the top of the route.

John Lyall was tasked to assess Ron's exact position on the cliff.

To avoid bringing down more loose rock he and Duncan Scott, one of the Team Doctors, abseiled down an adjacent route called Broken Gully and 'pendulumed' across to Ron's location. Duncan, John and Ron were then lowered to the foot of the route where Simon Steer was waiting to receive the casualty. The remaining Team Members stayed well clear of the crag until the manoeuvre was complete. By this time, Ron was close to exhaustion but managed to make his way through the boulder field to the helicopter before being airlifted to Raigmore Hospital.

John Lyall describes this call-out as one of the most dangerous he has ever taken part in, due to the loose rock which fell during the rescue and which bounced off some of the Team Members and the casualty. The whole operation took over 160 hours of Team time and was still only the first incident that week.

Ron would later say publicly: 'A big thanks to Cairngorm Mountain Rescue Team and, in particular, John Lyall and Duncan Scott for risking their necks in a particularly tricky and dangerously loose rescue.'

On the following day a rockfall from Pygmy Ridge inflicted a compound fracture on a walker's thumb. He was escorted out on foot in a rescue that took eight hours. On the 15th a climber fell on Lurcher's Crag and suffered a broken pelvis. This necessitated a close liaison with the helicopter service and a dramatic winch to safety. Eighty-five man hours were expended in this technical rescue. Two days later a fourth rescue involving the Team took place in the heart of the Cairngorms.

Shelter Stone Crag at the west end of Loch Avon is a flat-topped cliff, obvious from the plateau area on the north side of Loch Avon and holds a variety of hard winter and summer routes. To climb here requires a long walk in, either from the Braemar side of the mountains or from the ski ground car park on Cairn Gorm.

In the early afternoon of the 17th a pair of climbers were halfway up a hard technical route called The Needle when the lead climber fell approximately 10m, landing on a ledge. The Braemar Team, on the south side of the Cairngorms, took the call and arranged that a group of rescuers be airlifted with equipment to the crags above the accident location. This done, Kenny Lawson in Braemar Control called Willie Anderson, to inform him of the ongoing technical rescue in this area that is held in common, more or less, by both Teams. Because of the remote location and the complexity of the rescue, combined with the severity of the casualty's injuries, both Cairngorm and Braemar Teams were required and a massive operation ensued, taking up 240 hours of the combined Teams' time.

Kenny at Braemar asked if the Cairngorm Team could provide a receiving party at the base of the cliffs which are better approached from the north side. He reported that the casualty had a suspected broken pelvis. The Team Members, although wearied and physically depleted by the events of the week, responded to the call-out with their usual stoic enthusiasm. Due to the vertical nature and height of the rock face the Braemar Team, at the top, were unsure of the exact location of the injured climber. The helicopter pilots were asked to assist and hover-taxied up the cliff face until, when level with the plateau, they pointed their nose in the general direction of the casualty. The Braemar Team then set up belays and lowered two Team Members.

It is often difficult to locate a casualty who cannot be seen from above and, as sometimes happens, they missed him. Meanwhile, to keep things moving, the helicopter airlifted three Cairngorm Team Members with additional equipment to join the Braemar group at the top of the crag. John Lyall attached himself to a safety rope and, by hanging over the edge, was able to pinpoint the exact location of the injured climber. The Teams reset the belay and John Armstrong and Chris Robinson, another of our doctors, were lowered. The helicopter crew returned to Glenmore Lodge to await further developments.

Chris and John arrived at the casualty four and a half hours after his fall and Chris did his triage assessment *in situ*. Pain was felt in the pelvis and chest with even minimal body movement. Morphine and other analgesia were administered. John Lyall was then lowered with the stretcher and a vacuum mattress which was deflated to immobilise spine and pelvis. The stretcher was lowered to the foot of the crag. All this was achieved on a narrow ledge, at height and in difficult conditions. As the casualty was being lowered to the foot of the crag, the helicopter was recalled and flew into Glen Avon, setting down about half a kilometre from the foot of the route. This necessitated a stretcher carry with the casualty who was then transferred to the waiting helicopter and flown to Raigmore Hospital in Inverness. It was by now just after midnight although, thankfully, in summer conditions.

A 500m stretcher carry should not be underestimated. It was extremely demanding for the Team Members who were already tired at the start of the rescue. It was also rough on the casualty, to say the least, and risked exacerbating his pelvic and potential spinal injuries.

As was becoming all too frequent, service constraints that were sometimes interpreted differently by different crews added much unnecessary work to the already tired Team Members. In this case the aircraft put down in the safe location they had used earlier.

They were also obliged to decline a request to return to 'clean up the hill', which means assisting with the evacuation of the Teams and their equipment. It is usually accepted that a mission is not completed until all personnel are returned safely to base. This principle applies to most jobs but in mountain rescues the requirement is more acute.

The decision by ARCC to request that the aircraft must return to base in the above scenario would not have been an easy one for the crew to carry out. However, the chain of command and the contract restrictions would have to be followed.

The RAF would not have hesitated, they would also have been mindful that this was the fourth prolonged technical rescue in four days, and returning to the rescue base carrying all the equipment would involve a strenuous ascent of 2,000ft, a journey across the plateau, followed by a descent back to the ski area. Probably 25 minutes flying time but at least two and a half hours walking time for the Team Members, with further time required to sort and stow away equipment at the base.

I can only imagine the dismay of the Team Members at the head of Loch Avon, just after midnight, watching their hoped-for lift disappearing down the glen.

Willie Anderson's view, and my own, is that, in these circumstances, a second aircraft should have been sent. In previous times, the aircraft would stand by until the Team was back at base and ready to go again if necessary. Only then would the rescue be considered complete, and that would be the Team Leader's decision.

At the time of the helicopter service privatisation, the new service was promised to be 'the same or better'. Five years down the line, no Rescue Team in the new Independent Mountain Rescue (iSMR) Service would have said that this was the case.

Early in the life of the new search and rescue contract, Willie Anderson tells me he organised no fewer than 25 Team Members to gather at the Rescue Centre for a training exercise with the new Sikorsky 92 aircraft. It was a beautiful day with clear skies when the Team assembled at one of the car parks in the Cairngorm Mountain ski area. This helicopter training exercise, however, was called off with only 15 minutes' notice. The reason given was that 'triggered lightning' was shown as threatening in the Cairngorms.

Triggered lightning is caused by a static charge created by composite materials in the aircraft reacting to particular atmospheric conditions at certain times of the year. This can cause problems with the aircraft. These exact conditions are experienced every winter in the Cairngorms, Lochaber, Glencoe, and Tayside Team areas. There is a computer program used by pilots of S92 aircraft flying out of Shetland and elsewhere which shows areas where triggered lightning may happen, and they are forbidden to fly into these areas unless in cases of emergency. This applies to aircraft from all bases. Triggered lightning is not a new phenomenon, but only in recent years has it been recognised as a dangerous issue.

When the new contract was granted, civilian Mountain Rescue

Teams were not informed of this possibility. This lack of communication only exacerbated an already deteriorating situation. It could also be, however, that the contractor's attention was focused mainly on the sea. The contract was, of course, intended for both sea and mountain rescues. This 'one size fits all' may work better for offshore incidents, it seems, than for those in a mountain environment. Better mountain training and familiarisation for the crews could only improve the situation.

Sea and mountain rescues present very different challenges. Flying through steep-sided glens, or close to rock faces, as our colleagues in the RAF did routinely, maintaining stability while winds whip around mountains and through exposed passes, calls for different skills than those required to winch up from a sea vessel even in gusty conditions. A different approach from that of the RAF was bound to be taken by a commercial contractor. Perhaps a single contract for these two functions needs closer examination.

On a more positive note, the Sikorsky 92 is roomier than the Sea King and has a shelf suitable for a stretcher and casualty that means less discomfort and makes it easier for a doctor to monitor the casualty's condition.

Under the terms of their contract, the aircrew's focus is on 'persons in distress', rather than on co-operation with the Rescue Team under the Team Leader's authority. Therefore, when the 'person in distress' is handed over to a medical team and in a place of safety, their responsibility is at an end. Any further activity could be considered 'additional to the contract', but this is hardly conducive to a co-operative attitude. It also raises the next major point of concern about the privatised service.

The contractor has argued that crews have to be quickly back at base to prepare for the next call-out. This argument, of course, is more relevant to the Mountain Rescue Teams who, after a long rescue, must go back to the day job *as well as* be ready for the next call-out. They do not have the luxury of resting in the superb accommodation suite at Bristow's Inverness Rescue Base.

The idea of 'persons in distress' raises a further question: can a fatality, a casualty who has been declared 'deceased' reasonably be described as a 'person in distress'? Obviously not, and crews cannot fly such casualties out under the terms of the agreed contract, unless a liberal interpretation of the rules is applied. As a result the Rescue Teams have often been obliged to stretcher bodies out over considerable distances.

On this subject, murmurings of discontent were also coming from Lochaber Mountain Rescue Team. Scotland's Mountain Rescue Teams generally cover vast areas of remote mountainous regions. Lochaber MRT, Scotland's busiest Team, probably most famed for call-outs on Ben Nevis, is no exception.

The Knoydart Peninsula is part of its beat, one of the wildest and most inaccessible parts of the Scottish Highlands, with very few roads or Land Rover tracks but home to some of the finest Munros and Corbetts. To succeed in getting to the top of most of them requires more than one day and night. The small village of Inverie is only accessible by boat from Mallaig, or by the long walk in from the road end at the west end of Loch Arkaig or, again, from the road end at Kinloch Hourn. The Old Forge Inn, Scotland's remotest pub, sits at the mouth of Loch Nevis and is a popular starting point for some hillwalkers.

In the last ten years I have come to know this area well from the sea; sailing into Loch Hourn and anchoring near the remote Barrisdale Bothy or into Loch Nevis and up through the Kyles to Sourlie's Bothy, anchoring near Camusrory Lodge. Using Finlandia as a base, some of my friends have hillwalked on Sgurr na Ciche while I remained on board enjoying the view. I have enjoyed a completely different perspective of these mountains since my hillwalking days.

In May 2018, Lochaber MRT received a call from the police reporting a male hillwalker missing, possibly somewhere between Knoydart and Glenfinnan. He had been reported overdue from a trip to Sgurr a Choire-bheithe, a very remote Corbett in Knoydart.

The coastguard aircraft was already in the area on another mission when Lochaber asked them to overfly the area.

The S92 searched the approximate route and located a body in a gully which was inaccessible to the aircraft. The crew returned to the Lochaber base and four Team Members came on board to recover the body. At this point ARCC instructed the pilots not to continue. The dialogue was overheard by the astonished rescuers on board. The two pilots questioned the instruction which, if obeyed, would mean the Rescue Team undertaking a 14-mile (22km) trek to the location carrying an empty stretcher and the same length of return with a loaded stretcher. At least 20 more personnel would be required to assist. The time taken would have been eight to 12 hours and possibly more.

I am not sure of the further conversation between the pilots and ARCC but thankfully the aircraft flew the Team to Knoydart, returning with the body in an operation taking less than an hour. This was an extreme example but by no means an isolated one. In the not too distant past application of the same rule has meant a 20km carry from the Monadhliath hills at Laggan, rendering the Team Members unavailable to respond to any further call-out for the duration of the long walk.

As a result of these incidents, and others with sister Rescue Teams, the iSMR wrote a letter to the police in July 2018, which was not acknowledged although a reply came from the Department of Transport in September stating: 'No action possible'. This was perhaps not surprising as the MP involved in this decision, Nus Ghani, has a constituency in the well-known mountain area of Wealdon in East Sussex and cannot be expected to show an informed approach to the problem.

The Rescue Teams understood that the contract was unlikely to be altered within its current duration period. However, any subsequent contract, or contracts, could and should be drafted with a clearer understanding of the unique demands of the volunteer Mountain Rescue Service.

Frustrated in the extreme, in October of the same year, the iSMR distributed a carefully worded press release, also posting it on the Lochaber Team's Facebook page. The main thrust being that there was an unwillingness by the contractor to help recover dead bodies from the hill and also a further unwillingness to help Team Members to return safely to base with their gear.

The following extracts are worth including here regarding the removal of bodies from the hill. The italics are mine:

> '…one incident where volunteer teams had to undertake an incredibly dangerous lower of the stretcher down a narrow gully, dodging rockfall while the aircraft was instructed to stand by. *The helicopter was only to react in the event one of the rescuers was injured.*'

Again,

> '…one team had to carry all of the required equipment to access and then recover a body from thousands of feet up a mountain, surrounded by the constant risk of rockfall. Even though assistance was requested *it was again instructed not to assist*, not even to carry the equipment.'

Over the following weekend the Facebook post reached over 600,000 people with some 212,000 engagements.

As a result of this huge support, questions were asked in the Scottish Parliament, and a large amount of press attention was given. Bristows requested a meeting in their Inverness Airport Rescue Headquarters, which Willie attended with other iSMR Team Leaders, meeting senior pilots but not senior headquarters staff. Internal discussions had persuaded Bristows that the matter was better dealt with at local (in this case, Scottish) level.

It is not difficult to imagine the pressure that such strong negative publicity had exerted not only on the company and also on the crews, but frank talking and openness led to a better understanding between the parties and a resolve to interpret the contract in a more liberal fashion. Between then and my time of writing there followed a marked improvement in relations and service, with Team Leaders being respected as the experts on rescue requirements in the mountain environment, and support when clearing the hill.

Much later, after my visit to the Rescue Centre, I visited the private coastguard facility at Inverness Airport, and was shown around this impressive facility by chief pilot John McIntyre. From him I learned that two S92 rescue aircraft were due to be replaced by two Augusta Westland 189 helicopters. Although smaller, these aircraft have more powerful engines and are equipped with the latest state-of-the-art technology. Meeting and talking with John and his crew members, I was impressed by their professionalism and commitment, and felt confident that, with contractual and technical challenges properly met, a good partnership with the rescue service was at least possible. This impression was confirmed when, in January, two climbers got into difficulty in Coire an t-Sneachda.

The lead climber had fallen on the technical climbing route, Doctor's Choice, and sustained a leg injury. His companion remained on the crag and called the emergency services. Cairngorm Mountain Rescue Team and Rescue 951 both attended. Due to the high avalanche risk and turbulent conditions the aircraft could not venture too close to the cliff but instead hovered higher up. The pilot used all 90m of his capacity to lower the winchman. The injured climber was thereafter transported to Raigmore Hospital and the Rescue Team assisted the remaining climber off the hill.

In a press release the next day the coastguard helicopter crew said: '…this was a great team effort between us and the Cairngorm Mountain Rescue Team, who we think are real heroes for bearing the conditions so well and taking the second casualty off the mountain.'

This seems to me to be significant, and I look forward to the day when mountain rescue is given its own bespoke agreement with whatever service provider is chosen and hopefully a return to the sort of attitudes and relationships that led to my much appreciated gift from the Northern Constabulary.

2. New Technology

Of the many changes mountain rescue has undergone since I stepped down, none has surprised me more than the introduction of the Can-Am all-terrain vehicles. Usually known simply by its manufacturers name, the Can-Am is an enclosed, tracked vehicle, which travels on either small wheels or tracks, depending on the nature of the terrain. All earlier models of such snow-adaptable vehicles we tried were slowed and stopped by snow building up in the moving parts, by being unstable on steep ground, or by repeatedly breaking down. One such tracked vehicle had to be lifted twice from Coire an t-Sneachda by the Sea King. A second, eight-wheeled vehicle called an argocat (used on the grouse moors and nicknamed by gamekeepers as tupperware ponies) was of some use but left the driver exposed and was not capable of carrying sufficient equipment.

At last though, the Team has found machines it can trust, albeit in limited circumstances. Already used and recommended by others, the Cairngorm Team purchased two vehicles manufactured by Can-Am: the Commander and the smaller Traxter. On wheels, the Traxter is ideal for quickly bringing in a casualty from, say, Rothiemurchus Forest. This casualty might have suffered a heart attack or twisted an ankle or knee. Its best use though, is to get the Team and its equipment over rough or steep ground to where they can continue on foot to the accident site.

On tracks both can reach Point 1141 near Cairn Gorm. Point 1141 being 1,141m above sea level, a satellite summit of Cairn Gorm to the west, which is clearly visible from Aviemore High Street on a good day. The large cairn on the summit is an established landmark that serves to guide hill-goers down onto the safe route towards the ski ground car park. From this location the vehicles can provide both rescuers and casualty with a more or less comfortable downhill ride to safety. They would be taken beyond 1141 only with great reluctance as the likelihood of getting stuck would be too great. After 1141, it's quicker to walk.

The Traxter, unlike the larger Challenger, can take a stretcher so, sadly and all too often, the vehicle is used to recover bodies, for which its design adapts admirably.

When Donnie interrupted our discussion on helicopters, and tea and biscuits were duly consumed in best bothy fashion, Al took me into the Team's new extended garage to let me see these vehicles beside one of the Land Rovers, now decked out with the Team's new branding (more on that in the next chapter). Impressive to look at, they have almost the appearance of a Mars rover. The Traxter can carry six people comfortably, with equipment in the back, and if necessary seven, and it costs about half of the Land Rover. The Land Rover is still a tough vehicle though, that can reach most places, although not the lip of the Cairngorm Plateau in winter conditions.

The Traxter has already proved its worth, one such occasion being on the New Year holiday before my visit, when two experienced hillwalkers, a couple with their collie dog, bit off more than they could chew on a long holiday walk (the couple that is, not the collie). Their proposed route took them from their caravan at Glenmore campsite along the wide track from Glenmore Lodge to near Ryvoan Bothy. A southwards turn then took them, still on the track and good paths, along the approach to Bynack More through Strath Nethy.

This is where the real challenge started because this strath barely deserves the name. Usually, straths are wide U-shaped valleys, cut by glaciers, with plentiful views to either side. Strath Nethy is more of a downward slash through the mountains: narrow, well populated with heathers and stubby trees, scattered with boulders dropped by the retreating glacier. In summer it presents a real challenge to fit young walkers; in winter, an exhausting, time-consuming trek. The collie will probably have loved the rough going but would have burned off more energy than it could afford.

They intended then to climb to The Saddle between Bynack More and Cairn Gorm, a location that gives tremendous views into the glen and across to Beinn Mheadainn and Shelter Stone Crag. From there they planned to descend into Glen Avon to walk along the loch side path before re-ascending via Coire Raibert to the Cairngorm Plateau, returning over the mountain summit, past the ski areas, and back to the campsite. This would be a demanding walk for most people. Whether by good fortune or good foresight, they carried a bivvy bag.

When darkness fell and no lights came on in their caravan at Glenmore Caravan Park their neighbouring caravanners called the police and the rescue began at 18.00. No mobile phone connection could be made.

Under the new, privatised regime, the rescue aircraft is termed Rescue 951, and by 22.00 it was flying over Strath Nethy, Bynack More and Loch Avon. Low cloud meant that visibility was limited. Willie sent a Rescue Team up the hill on the Traxter via the ski area thinking, possibly, they would come across them on the ascent, but no. The police then gained access to the caravan but found no further illuminating information.

At 23.15, the crew of 951 flew over the area around the refuge at Fords of Avon, with the notion that the pair may have taken a wrong turn. Again, no joy, and they returned to the intended route. Not long after, they were able to report footprints (and paw prints) in the snow around Coire Raibert.

Confusingly, the Rescue Team found a dog lead at Point 1141, which proved to be the same dog's, left when the couple were there a few days earlier.

Wind was varying between 15 and 30mph, snow was described as 'dusting'. Footprints and paw prints were found and followed for about ten minutes before snow filled them in. The Team fired flares. Simon Steer drove the Traxter into Coire Cas to check for lights descending the hill. All to no effect. Even armed with 951's reports of footprints the Rescue Team drew a blank, and Willie eventually called them back to the Rescue Centre at 05.00 on the morning of the 2nd to take what rest they could.

At 08.00, before first light, to be on the hill as the sun rose, they were heading out again, not much rested.

At 09.45, the crew of 951 reported sight of walking poles near the top of Coire Raibert. Due to avalanche risk the aircraft could not land or winch, but at last the casualties had been located. Other elements of the search, around the corrie rims and on the plateau, were called off.

The walk up Strath Nethy had demanded more of them than they had expected, taking much more time than they had prepared for. To make things worse, in the course of this strenuous climb the woman's head torch failed. They then proceeded with the man advancing what he thought was a reasonable distance using his own head torch, before turning to light her way to him. This, of course, slowed them even more.

In this manner they made their way to The Saddle, now in a state of considerable fatigue but probably short of exhaustion, where they dropped to the loch side and followed the path to Coire Raibert. From there they ascended as far as they could before stopping to bivouac for the night in temperatures that would descend to minus 20 degrees, allowing for wind chill. They had spent the night in the bivvy bag, with their feet in their rucksacks and with the dog between them to keep them warm. The dog, in fact, may have saved their lives.

The Rescue Team escorted them to the summit of Cairn Gorm where the Traxter was waiting for them with food and hot drinks, a great relief for the woman especially. Our doctor diagnosed her as hypothermic and gave his opinion that she would not have survived a second night in the open, even with the help of the heroic collie. The Traxter probably did not save the couple's lives but it certainly shortened their ordeal and speeded their recovery. It also preserved the energy of our rescuers. Three hundred hours of mountain rescue time had been expended to good effect, much of it captured on the Team's new Go-Pro cameras.

The Traxter proved its value then, as it has on other occasions, but like all innovations it has its limits. The basic unit of mountain rescue, on which all else depends, is still the mountain rescuer, the individual within the Team, and always will be.

Before we left the garage, Al showed me the Team's Ski-Doo. Similar to a motor cycle, it takes one or two Team Members as driver and passenger and flies across the snow at a great rate. The public probably knows these vehicles best from when they were used to chase the Pierce Brosnan version of James Bond across a frozen lake in *Die Another Day*. They are less stable than a four-wheel or tracked vehicle and can turn over quite easily. Al said something else that was interesting in its implications: they can 'tempt into dangerous places'. They are not often used.

Video from the Team's Go-Pros, discreetly edited, was used to inform the public of the rescue and enlarge the Team's public footprint. Innovated since my departure, these cameras were purchased around the time that our sponsored walks came to an end. Costs for the walks, including such things as bus hire, had become too great against the amount of money raised. Considering the months of organising and effort, on top of normal rescue work, and an increase in income from other sources, the committee decided to end them.

The Go-Pros, surprisingly, take up at least some of the slack. Some wear them on their helmets, some on chest harnesses. Now, in the era of iPads and phones, of websites and podcasts, the moving picture is more valued than ever before, especially by BBC and ITV journalists with whom relationships remain very sound. The Team's relationship with the press has always been a positive one and I am glad it has continued after my departure. Willie shares a Dropbox with several media outlets and a quick edit, upload and download at the far end can put details of the rescue before a waiting public more quickly than ever before.

You might ask how this raises funds. The answer is that the

higher profile of the Team draws in donations. Trust funds are often looking for suitable charities to place their money with, and few are as public-friendly, sympathetic and easily understood in their purpose as mountain rescue. After a recent rescue, Al took a call from a fund executor and, as a result, a new radio system was paid for outright and almost immediately.

When Al and I returned from the garage, Iain Cornfoot joined us. One of the most committed rescuers of the present era, Iain is a lean six-footer in his mid-thirties. Mentored by Donnie Williamson as part of the Wee Team, he has now racked up many hundreds of hours of rescue time. He is Depute Leader to Willie and a likely candidate for the big job on that distant day when Willie decides to stand down.

Iain is a qualified helicopter pilot but has a number of other occupations: on North Sea oil rigs when rope access is required, with his own first-aid company which practises on the hill, as head of Cairngorm Mountain's winter ski patrol, flying his drone for television programmes. He is not often bored. His subject for the day though, was the new technology of drones. Its usage for mountain rescue, he says, is still in its infancy but also in rapid development.

There is no formal qualification for being a drone pilot, a fact that can make helicopter pilots more than a little nervous. That is, pilots such as Iain himself; he is both poacher and gamekeeper. Not every drone enthusiast appreciates that a drone striking a helicopter could bring the craft down. Shared space is therefore risk space. In the absence of any formal qualification to fly an Unmanned Aerial Vehicle, some of the manufacturers run their own courses. Iain has been through one with a particularly stiff written section, one of three in the Team to have done so. He also has his own drone, as has Chris Stewart, who generously supplied the photographic image used on this edition's jacket. An excellent photographer, particularly of wild places, Chris acquired his for that purpose.

Coming from an aviation background, as Iain does, assists in the understanding of the drone's place in the aerial environment and, when using them for mountain rescue purposes, a combination of aviation and mountaineering experience such as his is vital. An inexperienced drone owner turning up to 'lend a hand' would be turned away politely.

Willie strongly insists that the drone is just another tool in mountain rescue, and certainly not the grand answer to all search and rescue. He suspects they may be better suited for non-mountain searches, such as for missing persons in forests, or drowned persons in rivers, where weather conditions are likely to be less extreme.

A drone can be controlled remotely, to a distance of about 8km, but safety requirements demand that they never be out of the pilot's sight, regardless of what can be seen from the camera. Were this not so, certain kinds of search, in good weather conditions, could be carried out from the safety and comfort of the Rescue Centre. Five hundred metres distance and 100m above the ground are the effective limitations. Allowing that much mountain rescue is necessarily carried out in difficult conditions and remote locations, drone searches are more limited than most members of the public realise.

Within those limitations though, they can perform wonders. For example, filters can be applied to the cameras to search out individual colours. If a casualty is known to be wearing a red jacket it can pick out red. Soon, according to Iain, they will be able to navigate through trees and so search in forests more quickly and thoroughly than a team of rescuers. Already they can lock onto phone signals, provided that the phones are turned on. Also, they can detect their own radar signals when they bounce back from the Recco (reflective) strips already featuring on many weatherproof jackets. Several metres of snow present no barriers to this amazing technology. By measuring the decay of the reflected radar they can estimate the depth. With this facility, many hours of probing can be saved.

The Cairngorm Mountain Rescue Team uses drones only with considerable caution, and not at all where helicopters have already been called out. Weather is the great limitation, with a wind speed

limit of about 20mph (32kph) and within the pilot's circle of visibility which may not be all that wide. Iain's personal drone weighs
less than a kilogram and can be carried in his rucksack. With 951
on the ground, it would have been ideal for the Shelter Stone Crag
rescue described in the previous chapter. Iain could have flown
it over the edge while watching its progress on an iPad, possibly
even a phone, and located the casualty precisely. Time would have
been saved in both the first descent, which missed, and John Lyall's
exploratory descent.

It doesn't take a lot of imagination to see future drones establishing communication and even carrying in supplies. Perhaps
they will deliver those missing maps that might have 'blown away'
and stay to watch the casualty navigating out. 'Your map, sir! Hot
drinks, ma'am!' That day might come but has not yet arrived.

Already some are in use that are as big as cars. Smaller drones,
such as Iain's, are quite vulnerable, where larger drones are more
robust and might deploy two cameras. So, they can deploy both
night vision and infrared, bringing some helicopter qualities to a
handier, not to say Lilliputian, size. Regulations are developing
along with the technology and, from March 2019, larger drones
must be registered. New restrictions are being brought in, such as
no deployment near airports.

On the necessity of maintenance, Al points out that the drones
need frequent attention particularly after use. Therefore, it seems
that an individual pilot is best to maintain his or her own drone,
keeping it in tune for immediate use and having the best 'feel' for
his or her machine.

I came out of our discussion feeling that the future had been
pointed out to me but that much development and practice were
required before unmanned aircraft would replace rescuers and
helicopters. Unlike the next modern miracle Iain would introduce
me to, they had not arrived fully formed.

The four of us, Willie, Iain, Al and I adjourned to the control room,
with its two pilots' chairs and array of screens and microphones,

to discuss the software known as SARLOC: Search and Rescue Location. Devised by a rescuer named Russell Sore, in Wales, it can fix on a casualty's smartphone if they will only click on a link that the Team sends by text. With that done the casualty's location can be tied down to a 100m square. Willie has, on more than one occasion, talked casualties off the hill. If they have a compass, he can give a bearing from their location (which they will be unsure of) to the nearest path. Otherwise, the Team can go directly to them. If this could have been deployed on the New Year rescue described earlier in this chapter, the couple would have been saved many hours of distress and the Team would have been saved nearly 300 hours of rescue time.

The requirement for the casualty to click on the text is not due to a technical necessity incidentally; it is in recognition of data protection legislation. The Team can circumvent this legislation by appealing to the police authority much higher up the chain than the officers they normally deal with, but time and trouble, as well as uncertainty over the outcome, mean it is not normally worthwhile. The value afforded to data protection in the modern era, means that phone apps have been a mixed blessing.

As well as providing that vital lock-on capacity, with immediate voice connection, almost all climbers and walkers now carry phones with map software included. With a touch sensitive screen, scale can be distorted. Batteries have limited life, especially in cold conditions. With all this technology, map and compass skills are as necessary as ever. The more things change the more they stay the same, except that climbers now are of a generation that has its nose pointed at a phone screen all the time and puts its trust in what it sees.

More than a little impressed by the technological wonders that were carrying mountain rescue on from where it was when I left, I asked the group if they thought that any lives had been saved by these developments. Lives that would have been lost ten years before. The answer from all four was, 'probably not', but many hours of search time and casualty discomfort had undoubtedly been saved, and more technical improvement would surely come along.

What then, have the most significant developments been? Al replied for all: none of the above.

'The most significant developments are the improvements in mountain weather and avalanche forecasting, which become more accurate with every passing year, and the constant revision of information available on websites and phone apps. The great thing is for walkers and climbers to build regular, daily and more often, visits to these sites into their planning, and to build this information into their choice of targets, means of approach and the equipment they carry.

'They might keep in mind the famous "Three Ds": Description (of the journey), Distance (how far there; how far back), Direction (map and compass, of course). To those they might add another two: Duration (how long there; how long back), and Destination (don't forget just what you are trying to achieve). Use these to plan before you go on the hill and keep an eye on the conditions, day by day, as your adventure approaches.

'There are several constantly revised weather websites and apps available, such as those of the Mountain Weather Information Service and the Scottish Avalanche Information Service, that should be referred to every day on the run-up. They are tremendously specific to area and location, so don't rely on someone else's experience from the previous week. Your experience will be different. Don't rely on an account you read on a website. If the weather was wonderful then, and gave fine views, you may be faced with wind-driven rain or even white-out. Real guidebooks, such as those published by the Scottish Mountaineering Club are more reliable than websites. Expert opinion will always be better than hearsay.

'Build all this into your systems, it gets easier every time you do it, and your interpretation of the information will become increasingly refined. Regularly consulting these websites, added to direct experience and reading makes you a more self-reliant mountaineer or hillwalker.'

He went on to tell another story, again from that busy October, which effectively closed what had been for me a very rewarding visit:

'The young couple had come from the south, enthusiastic but inexperienced hillwalkers who were accustomed to a softer land-scape than the Cairngorms. Nonetheless, they had read website accounts and saw nothing especially daunting in an ascent of Ben MacDhui from the car park at the ski area on Cairn Gorm. Their planning was minimal and mostly reliant on an account they had read on a website that told of fine views from one special location. Intending to set out from the car park at 09.00 they in fact left nearer 13.00 without maps, compasses or torches. Simple arithmetic on the basis even of the time given on the website would have told them they would be out in darkness. They did have Google Maps on their phones.

'They succeeded in reaching the summit but became disorien-tated and exhausted on the way back. In the woman's words during our debrief at the Rescue Centre, "We went up the tourist route and came back the professional route. We were supposed to be coming down, but there were a lot of ups", which would confuse the inexperienced. In low visibility they had found themselves (unknowingly) in Coire Raibert in darkness. Already worried, they phoned the police who asked us to help. Thanks to their phone we were able to locate them on SARLOC and a Team was sent to walk them out, which they did under their own steam.

'They had come to the Cairngorms with inadequate gear, without maps or torches, and set out late without considering the likelihood, certainty in this case, of being benighted. A week before, they had checked the weather for their prospective day but not checked it again. This is my point about easily accessible information: forecasts should be checked every day on the run-up. In fact, the weather they encountered had been exactly as expected on that day, but they chose to rely on week-old, stale information.

'It was a classic case of enthusiasm without ability, but thankfully no lasting harm and, you know, there was a delightful naivety about their approach. We all liked them. I think they reminded us of the hillwalkers that many of us have been, respectful to the landscape and wildlife, a pleasure to speak to and properly appreciative of our help. They had a lot to learn but were exactly the sort of people we would want to meet on the hill and to encourage. I hope they come back many times.'

3. A new beginning

Late in the year 2015 an event took place which largely went unobserved by the Scottish public. However, in Scotland's mountaineering circles, blogs mushroomed discussing it, stating conclusions informed and uninformed on the subject. I will in this chapter try to give my take on the subject.

Several of the Highland Teams made the decision to form an independent group to better manage their own specific requirements. Independent Scottish Mountain Rescue (iSMR) was founded as a non-profit seeking limited company by the Cairngorm, Lochaber, Glencoe, and Tayside Mountain Rescue Teams.

The motivations for this decision were primarily related to funding and decision-making at committee level of Scottish Mountain Rescue. There was also the increasing separation of roles between the Highland Teams, mainly involved in search and rescue activities in challenging environments, and those Teams more usually concerned with search and rescue in lowland and urban areas. The Highland Teams were outnumbered and often outvoted by the larger committee and therefore felt disenfranchised.

Some of Scotland's Mountain Rescue Teams give the greatest part of their time to literal 'mountain rescue'. That is to say, the activity of accomplishing the rescue of casualties in mountains, frequently by technical means involving ropes, stretchers, helicopters, and long exposure to the elements in hostile environments. Along with these technical rescues would be a fair number of simple walk-outs, a few searches for missing children, and other low-risk activities. The Cairngorm Team is such a group, as are the Glencoe, Lochaber and Tayside Teams, who together now make up Independent Scottish Mountain Rescue (iSMR).

Elsewhere in Scotland some of the other Teams are involved in a greater proportion of rescues which are relatively non-technical and include valley or urban search and rescue. In recent years I watched on television, along with much of the rest of the nation, while Mountain Rescue Teams were deployed by the police to search the Argyll forests in vain for the remains of a suspected murder victim. Again, I watched as another Team was deployed in a search around Edinburgh for a missing child whose remains were later found far distant in Fife. Together, these searches must have consumed many hours of mountain rescue time.

This work is important and obviously of great value to both police and public but is it mountain rescue? Clearly not. With regard to the tension between 'mountain rescue' and 'search and rescue' there is a clear difference between those many hours of searching woodland and urban locations and the many hours expended in actual mountain rescues.

When I joined Cairngorm Mountain Rescue Team in 1972, it had little funding and was very poorly equipped for its growing role. We did, however, receive limited funds from the then Northern Constabulary which helped with expenses for fuel and equipment. Separately from the above, the Teams were, and still are, supplied at no cost with some items of vital equipment such as McInnes stretchers, vacuum mattresses, oxygen equipment and medicines.

As well as my limited mountaineering skills, I brought my well-developed business skills to the Team, and it is a matter of personal satisfaction to me that when I left the Team it had been for many years in a strong financial position. This was achieved initially by applying various fundraising methods and later supplemented by the granting of a modest amount of funding from the Scottish Government which is allocated to and distributed by Scottish Mountain Rescue. The Cairngorm Team takes some credit for this as we initiated and progressed the meetings with the then First Minister of Scotland, Jack McConnell, which led to the awarding of this funding in November 2003.

These joint funds are administered by Scottish Mountain Rescue and distributed to the Scottish Teams using a complex formula which takes account of the number of hours spent on 'search and rescue' among other factors. This seems reasonable but on closer examination it can be seen to be unworkable. The high number of hours logged in searches in urban and woodland areas by some non-Highland Teams completely distorts the funding formula. This had become a source of disagreement at committee level of Scottish Mountain Rescue.

Police Scotland are responsible for all search and rescue activities in Scotland and they rely heavily on the civilian Mountain Rescue Teams to support them in some of their duties. Mountain Rescue Teams throughout Scotland can provide a useful service. They have their own off-road capability, their own radio communications, they are skilled in emergency first aid and are trained to operate independently in hostile environments and weathers.

It is perfectly appropriate therefore that the police will use Mountain Rescue Teams in certain situations as they are a very valuable resource. However, the prime function of Scottish Mountain Rescue Teams is first and foremost rescue in the mountains.

Some teams, including Cairngorm, are highly active and effective fundraisers. Others in Scottish Mountain Rescue are less so and therefore require more from the Scottish Government funding. Funding also comes directly from the public whose generosity when it comes to a cause like the Cairngorm Mountain Rescue Team is extraordinary. As a suitable target not only for individual donations but also for bequests, legacies and corporate donations, mountain rescue stands out as a completely deserving candidate.

This gives rise to a further dilemma. If the generous public, prompted to donate specifically by the reporting of genuine mountain rescue incidents, finds its donations being used to reinforce the search resources of the police when investigating possible criminal activity, how should they view that? It is undoubtedly worthwhile and necessary, but is it what was intended? The CMRT committee suspected otherwise.

Such discussions are far from new, and I admit to having considered these matters keenly over the decades. In Chapter Twenty-two of this book, I commented on the potential difficulties associated with the slippage of mountain rescue resources into non-mountainous search and rescue, saying, *'Manipulation of mountain rescue resource, into general search and rescue, risks division between the Highland and Lowland Teams and could possibly provoke a breakaway by the Highland Teams at some future time.'* Ten years later this prediction has finally come to pass.

In 1988 I contributed an article to the Scottish Mountain Rescue magazine, *Cas Bag*, in response to the Struthers Report which had been commissioned by the then Mountain Rescue Committee of Scotland and which had informed us of 'things to be done to improve funding' by citing a long list of activities that Cairngorm Mountain Rescue Team were already carrying out and had indeed, often originated. As an indicator not only of the thinking at the time but also the depth of feeling, I can do no better than repeat that short article here with a few amendments. It is still relevant.

RAISING SOME FUNDAMENTAL ISSUES

There has been some debate recently in mountain rescue circles, about whether Teams should continue to fundraise individually as at present, or join together and fundraise collectively under the banner of the Mountain Rescue Committee of Scotland, on a national scale.

As present Leader and long-serving member of the Cairngorm Mountain Rescue Team it has been my experience that the existing methods of fundraising are perfectly adequate if properly used, and therefore as a supporter of the time-honoured belief that a thing should not be 'fixed' unless it is broken, I wish to put forward my arguments in favour of retaining the status quo.

Some teams seeking centralised funding have put forward the argument that the larger and busier Teams such as Lochaber, Glencoe, Skye and Cairngorm find it easy to raise funds – because they are busier they receive more publicity and consequently the money just pours into the Team bank accounts. THIS IS SIMPLY NOT TRUE. The Cairngorm Team are proud of the fact that they work very hard for every penny which is donated to them.

When I joined the Cairngorm Team in 1972, we had no funds, very little equipment and no vehicles. In the early months of 1972 there was a great deal of publicity about mountain rescue as a result of the Cairngorm Plateau Disaster of November 1971. At that time Cairngorm became almost a household word, but this did not have the suggested effect of causing funds to roll in unsolicited. In fact for some 18 months following this incident, the Team continued in the same position as before with no funds, no vehicles and very little equipment. It was not until Team Members themselves decided to get their act together to raise our own funds and profile that things started to improve.

We had at that time a distinct advantage in the person of our Team Leader, Mollie Porter. She was the first woman Leader of a Scottish Mountain Rescue Team, and this fact led to TV coverage, radio interviews and a great deal of publicity for the Team. One can argue the ethics of using this sort of exploitation, but Mollie certainly did the image of the Cairngorm Team a great deal of good.

We raised funds as follows:

- We targeted companies for donations of cash.
- We targeted companies for equipment.
- We targeted companies for vehicles.
- We held a sponsored walk to the Shelter Stone.
- We put collection bottles in the pubs in upper Strathspey.

In fact in 1973 and 1974 we had anticipated and acted upon the 'NEW' ideas on fundraising and profile raising which have now been put forward by the Struthers Report 15 years later.

Our efforts were rewarded, and like many other Teams we have continued to be successful at fundraising, but please note that it did not just happen – WE MADE IT HAPPEN, and without seeking help from the Mountain Rescue Committee of Scotland.

It has been argued that some Teams in remote areas have difficulties with fundraising due to their locality, but WHERE ARE THOSE TEAMS? It should be remembered that Mountain Rescue Teams usually operate in areas of great scenic beauty. HOW HARD HAVE THEY TRIED TO RAISE FUNDS? It is up to each Team to use the unique advantages of their own area when planning their fundraising activities.

One of the best examples of using such an initiative in a remote area is demonstrated in Kintail and Glen Affric. In 1983, the Highlands and Islands Fire Brigade ran an invitation event for emergency service personnel including Mountain Rescue Teams. This event took the form of a biathlon of 50 miles from Morvich to Kintail, through Glen Licht and Glen Affric to Cannich, then down Strathglass, along the Beauly Firth, finishing in Inverness. The event was titled the Midsummer Madathon and even though not highly publicised raised large sums of money. That event, renamed the Highland Cross and open to all, is now so popular that each year hundreds of would-be entrants from all over the UK are disappointed due to limitation of numbers. Many thousands of pounds have been raised by this event in an extremely remote and poorly populated area of Scotland. There are lessons here for us all.

Each Mountain Rescue Team has within its membership a unique mixture of individuals, each with their own particular skills and talents. It is my belief that membership of a Mountain Rescue Team involves a high degree of personal commitment to that Team and to all of its activities, including those of fundraising. The fundraising potential of the Team is greatly increased by the involvement of those individuals, but it is unlikely that the same degree of commitment would be available if the fundraising became centralised and anonymous.

It is our experience that when appeals are being made for funds or equipment it is usually the ones made by personal contact which raise the best response. If you ask the right person at the right time using the right contact, then the chances of success are greatly increased.

A classic example of being in the right place at the right time comes from a Team Member who in his professional life practises as a dentist. For the sake of anonymity we will call this dentist – Hamish. On being called out to an unknown patient suffering with toothache, Hamish proceeded – as is the habit with dentists – to cram his mouth full of instruments before engaging him in conversation. In the course of this one-sided exchange Hamish somehow discovered that the stranger was an employee of W Gore Ltd and that he was in the area testing a new Gore-tex fabric. Seizing his opportunity and (rumour has it) his patient, Hamish offered the services of the Team. A deal was struck before the unfortunate patient struggled free of the chair, and a few weeks later the Team received enough of the new material (Taslan Gore-tex) to make up to 40 sets of jackets and trousers. It is our experience that companies much prefer to be associated with a particular Team than with an unknown committee.

Having put forward these views on the desirability of personal fundraising by individual teams, I wish to comment only briefly on the possible results of a policy of central fundraising. Commonly held funds would create great difficulties with administration. Who would make the decisions on which Teams were most in need of funding? The allocation of funds would require the creation of yet more unnecessary sub-committees thus requiring still more funds. Ponder for a moment the scene of Team Leaders and treasurers meeting at dawn, with ice axes drawn and avalanche probes upraised, each staking a claim on the funds available. The committee meetings of the Mountain Rescue Committee of Scotland would certainly become more lively.

It is my belief that mountaineering is a very personal activity and that commitment to a Mountain Rescue Team is a very personal commitment. Each Team has a strong feeling of individuality and I do not believe that many Teams would be willing to relinquish any of their identity in order to become involved with this communal activity.

The Cairngorm Mountain Rescue Team will resist any such interference with its own fundraising activities, as it is our belief that fundraising is a matter for each individual Team.

In my time in the Team there was a feeling that Scottish Mountain Rescue had lost its way. There were other issues which irked also.

One of the Cairngorm MRT members was a physics teacher at Millburn Academy, Inverness, named Nick Forwood. Nick's skill set included electronics, which led to him filling the post of radio officer not only for the Cairngorm Team but also for the Mountain Rescue Committee of Scotland. This position eventually took him into covert activity associated with the British Government and the purchase of an all-terrain Unimog vehicle. The secrecy and manipulation around the purchase and use of this vehicle sadly fuelled discontent among the members of Scottish Mountain Rescue and although well intentioned confers no credit on the government agencies involved.

In 2018, now retired after 22 years as a Cairngorm Team Member, Nick agreed to talk to me about the reasons behind the purchase.

In 2003, at a time when we were all pressing the Scottish Government for additional funding, Nick was invited to a meeting, subject to a confidentiality agreement, with a senior civil servant at St Andrews house in the offices of the Secretary of State for Scotland who was, of course, a United Kingdom (not Scottish) government minister. There he learned that, after the Lockerbie Pan Am jet disaster in 1988, the UK Government became aware that it did not possess a disaster command and control vehicle suitable for the new millennium. In the light of this understanding they decided to commission a multi-agency response vehicle which they would badge as a mountain rescue vehicle and give to the Mountain Rescue Committee of Scotland. This course of action would bring the UK Government additional credibility by apparently giving assistance to those highly voluble Mountain Rescue Teams, but would also, in reality, fill what was by then seen as a resource gap for the police and army in the case of a major incident.

The vehicle design was based on an off-road Mercedes Unimog Chassis which would deliver direct drive to all wheels. It had a large rear cabin fitted with desks and chairs, the internal specification was very high and, externally, it positively bristled with communications equipment. With massive large off-road tyres, blue lights and mountain rescue badging it was a very impressive vehicle.

However, due to the secrecy, the receipt of this gift had never been properly aired or explained at any full committee meeting. Security requirements meant that the members had been kept in the dark, and when the vehicle arrived it was seen to be different from all expectations. Such a magnificent resource at no capital cost seemed generous beyond belief but, faced with a fait accompli the members asked questions.

In fact, the idea had not been properly thought through. Where was it to be garaged? No Team had premises capable of accommodating it, drivers would have to be specially trained. What would be its maximum speed? If garaged in Inverness how long would it take to travel to, say, Oban? What would its fuel consumption be, and what, anyway, was its functional suitability for mountain rescue?

I do not recall being told that it came as a 'gift', and neither I nor the other Team Leaders were aware that a blanket of state secrecy had been thrown over the matter. Misinformation and confusion were compounded when, for insurance and road tax purposes, the Mountain Rescue Committee of Scotland was declared to be the owner.

Although funding did not come out of the police budget they, as the body responsible for the lives of persons on land in the UK, would have access to it. This, as it can be seen now, would be required should that extreme national emergency arise. None of this was known though, and we were left to wonder why we had purchased (as we thought we had) such a vehicle, and where the money had come from? I admit that, at the time, I was extremely cynical about our parent organisation spending money in such a cavalier manner.

Of course, in the matter of finance it later became clear that it had not cost the parent organisation any money at all. The unfortunate Nick, having been sworn to secrecy until the vehicle was ready to be commissioned, could not enlighten us and received criticism from other committee members that, in the light of this revelation, they may now regret. Unhappy with the support he received from the Council Executive, he resigned.

The vehicle became, inevitably, a white elephant, but the Scottish Government needed an organisation to take responsibility and to ensure that *someone* was trained in its use. Garaged initially at Inverness Airport, it was ultimately transferred to the Red Cross. This unfortunate and poorly managed affair increased the tensions within the Mountain Rescue Committee of Scotland. Certainly, such machinations did not endear it to me. As collateral damage, Nick received no credit for doing much work that he believed was to the benefit of our national security.

Within this amazing story the major point of dissatisfaction was with communication and trust. The Teams did not feel adequately consulted before these actions were taken.

However, not all expenditure by Scottish Mountain Rescue was felt to be unwise. Time spent on training ventures was usually well spent, and peripheral contributors could sometimes benefit.

The A&E department of the nearest hospital is often put on alert when a rescue is proceeding but sometimes left in ignorance of the casualty's condition until they arrive. When Paul Hyett fell on Ben Alder (Chapter Twelve), we were with him from around midnight with the police radioing in regularly to update A&E at Raigmore Hospital. It was not until after 04.30 that the badly injured Paul was airlifted from the scene and flown to where expert help was not only waiting but prepared for him.

On an occasion not too many years ago, from the hills above Glenmore Lodge there arrived a report of climbers lying among the boulders below the steep slopes of Coire na Ciste. Multiple casualties, blood and twisted limbs were mentioned. Fresh snow lay on the ground.

A rescue party left from the lower of the two car parks in the Cairngorm ski grounds, near the mouth of the corrie. The weather was forecast to deteriorate later in the day but, by a stroke of luck, a number of accident and emergency surgeons were attending a seminar (funded by Shell UK) at nearby Glenmore Lodge. The search and rescue party therefore consisted not only of experienced Team Members, but also included some highly qualified surgeons, one of whom was Dr David Sedgwick, the A&E surgeon at the Belford Hospital in Fort William. For years, David had been attending the trauma injuries of climbers who had fallen or been avalanched on Ben Nevis. With snow now falling heavily, the rescue party located the four climbers and left the A&E surgeons to diagnose, treat and stretcher the 'casualties' off the hill. Have you guessed? This was a training exercise organised by MRCS as part of the Shell UK seminar.

David Sedgwick at the time said, '…as non-mountaineers we were treated to the quite difficult conditions that teams routinely have to deal with. Applying first aid to casualties lying in difficult positions, in low temperatures, and with a wind blowing snow in your face proved to be very challenging. Carrying them off the hill, we quickly understood the extreme effort required to move an injured person on a stretcher downhill over rough terrain, even for only a few hundred metres. The exercise was very informative and gave us an insight into the difficulties of applying first aid by the book in a mountain environment.'

Notwithstanding these undeniably good seminars, our committee eventually found itself experiencing increasing difficulty in finding members willing to attend SMR meetings. In much earlier times, Teams such as Cairngorm, Glencoe and Lochaber had two votes to cast to the Lowland Teams' one each. This was, in some way, a recognition of the differences between 'search and rescue'; and more concentrated 'mountain rescue' as outlined earlier.

In recent times this was altered to each Team having a single vote. This meant that the small number of Highland Teams who were involved in the bulk of actual mountain rescues and who had different needs were consistently outvoted, not least when it came to the allocation of funding. In 2013 Scottish Mountain Rescue appointed a salaried Chief Executive, a move that was not approved unanimously and only served to increase the sense of disassociation.

Matters came to a head when, with Scottish Mountain Rescue in receipt of a large legacy donation, the Lochaber Team applied for a new radio system, badly needed to replace their own, that by now, was less than fully effective. They were turned down. Our own Team's radios were not much better and our request for similar funds would probably have been next. Underlying all this was the feeling that the Lowland Teams suspected that the larger Teams had more than adequate funds anyway.

Willie Anderson attended this meeting and saw this decision about the radios as the last straw. He called Miller Harris of the Lochaber Team on his return and what had been no more than mutterings of general discontent became reality. Independent Scottish Mountain Rescue (iSMR) was founded in late 2015. Funding for new radio systems for both Cairngorm and Lochaber Teams would come later in a direct deal from Viridor, a company much involved in sustainability, which takes us into a new but related subject.

A new development in fundraising, since my time, is the advent of social media utilising some of the new technology described in the previous chapter. Cairngorm Mountain Rescue Team committed heavily to its own website and to Facebook. Through these platforms and with the use of Go-Pro cameras, it can inform and involve both the media and, more directly, its many thousands of followers.

A visit to our website will show that the Cairngorm Mountain Rescue Team proudly displays the logos of its new sponsors on its Partners page, a thing unheard of in my time. These are supportive companies that supply equipment and sometimes money. The Partners page also has a means of receiving individual donations, although the greater part of modern funding now comes from corporate donors and legacies.

It is a simple fact that the greater the presence of the Team in the media, whether in conventional journals and broadcasts, or social pages, the more attractive it becomes to donors. The more exposure the rescues get, the more deserving a beneficiary the Team is seen to be.

Now, at my time of writing, and as a direct result of the formation of iSMR, a charitable trust is in the process of being formed with the express purpose of additional fundraising for mountain rescue in Scotland and possibly across the UK. Trust meetings will be chaired by a representative from each of the iSMR teams on a rolling basis.

The possibilities are far-reaching, and I look forward to advances that cannot yet be visualised but that will lead to a more effective Mountain Rescue Service.

Under consideration by the new Trust is a benevolent fund for injured Team Members who are presently covered by the current police insurance which is not always satisfactory. After an accident, it can take time before payments are approved by the police insurers and, as has been proven by painful experience, it is also necessary for each claim to fit exactly the specification of the policy, which was not designed for mountain rescue but for routine police work. The benevolent fund would bridge the gap between the time of an accident and the time of funds coming from the police insurance. This policy would be available not only to iSMR members but to all Team Members in Scotland

Recently I met with Damon Powell, the current Chair of Scottish Mountain Rescue to seek his opinion on the split between the two organisations. We could not agree on the subject of paid officials. I raised the point that Scottish Mountain Rescue, in addition to their paid Chief Executive, had added a full-time paid fundraiser to their staff and that at their AGM in 2018 their medical officer had recommended that in the future the medical officer post should also become a full-time paid post. The funding for these posts would presumably come from the pot of donations to Scottish Mountain Rescue. Comparing the successful voluntary and unpaid management of both Lochaber and Cairngorm, I did say that I found it hard to understand the need for these posts to become paid positions. We did agree that it would have been much better if the split had been avoided but we did not see any prospect of reconciliation for perhaps a generation at least.

I am pleased, however, to conclude that there is little if any animosity or friction among the Teams themselves, and both organisations continue to work together harmoniously on rescues and where necessary hold training exercises together.

One other matter arises from the departure from SMR, relating not only to funding but also to the Team's sense of identity. On finding themselves exposed on a new, rather airy ledge the suggestion arrived from some quarter that the Cairngorm Mountain Rescue Team logo was actually copyright of Scottish Mountain Rescue. To avoid confrontation on the use of the logo the committee of iSMR put its collective head together and found unanimity.

An Inverness-based company, Tide Design, was appointed to develop the brand, and after much consultation came up with the new logo that now adorns all the CMRT vehicles and equipment, and which can be seen in this volume's second plate section, and also on the CMRT website at *www.cmrt.org.uk*. The design was supplied by Gregor McNeish, a man of considerable outdoor pedigree, who has provided the Teams with a symbol to gather around and wear with pride.

4. Safety in the mountains

On 13th March 1951 at around 18.00 hours a Lancaster Bomber converted for reconnaissance took off from RAF Kinloss on a navigational exercise, a routine, scheduled seven-hour flight. Just after midnight the crew sent what proved to be their last message from a location to the north of Cape Wrath. They never returned and it was to be three days before the wreckage was found in Coire Mhic Fhearchair on the North Face of Beinn Eighe, deep in the Torridon Mountains. It took a further day for a Rescue Team from RAF Kinloss to reach the crash site and many more before the bodies of the eight crew members were recovered.

There were no civilian Mountain Rescue Teams then, and the RAF Teams were very much in their infancy. The search for this missing plane and subsequent recovery of the bodies were not only instrumental in the development of the RAF Mountain Rescue Service but also a motivating factor in the formation of organised civilian teams. Among the rescuers working on Beinn Eighe, was a young serviceman named Donald Rich who was doing his national service at the time and was based at RAF Valley.

Torridon is a magical place which I first visited on my bicycle in the late 1950s. Having spent the night at Ratagan Youth Hostel on the shores of Loch Duich, I travelled over the steep, single-track road from Auchtertyre to Strome, crossing Loch Carron on the ferry. This ferry service was discontinued in 1970 leaving only the two slipways at North and South Strome. For many years, visitors to this part of the world were amused and puzzled by the road sign on the A890 which stated 'Strome Ferry No Ferry'. The sign achieved global notoriety and for four decades became a talking point with any visitor to this part of the Highlands until it was removed in 2015.

More recently in 2012 the ferry was reinstated for a time when a landslide closed the A890 road along the south side of Loch Carron. Pupils from Loch Carron village and the surrounding area who attended Plockton High School were faced with a 140-mile detour via Inverness to get to school. The Glenachulish is the last sea going car ferry in the world operated by a manual turntable and normally operates in the summer across the fast flowing Kylerhea narrows between Skye and the mainland at Glenelg. It was brought into service while the road was repaired and once again there was a ferry at Strome.

From North Strome I continued my journey to cycle to the remote village of Shieldaig, meaning to spend time at Inveralligan Youth Hostel and the isolated Craig Youth Hostel on the peninsula beyond Diabeg. The mountains here are among the most dramatic in Scotland, whose hidden grandeur I only discovered later in life when I started winter hillwalking and snow and ice climbing.

By this time, Donald Rich, the airman from North Yorkshire, had developed a great love of the Scottish Hills, eventually completing his Munros on Beinn a'Bheithir, also known as the Ballachulish Horseshoe. He took great pleasure in introducing his family, including his young daughter, Heather, to the mountains of the Highlands. Heather Morning, as she now is, takes up her father's story:

'I was eight years old when we visited Torridon for the first time together, and my father shared his story about the extensive search for the lost aircraft.' Heather remembers him describing a 'foot in a boot', which could be seen as a surprising bedtime story for an eight-year-old girl, but perhaps it was this which inspired her to join Cairngorm Mountain Rescue Team in 2000. For 16 years she was a valued member, taking part in and leading many rescue parties.

Heather holds the Mountain Instructor Certificate, achieved after about ten years of training and was the first female mountaineering instructor with the military Joint Services. She spent three seasons in Antarctica with *Antarctica Logistics* and made the first female solo ascent of Mount Vincent. With such a wealth of experience, supplemented by her hands-on experience in the Cairngorm Team, I could not think of a better person to be safety advisor for Scottish Mountaineering.

Mountain Rescue Teams, although always at the sharp end of rescue activities, seldom issue safety messages. Few Teams see this as their brief, and fewer still have the time to do it. As volunteers they already devote huge amounts of their time to the rescue service and, when the rescue is over, are only too glad to return to their families and jobs, to continue whatever was interrupted by the call-out.

As Leader of the Cairngorm Team I was very conscious of a need to provide more information to the hillwalking and mountaineering public concerning the serious potential consequences of poor planning, poor equipment, and inexperience. That said, it was a void I did not feel was mine to fill. There is a limit to how much a mountain rescue volunteer can contribute while pursuing a normal life elsewhere.

As the Scottish Government continues to create National Parks and encourages healthy lifestyles, including walking and cycling in the great outdoors, it seems appropriate that it should concern itself with these safety issues while also providing some of the funding for the Rescue Teams.

The safety advisor for Scottish Mountaineering is a full-time position, and soon this solitary post will be added to as the workload increases. Heather has been in post for ten years, funded by the Scottish Government through Sports Scotland, and operates from an office at Glenmore Lodge. She teaches courses on mountain safety in summer and winter that are so popular they are generally fully booked for months in advance.

Heather has learned, as I have, the value of storytelling in getting her message across, and often refers to an incident in 2013 which resulted in the death of a student. Her purpose is to illustrate how easily a party can get into serious trouble by not making proper preparations. For the same reasons, here is the story.

Team Members Dave Rutledge and Iain Cornfoot, who work at the ski grounds on Cairngorm Mountain, were on ski patrol duty when, one early afternoon in February, they received a call warning that, due to the worsening weather conditions, there was a possibility that the ski road would have to be closed. All skiers on the slopes were therefore to be cleared.

Dave was the senior Cairngorm Rescue Team Member on the call-out list that day and, just as that call ended, he received another. This was from the police in Aviemore stating that a party of students had requested assistance in navigating off the Cairngorm Plateau. Their reported position was 'somewhere near Spot Height 1141'. As Dave was already near the summit of Cairn Gorm, he decided to take two other patrollers and ski towards 1141, alert for any sign of the missing group. Visibility was poor and, with the rising wind and increasing snowfall, it was not an easy task. From the cairn they had a fruitless look south across the plateau but, with wind speed still increasing and visibility down to just a few metres, they had no choice but to return to their main task of assisting in the evacuation of the hill.

At about 16.30 at the Day Lodge, Dave met two climbers who said they had assisted a hillwalker who was lost in Coire an t-Sneachda. The walker was from Leeds University and, although apparently uninjured, he had told them that he had fallen from the Cairngorm Plateau into the corrie which runs parallel to the ski area of Coire Cas. He confirmed that he had been with a group of seven students who had earlier phoned for help.

At this point Dave realised that the incident was escalating. He drove to the rescue base to instigate a full Team call-out and a search for the remaining six climbers.

Heather left work at about 17.00, as usual, and was heading for home when she received the call-out and was tasked to lead a search group into Coire Cas, a likely area for the missing group to have reached. High winds from the south-east meant that avalanche risk in the Northern Corries had increased dramatically and there was concern that, if the group had been unable to locate 1141, they could easily have drifted into the high avalanche risk areas. Even for Heather, the simple act of navigating from the car park into the corrie was extremely difficult so low was the visibility.

If the group had reached Point 1141 they could already be making their way down. A grimmer consideration was that some other members of the party had fallen from the ridge. With these possibilities in mind, Al Gilmour and a group were tasked to search in Coire an t-Sneachda and, if possible, climb to 1141. The search was well and truly on, but gale-force winds, driving snow, temperatures well below zero and increased avalanche risk made activity of any kind difficult. The search was called off around midnight. To resume at first light, additional Rescue Teams and extra personnel were recruited from groups who were training in the area and who offered to assist.

To extend the cover, the Braemar Team was asked to search on the south side of Cairn Gorm, allowing for the possibility that the group had gone south. This was considered unlikely as the wind was from the south-east and they would have been walking into the teeth of the gale in white-out conditions.

Heather was now tasked with the search of Coire an t-Sneachda, including the use of probes. Her large group included policemen from Northern Ireland who had been training in the Cairngorms and offered to help. This corrie was a likely spot but also a dangerous one as the avalanche risk at the head would be high. Progress was inevitably slow and extremely hard work in the fresh snow. Probing in avalanche debris on the slopes below Point 1141 was very time-consuming.

The weather cleared somewhat at 14.00, and a 999 call was received from the missing group, confirming that they were lost. From the description given, Braemar Control was now able to approximate their position. A Sea King aircraft was tasked to search over the area and found five of the group of six on the top of Carn Tarsuinn, approximately 10km from their starting point. This was the search co-ordinator's first indication that the search had reached a higher order of seriousness with one member of the party apparently missing and alone.

At this time, Heather's group, having found nothing in the avalanche debris, commenced a sweep search towards the bottom of the climbing route known as Jacob's Ladder. Here they discovered a body lying in the snow behind a boulder. The missing member of the party was found, but tragedy had struck. It appeared that, after falling from the ridge above, he had walked to this location before succumbing to his probable injuries and hypothermia.

Over the following days an analysis of the incident was made considering what was known for sure.

The party of seven had left the ski ground car park in Coire Cas on the Sunday morning, intending to reach Point 1141 and the plateau where they would practise their winter skills.

The weather was 'reasonable' but a deterioration was forecast for the afternoon. They remained on the hill. In the early afternoon wind speed increased dramatically and the falling temperature brought snow. With reduced visibility, the seven became disorientated and decided to phone for help. They suspected that they were near 1141 but were unsure.

One of the party ventured too near the edge of Coire an t-Sneachda and slipped, possibly falling through a cornice, and disappeared from view. In fact, he fell hundreds of feet to the corrie floor but, by some miracle, survived and was not seriously injured. He walked out slowly until he was met by the two climbers who took him to the Day Lodge at the car park.

With the wind now increasing to gale force another member of the party also disappeared over the edge but was less fortunate and died. His was the body found by Heather's party the following day.

It transpired that the remaining five did not have any real experience of mountain navigation. Not only did they lack maps and compasses, but they were overwhelmed by the weather. With no idea of where they were, they believed that the way to safety began only one or two hundred metres from where they had phoned for help. With no maps or compasses, or the ability to use them, they retreated in what turned out to be the wrong direction. To their credit, they walked all day and night to keep warm and, as the weather cleared the next day, made their way to the top of Carn Tarsuinn where they were subsequently found. This was many miles from Spot Height 1141. They were hungry and cold, but by moving had avoided hypothermia.

In many of her safety lectures, often to student groups, Heather uses this incident to illustrate some of the things that can go wrong. Most of them – confirmed by my discussions with Willie and Al in the rescue base – still come down to bad planning.

In this case, the group had not taken a close look at the forecast for the day. It was clearly stated that snow would arrive and wind speed increase in the early afternoon. In such conditions, competent navigation would be vital on the featureless Cairngorm Plateau. With the wind from the south-east, avalanche conditions would quickly develop on the north-west slopes with cornices on the upper slopes. White-out conditions would be likely, which are not unusual in the winter Cairngorms, and should have been anticipated and planned for. In fact, no one in the group had experience of this level of navigation.

More generally, they underestimated the navigation skills required in Scottish winter mountaineering, especially on this unique terrain. Each member of the party should have had a map and compass and knowledge of basic navigation. Mobile phones loaded with maps in these conditions are no substitute for OS maps and Silva type compasses. The party leader should have been aware of all this and, in addition, had some experience of severe weather conditions. Sub-zero temperatures, gale-force winds, blowing snow all make navigating in featureless terrain extremely difficult. There is a plentiful supply of similar incidents in the records of the Cairngorm Mountain Rescue Team.

Mountaineering Scotland already broadcast, lecture, write and generally try to spread the message that smartphones have their limitations in hill navigation. If we can increase the effectiveness of this message, then perhaps we can reduce the number of these incidents.

One of the major changes affecting mountain rescue in the last ten years is an increasing reliance on the mobile phone. To quote Heather, 'They have taken over our lives, but they do give a false sense of security. They are an awesome tool of the trade with high functionality, but this has to be underpinned by the correct use of a map and compass.'

It seems that growing numbers of inexperienced walkers are using their phones for navigation without knowing the rudimentary principles of navigation. The question is: how do you persuade the modern generation who rely so closely on their phones for communication that, if you go into the hills, you must also learn the old-fashioned but life-saving techniques of navigation?

There are other major disadvantages in their use, for example battery power. Even when phones are fully charged extremely low temperatures reduce the duration of usage. Obviously, there must be an available signal if the casualty is to dial for help, but this is not always the case in remote areas. Direct sunlight on the screen reduces visibility. They are awkward to use when wearing gloves. Phone maps do not give the bigger picture of what is around you.

It is interesting to note that in October 2018 four incidents occurred, each involving parties of two climbers, each incident taking place on the Cairngorm Plateau and each involving the use of mobile phones.

One of these occurred on 23rd October 2018 after two walkers set off from the car park at the ski grounds on Cairn Gorm, hoping to reach the summit of Ben MacDhui. On the plateau they encountered mist and deteriorating weather and decided against proceeding. Unsure of conditions, or exactly where they were, they became rightly alarmed and dialled 999.

The Cairngorm and Braemar Teams were unable to use SARLOC to locate the casualties so they went out in winds of 70 to 90mph. The Cairngorm Team committed 15 searchers to the north side of the hill and Braemar, on the south side, 18. Eventually the casualties were found close to Linn of Dee, many miles from their start point. Willie Anderson reported that they did not have a map, compass or torch but they did have a phone app.

Team Leaders are deliberately non-judgemental but one newspaper quoted Willie Anderson as follows: 'they did not have a scoobie' (which translates as 'they were clueless').

Relying on a phone app has major disadvantages, and this message needs to be broadcast loud and clear to all potential hillwalkers and climbers. Maps on smartphones are progressively improving but they will not give the bigger picture of where you are in the wider landscape. You need the OS map 1:50000, or a relevant piece cut out or printed off from a map program and protected by a good-quality map case, a freezer bag, or similar. It is also worth noting that it is now possible to download and print out only that part of the map you need, which makes it more sensibly sized in the map case, and gets around the problem of walking off the limits of the map in use.

Weather forecasts have improved dramatically in the last ten years. There are a lot of good forecasts out there and they are becoming increasingly accurate, as I have appreciated when sailing. Storms can usually be predicted on the west coast of Scotland at least 48 hours in advance and I would have no excuse for being caught out at sea in bad weather. Mountain weather is just as predictable.

The Mountain Weather Information Service (MWIS), sponsored

by Sports Scotland in association with Mountaineering Scotland, puts out a forecast each day at 16.30 predicting likely weather conditions for each mountain area in the Scottish Highlands. This service is available seven days a week 365 days of the year. It is an excellent forecast, and hillwalkers visiting Scotland should be aware that it exists and should make use of it.

Avalanches are a continuing problem. In winter the Scottish Avalanche Information Service gives hillwalkers an up-to-date forecast on snow conditions with an alert system indicating the likely areas of avalanche. Winter climbers should have a basic understanding of the nature of avalanches, and by logging on to the SAIS website can improve the odds of avoiding one.

Good navigation in winter in all the Scottish hills is essential as, with the wind in the right direction and snow being blown, cornices can build quickly. It is very easy to miscalculate and walk onto a cornice with disastrous results. Mountaineers in bad visibility should allow a safe wide margin (sometimes called 'hand railing') when walking round a corrie rim.

In concluding this chapter on safety, I must mention personal locator beacons. There are a variety on the market and it is, of course, a matter of personal choice whether to carry one. A highly positive example of their worth was demonstrated near the Lairig Ghru in early 2019.

The Lairig Ghru is probably the best known of the great passes through the Cairngorm Mountains, in days gone by providing a route for cattle droving between Speyside and Deeside. This great cleft cuts the Cairngorms in half and for more than a century has been an attraction to hillwalkers and climbers. Start walking from either end and there are very few ways out, but the March Burn is one.

The March Burn begins its journey high on the central Cairngorm Plateau near Lochan Bhuie at a height of 1,125m. It falls steeply, arriving near the Pools of Dee in the Lairig Ghru. In good conditions it can be used as an escape route from the plateau.

On 27th January 2019 a hillwalker from Surrey who had bivouacked somewhere on the high ground near Lurcher's Crag arrived near the start of the descent of the March Burn. Near the top, as the ground began to descend and with the wind increasing to gale force, he was blown into the top of the gully, injuring his legs and back. With temperatures falling and blowing snow he was in a serious situation.

He was well equipped with good waterproof protective gear and, unusually for mountaineers in Scotland, had a personal locator beacon. These work by satellite signals, and therefore in an emergency where the phone signal is weak or non-existent they can notify the police that you need help. He pressed the SOS button, the signal went to the USA, then back to ARCC Farnham, and from there to Police Scotland. The coordinates showed his position somewhere near the top of the March Burn.

Due to the urgency of the call, appalling weather conditions and the fact that a stretcher would need to be used, the following Rescue Teams were called out: Cairngorm, Aberdeen, Braemar, Glenmore Lodge, and RAF Lossiemouth. The coastguard was asked to provide air support, and an S92 was tasked to assist.

Once near the top of the March Burn, and with the coordinates to hand, it took the rescue parties only around 30 minutes to locate the casualty. He was in a bivvy bag covered in snow, but there is no doubt that, if he had not been found and stretchered off the plateau, he would not have survived the night.

It was a long arduous stretcher carry across the plateau, but the good outcome achieved shows again that, although there may be differences of opinion at committee level, when there is a life at risk all agencies come together. Party politics have not affected 'boots-on-the-ground' mountain rescue.

It is ten years since I first started to write my stories about Scottish Mountain Rescue, especially in the Cairngorms. In that period, many things have changed but much remains the same. There is no doubt that the use of smartphones has been a factor in an increasing number of incidents, but this is not exclusively a Scottish problem. The Leader of the Wasdale MRT in the Lake District recently stated that a huge number of man hours was now being spent on call-outs for parties relying on their phone for navigation. It is an issue that the British Mountaineering Council should continue to highlight.

Accidents still happen, and cannot always be avoided, but their frequency and severity can be reduced by preparation and planning undertaken by the mountaineers. This is not a new principle, but its processes are now supplemented by weather forecasting and avalanche conditions assessment, freely, easily and constantly available to all, that have advanced immeasurably in the years since I led the Cairngorm Mountain Rescue Team.

AFTERWORD:

THAI BOYS

The global news story that broke in July 2017 gripped the whole world. Twelve young members of a Thai boys' club football team and their coach were missing. Their bikes were found outside a notorious cave system that snaked many kilometres into a mountain side.

The cave system was known to flood and it was thought that the boys were trapped. The world watched as the Thai rescue services searched the cave system. Hopes dwindled when they were initially not found. Offers of help from experienced cave divers came from around the world. Cave divers from the UK were major players in the search and it was two UK cave divers who found the group trapped on a ledge by the flood water. Although now located, the group were in grave danger as the cave system was beginning to flood and their only exit would involve some underwater passages. A massive rescue effort unfolded.

These unpaid, experienced divers from both the UK and Australia were used in the most difficult underwater passages to shepherd the boys to safety. Watching the drama unfolding I reached the conclusion that the scenario being played out in Thailand was similar to the rescues which take place regularly each winter in the Scottish Mountains. Unpaid experts in Mountain Rescue Teams use their skills and experience to rescue climbers who have suffered an accident or become lost in bad weather.

In Thailand It took the help of unpaid amateur experts in their own sport of caving to bring the rescue to a satisfactory conclusion. In Scotland unpaid amateur experts in the Mountain Rescue Teams offer the same service, mostly with the same highly satisfactory outcomes. There is no one better to do the job.

MAPS

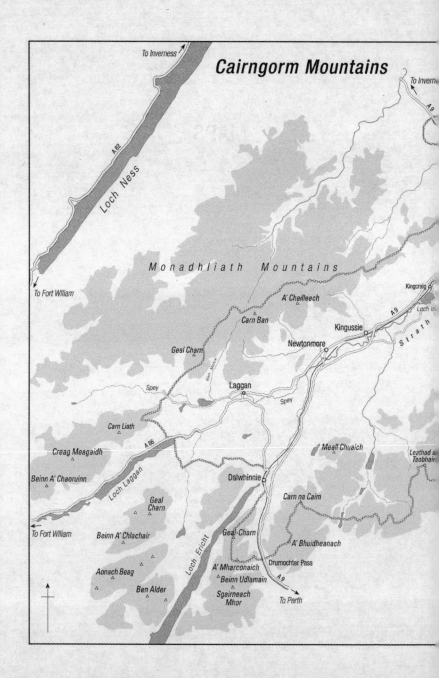

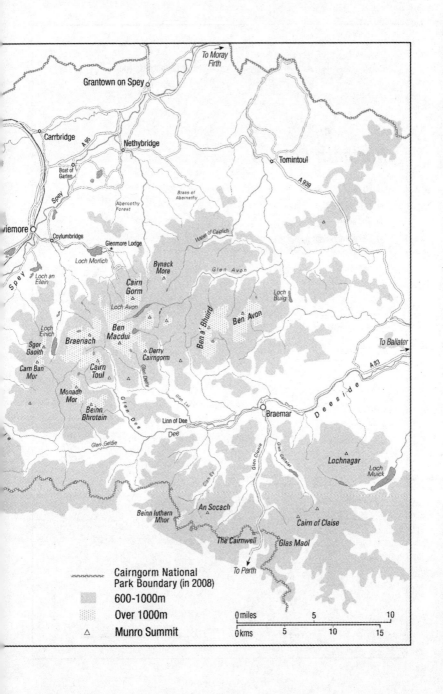

To Moray
Firth

Grantown on Spey

Carrbridge

A 95

Nethybridge

Tomintoul

A 939

Boat of
Garten

Braes of
Abernethy

Spey

Abernethy
Forest

Water of Caiplich

Aviemore

Coylumbridge

Glenmore Lodge

Loch Morlich

Bynack
More

Glen Avon

Loch
Builg

Loch an
Eilein

Cairn
Gorm

Loch Avon

Ben a'Bhuird

Ben Avon

Spey

Loch
Einich

Braeriach

Ben
Macdui

Sgor
Gaoith

Derry
Cairngorm

To Ballater

A 93

Carn Ban
Mor

Cairn
Toul

Glen Derry

Monadh
Mor

Glen Dee

Glen Lui

Deeside

Beinn
Bhrotain

Braemar

Linn of Dee

Dee

Glen Geldie

Glen Ey

Glen Clunie

Glen Callater

Lochnagar

Loch
Muick

An Socach

Beinn Iutharn
Mhor

Cairn of Claise

The Cairnwell

Glas Maol

To Perth

〰〰〰 Cairngorm National
Park Boundary (in 2008)

▨ 600-1000m

▦ Over 1000m

△ Munro Summit

0 miles   5   10

0 kms   5   10   15

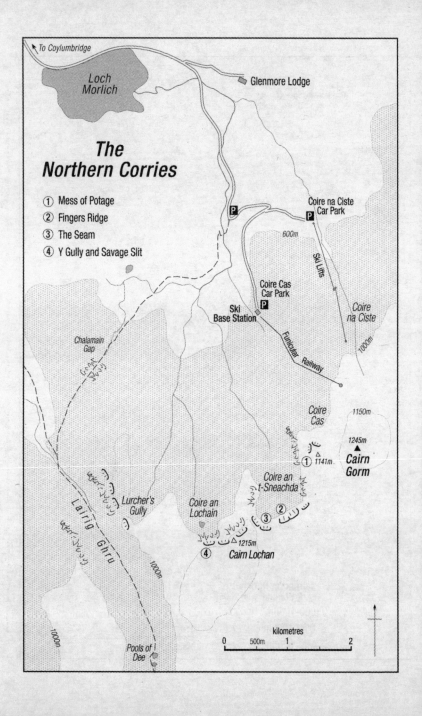

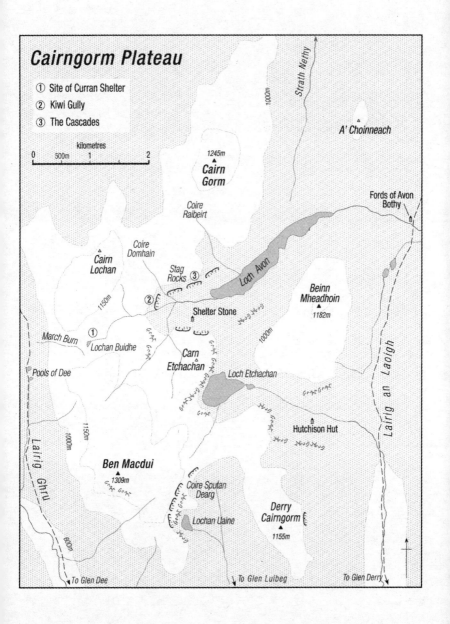

Cairngorm Plateau

① Site of Curran Shelter
② Kiwi Gully
③ The Cascades

kilometres
0   500m   1   2

Strath Nethy

1000m

A' Choinneach

1245m
Cairn Gorm

Coire Raibeirt

Fords of Avon Bothy

Coire Domhain

Cairn Lochan

Stag Rocks   ③

Loch Avon

Beinn Mheadhoin
1182m

1150m

②

Shelter Stone

March Burn

① Lochan Buidhe

Pools of Dee

Carn Etchachan

Loch Etchachan

Lairig an Laoigh

1150m

1000m

Hutchison Hut

Ben Macdui
1309m

Coire Sputan Dearg

Lochan Uaine

Derry Cairngorm
1155m

Lairig Ghru

600m

To Glen Dee   To Glen Luibeg   To Glen Derry

GLOSSARY
of climbing terms

ABSEIL: A technique used by climbers to descend the rope, usually to retreat from a climb.

BELAY: The purpose of belaying is to provide mutual protection for the members of a party by the use of a rope. The theory is that only one person is moving on the cliff at any one time but that person is secured by a rope to his partner who is himself stationary and secured by various anchors to the cliff face.

COMPASS: Silva type compass; one that can be placed on a map to work out your direction of travel.

CRAMPONS: Spiked devices which clip on to boots to aid traction on snow and ice slopes.

FIGURE OF EIGHT: A braking device used by climbers for abseiling or belaying.

FLARES: These are essentially large fireworks and are used by Teams to light up the area they are searching or to attract the attention of a missing person.

GPS: Portable Global Position Satellite system. Effective in some cases for locating your position on the hill. Can only be used as an aid to navigation. No substitute for map and compass. Like a mobile phone it does not need to be on all the time. Switch it off to conserve battery power. It will then be ready for use when you really need it.

HARNESS: A belt with leg loops worn by a climber. A full body harness will include protection for your chest. The climbing rope will be attached to the harness.

ICE AXE: A basic tool for walking and climbing on snow and ice.

ICE HAMMER: A device used by climbers similar to an ice axe but with a hammer head which can be used on steep technical snow and ice routes.

KARABINER: A metal D-shaped ring with a spring-loaded gate used in conjunction with the climbing ropes to aid protection.

MAP: Ordnance Survey scale 1:25000 or 1:50000.

MAP CASE: Clear plastic cover for map: Cheap simple solution – a freezer bag.

MOBILE PHONE: A useful emergency device for hillwalkers and climbers but only if it is charged. Charge the battery on your mobile phone and switch off when you go out on the hill. This means it will be of some value in an emergency. Try texting if signal is weak. It may seem out of place to list this here but in my experience there have been many frustrating calls from climbers in trouble on the hill who start by saying, 'I am down to only one bar.'

MUNRO: A hill in Scotland over 3,000ft (914.355m) above sea level.

NVG: Night-vision goggles used by RAF pilots.

ROPES: Climbers do not climb up ropes. Their primary function is to give some support between the climbers such as holding a fall. They can be also be used to give direct support, or to abseil off the route.

ROUTE NAMES: Climbers who make a first ascent of a technical route have the right to give that route a name of their choice.

RUNNER: Between belay points further protection can be put in by a lead climber and the rope runs through these; loosely called runners. Runners come in different forms and their use is determined by the type of climb that the climber is attempting. These runners can be in the form of pegs, nuts, friends, wires, ice screws.

SHELL GEAR: Outer waterproof and windproof jacket and trousers.

TECHNICAL ROUTE: A route on steep ground, usually a rock face in summer or in winter a cliff covered in snow and ice.

NB: In-depth descriptions of climbing terms and their uses can be found in the book *Mountaincraft and Leadership* by Eric Langmuir.

GLOSSARY
of Gaelic place names

Braeriach (*brigh'reeach*): Brindled Upland

Cairn Gorm (*from An Càrn Gorm*): The Rocky Blue Hill

Beinn Mheadhoin (*ben vae'in*): Middle mountain

Ben MacDhui (*ben mac'doo'i*): possibly Mountain of the Black Pig

Coire Etchachan (*corri'etch'a'han*):

Coire Raibeirt (*corri'raebert*): Robert's Corrie

Coire an t-Sneachda (*corri'an'trecht*): Corrie of the Snow

Glen Avon (*glin'a'an*):

Glen Einich (*glin'aineech*):

Glen Feshie (*glin'faishee*): glen of boggy haugh.

Lairig an Laoigh (*laarig'an'looee*): Pass of Lui (also calf)

Lairig Ghru (*larig'groo*): possibly the Red(ish) Pass, possibly referring a stream at the north end.

Mullach Clach a'Bhlair (*moolach clach a'vlar*): Peak of the Stone of the Field.

Sgoran Dubh Beag (*skoran' doo'beg*): Small black peaklet.

Sgoran Dubh Mor (*skora' doo'more*): Big black peaklet

Sgorr Gaoith (*skor gooee*): Peak of the wind.

Sgurr Dubh Mor (*skoor doo more*): Big black peak.

Sgurr Dubh an Da Bheinn (*skoor doo an da vane*): Black peak of the two ridges.

SELECT BIBLIOGRAPHY

Barton, Bob & Wright, Blythe, *A Chance in a Million*, SMT, 1985

Barton, Bob, *Safety, Risk and Adventure in Outdoor Activities*, Sage, 2006

Bonington, Chris, *Mountaineer*, Baton Wicks, 1996

Bonington, Chris, *Boundless Horizons*, Mountaineers Books, 2000

Brown, Hamish, *Poems of the Scottish Hills*, AUP, Aberdeen, 1982

Brown, Hamish, *Climbing the Corbetts*, Gollancz, 1988

Cliff, Peter (Ed), *Friends in High Places*, CMRA, 1988

Cliff, Peter, Mountain Navigation, Menasha Ridge Press, Birmingham, 1991

Craig, David, *On the Crofters Trail*, Jonathan Cape, London, 1990

Drummond, Peter, *Scottish Hill Names*, SMT, Edinburgh, 1991

Duff, John, *A Bobby on Ben MacDhui*, Leopard, 2001

Fyffe, Allen, *Winter Climbs in the Cairngorms*, Cicerone, Cumbria, 1982

Gray, Affleck, *Legends of the Cairngorms*, Mainstream, Edinburgh, 1987

Kempe, Ed & Wrightham, Mark (Eds), *Hostile Habitats*, SMT, Edinburgh, 2006

Krakauer, John, *Into Thin Air*, Pan McMillan, London, 1998

Langmuir, Eric, *Mountaincraft and Leadership*, Scottish Sports Council, Edinburgh, & Mountainwalking Leader Training Board, Manchester, 1984

McNeish, Cameron, *There's Always the Hills*, Sandstone Press, 2018

Murray W. H., *Mountaineering in Scotland*, J M Dent & Sons, London, 1947

Shepherd, Nan, *The Living Mountain*, AUP, Aberdeen, 1977

Watson, Adam, *The Cairngorms*, SMC, Edinburgh, 1992

Whyte, AF, *A Cairngorm Chronicle*, Millrace, Cheshire, 2007

Useful websites

Cairngorm Mountain Rescue Team: www.cmrt.org.uk
British Mountaineering Council: www.thebmc.co.uk
British Mountain Guides Association: www.bmg.org.uk
Cairngorms National Park Authority: www.cairngorms.co.uk
Cairngorm Mountain: www.cairngormmountain.org.uk
Glenmore Lodge: www.glenmorelodge.org.uk
John Muir Trust: www.jmt.org
Mountain Bothies Association: www.mountainbothies.org.uk
Police Scotland: www.scotland.police.uk
Scottish Mountaineering Club: www.smc.org.uk
Search and Rescue Dog Association (Scotland):
    www.sarda-scotland.org.uk
Search and Rescue Dog Association (Southern Scotland):
    www.sarda.org.uk

Weather and avalanche

Scottish Avalanche Information Service: www.sais.gov.uk
Met Office Mountain Weather Forecast: www.metoffice.gov.uk/
    weather/specialist-forecasts/mountain
Mountain Weather Information Service: www.mwis.org.uk